The Politics of Is

Decolonial Studies, Postcolonial Horizons
Series editors: Ramón Grosfoguel (University of California at Berkeley),
Barnor Hesse (Northwestern University) and S. Sayyid (University of
Leeds)

Since the end of the Cold War, unresolved conjunctures and crises of race,
ethnicity, religion, diversity, diaspora, globalization, the West and the
non-West, have radically projected the meaning of the political and the
cultural beyond the traditional verities of Left and Right. Throughout this
period, Western developments in 'international relations' have become
increasingly defined as corollaries to national 'race relations' across both
the European Union and the United States, where the reformation of
Western imperial discourses and practices have been given particular
impetus by the 'war against terror'. At the same time hegemonic Western
continuities of racial profiling and colonial innovations have attested to
the incomplete and interrupted institutions of the postcolonial era. Today
we are witnessing renewed critiques of these postcolonial horizons at the
threshold of attempts to inaugurate the political and cultural forms that
decolonization now needs to take within and between the West and the
'non-West'. This series explores and discusses radical ideas that open up
and advance understandings of these politically multicultural issues and
theoretically interdisciplinary questions.

Also available

Rewriting Exodus
American Futures from Du Bois to Obama
Anna Hartnell

The Dutch Atlantic
Slavery, Abolition and Emancipation
Kwame Nimako and Glenn Willemsen

Islam and the Political
Theory, Governance and International Relations
Amr G.E. Sabet

The Politics of Islamophobia

Race, Power and Fantasy

David Tyrer

PlutoPress
www.plutobooks.com

First published 2013 by Pluto Press
345 Archway Road, London N6 5AA

www.plutobooks.com

Distributed in the United States of America exclusively by
Palgrave Macmillan, a division of St. Martin's Press LLC,
175 Fifth Avenue, New York, NY 10010

British Library Cataloguing in Publication Data
A catalogue record for this book is available from the British Library

ISBN   978 0 7453 3132 4   Hardback
ISBN   978 0 7453 3131 7   Paperback
ISBN   978 1 8496 4873 8   PDF eBook
ISBN   978 1 8496 4875 2   Kindle eBook
ISBN   978 1 8496 4874 5   EPUB eBook

Library of Congress Cataloging in Publication Data applied for

This book is printed on paper suitable for recycling and made from fully managed
and sustained forest sources. Logging, pulping and manufacturing processes are
expected to conform to the environmental standards of the country of origin.

10   9   8   7   6   5   4   3   2   1

Typeset from disk by Stanford DTP Services, Northampton, England
Text design by Melanie Patrick
Simultaneously printed digitally by CPI Antony Rowe, Chippenham, UK and
Edwards Bros in the United States of America

I fy rhieni: diolch am bopeth

Fear is a bad advisor. Its companion is hate.
Aneurin Bevan

.

Contents

Acknowledgements

In *Breakfast at Tiffany's* there is a scene in which, by way of explaining that writing is a slow process, Paul Varjak tells Holly Golightly, 'Well, the idea is I'm not supposed to fritter my talent on little things. I'm supposed to be saving it for the big one.' Those of us who lack the talent (and style) to waste or save just have to make do with what we've got and it makes a huge difference to have the support of an excellent editorial team. I therefore thank David Castle, Jonathan Maunder, Robert Webb and all at Pluto Press for their incredible support and advice, and Thérèse Wassily Saba for her expert copy-editing. I also wish to express gratitude to the series editors, Ramón Grosfoguel, Barnor Hesse and Professor S. Sayyid. I wish to thank Ian Law for reviewing the manuscript.

I am also indebted to a great many others who have in various ways contributed to my experience of writing this book. Katherine Harbord: thank you for the politics and the Politics, and for medicinal diversions over in HQ after a hard day's teaching that you invariably made more enjoyable and stimulating. Gillian O'Brien: thank you for all the wisdom and intellectual stimulation you have shared, not to mention the odd bottle of Connemara Peated and the joys of ICSN. Rob Jones: thanks, mate! Gilda: I put the blame on Mame (Rita Hayworth says so), but thank *you* (teas, tattoos, proof-reading …). Mike Benbough-Jackson: *diolch yn fawr*. The girl with the dragon tattoo: *diolch yn fawr*. Katy Pal Sian: I owe you an especially big thank you for everything. It would be remiss not to mention the infectious enthusiasm of Emily and John for bamboozling me with Aristotle and Anoximander, running, and tales of Paris life. When things got lost in translation, Amal Sheiko was a great help – *dank je wel*. A number of other people provided much needed moments of escape along the way that kept me fresh: you all know who you are, but thank you from the bottom of my heart. I need to thank colleagues at Liverpool John Moores University including Liz Sperling, to whom I am especially indebted, Helen Churchill, Joe Yates, Lucie Mathews-Jones, Lucinda Thompson, the history boys and all in HSS. Professors Nick White, Joe

Sim, Steve Tombs, and Joe Moran always inspire those around them to retain their faith in academia and I am grateful for their support and encouragement. I wish to thank Amrit for friendship and intellectual generosity during the development of this project. Michaela: *go raibh mile maith* agait (there – I think I got it). Hussein Ali Agrama provided insightful comments as a discussant when some of these ideas were presented at a conference. I am also grateful to Frank Peter, Sarah Dornhof, Alexandre Caeiro, AbdoolKarim Vakil, Tina Patel, and Scott Poynting. Steve Lawler and Cheryl Connor put up with my analogue fascination for typewriters, old cameras and the obsolete, and kept me plugged into the matrix and on the straight and narrow (dammit), and for this I am grateful. I am indebted to the following people for providing hospitality and stimulating intellectual exchanges when they invited me to present at seminars and conferences: S. Sayyid, Shvetal Vyas, Gilbert Caluya, and Kam Kaur at the University of South Australia (who also published an early version of some of the themes in this book as an occasional paper); the organisers of the University of Salford Criminology Research Seminar Series; Tania Saeed and colleagues at St Antony's College Oxford; Nina-Clara Tiesler and colleagues at ICS at the University of Lisbon; Elena Arigita and colleagues at Casa Arabe e Instituto Internacional de Estudios Arabes y del Mundo Musulman in Cordoba; and Frank, Andreas and Colleagues at the University of Bern. I have enjoyed and benefited from the opportunity to test some of these ideas in the Blackboard Jungle and through supervision, and thank students for always speaking back and keeping the beat going. I should thank those who have ensured the spirit is willing even when the flesh is weak; here a number of hostelries spring to mind for their sterling work. My greatest debt of gratitude is to my family for putting up with me while writing this book.

David Tyrer
May 2013

Prologue

All this happened, more or less
Kurt Vonnegut, *Slaughterhouse Five*

As I write Lieutenant Columbo shuffles affably around the small screen, solving a murder in the movie industry in his own inimitable fashion. There is really no need to pay attention for it could be pretty much any one of sixty-nine different episodes which all hinge on similar logical devices in which befuddlement and harmless curiosity conceal what he *really* knows. The knowing *at-stakeness* of this kind of inquiry makes me mindful of the formulaic ways in which we tend to tell our tales, heavily reliant upon a set of stock character clichés and a reliable set of assumptions on which to base them. But as we wind towards the predictable climax of one of those and-now-what-I-brought-you-all-here-for moments when all will be revealed, I find myself more concerned with the rules of the game, and with the question of what happens when the conventions through which our tellings are organised are placed into question by the content of our tales.

We all tell our stories using certain vocabularies that are organised through grammars that establish rules to structure our narrations (Laclau 2000: 283). Most of the time this serves us well in putting into words, and integrating into memories, the events that occur as we go through life. But on rare occasions events can rise up on us as though they somehow burst through from beyond language itself, and can seem difficult to organise or express through language. The atrocities that took place on 11 September 2001 were such an example, and the mantra of the time that 'everything changed' on 9/11 seems to summarise not only the seismic geopolitical shifts that seemed to be set in train by the atrocities, but also the emergence of new ways of being able to incorporate certain types of unthinkable acts and events into the symbolic, or at least to find new ways of reorganising the old ways in which we tended to tell our tales.

Around 3,000 died in the attacks and it often appears as though in this ugly context, Muslims seemed to provoke particular fears and anxieties, not only about the threat posed by the few, but also questions about how they could be understood and narrated. Were the Islamist extremists, the anti-Semites, the homophobes, the bigoted thugs like Abu Qatada or Omar Bakri, just an aberration, or were they a more general reflection of the ways that Muslims feel about *us*? The events of 9/11 foregrounded a range of possibilities for narrating Muslims and opened what Norton (2011) has termed 'the Muslim question'. In the days, months and years that followed, attempts to answer that question, and even to work out what it was asking in the first place, took competing forms. For example, in 2011 the chairman of the House Homeland Security Committee convened hearings to explore Islamic radicalisation in the United States in the context of persistent fears and uncertainties surrounding these minorities within. For example research Kurzman (2012: 2–3) cites three senior figures on the terrorist threat: Robert Mueller, Director of the FBI told Congress that 'FBI investigations have revealed militant Islamics [sic] in the US. We strongly suspect that several hundred of these extremists are linked to al-Qaeda'; in March 2011 Mueller testified to Congress that 'we are seeing an increase in the sources of terrorism, a wider array of terrorist targets, and an evolution in terrorist tactics and communication'; and Janet Napolitano, Secretary of the Department of Homeland Security, said in a 2011 address that 'the terrorist threat facing our country has evolved significantly in the last ten years – and continues to evolve – so that, in some ways, the threat facing us is at its most heightened since those attacks'.

But on the other hand, Kurzman's research discovered that these fears were not borne out in the actual numbers of Muslims indicted on terrorism in the United States, and that although radicalisation exists, '[t]he limited scale of Muslim-American terrorism in 2011 runs counter to the fears that many Americans shared in the days and months after 9/11, that domestic Muslim-American terrorism would escalate' (Kurzman 2012: 8). Despite this, reports suggest that there will be further congressional hearings on home-grown Muslim radicalism (Kim 2012). Similarly, in the face of widespread concerns about the ability of Muslims to integrate into Western democracies, from a survey of 1,033 American Muslims the Pew Research Center

(2011) found that Muslims in the United States are far from being radicalised, alienated, or poorly integrated. The study also found that the percentage of American Muslims who believe there is no conflict between being a devout Muslim and modernity was almost to the number of Christian Americans who felt the same way about conflicts between faith and modernity in an earlier survey (Kim 2012: 36). Similarly, the percentage of American Muslims who thought of themselves as Muslim first and American second was only 3 per cent higher than the number of American Christians surveyed earlier who thought of themselves as Christian first (Kim 2012: 34).

It seems that what is at stake in the different positions is not primarily the strength of one set of empirical claims versus another, but rather the very terms on which we can make our claims – that is, the way we can tell our stories. Nor are these workings-through limited to academics, politicians, or security tsars. In a world in which surveys find startling numbers of US citizens who actually believe the conspiracy theories that their President, Barack Obama is a foreigner and, worse, a secret Muslim, these attempts to find a language for the Muslim question are being worked through all kinds of surprising narrations. In some way, we can all be affected or involved in these struggles over language. Nor is there a benign or responsible uniformity in the attempts to find a way to narrate the Muslim question, as became obvious through the emergence of an increasingly visible 'backlash' against Muslims across Europe (cf. Allen and Nielson 2002) and the United States (cf. Esposito and Kalin 2011). This backlash is often termed Islamophobia, and it cannot be easily exceptionalised; some even suggest that it has been reproduced on an industrial scale in the media to feed wider patterns of racial hate against Muslims (Steuter and Wills 2008).

No case more clearly illustrates this problem than the attacks launched by Anders Behring Breivik in July 2011. With two related terrorist attacks, the London-born Norwegian launched his war against what he saw as the Islamisation of Europe. Breivik's first attack was a bombing in Oslo; disguised as a policeman he then made his way to Utoya island, where he beckoned young Norwegians attending a left-wing liberal youth camp to gather round him for safety. Breivik then produced an automatic weapon and began indiscriminately mowing down the youngsters, calmly walking around the island to hunt them down. Sixty-nine were killed. This was not an attack against

Muslims, but it was a strike against the left-wing multicultural elites that he claimed were tacitly responsible for the stealth Islamisation of the West, and it was the first strike in what Breivik termed a civil war. Breivik's background was unremarkable; the son of a diplomat he was well educated and seemingly a model citizen – if one is able to ignore his bizarre claims about his mother having venereal disease, his resentment towards feminists, his hatred of immigrants, Muslims and multiculturalists, and his addiction to computer games. In his teens he had joined the right-wing Progress Party, later claiming to have been attracted by its anti-immigration stance. The attacks he launched at the age of 32 had taken up to a decade of planning and meticulous preparation. That same attention to detail would later resurface during police questioning, when Breivik recounted details of the youths he had hunted down, apparently ensuring his work would be recorded (Heyer and Traufetter 2011). Breivik detailed some of his planning in a diary and rambling manifesto in which he drew attention to the NATO bombing of Serbia, the Rushdie affair, the furore over the Danish cartoons featuring caricatures of Muslims as terrorists and depicting Muhammad with a bomb in his turban, and highlighting Muslim immigration to Norway (Friedlander 2011). Breivik's case tells us a story about far-right Islamophobia; his conspiracy theories about a threat of Islamisation fuelled by multiculturalism and left-wing elites are rehearsed across the blogosphere and resonate with views held by the organised far right across Europe and the United States, as well as those held by some more mainstream figures (Fekete 2012). Breivik claimed to have links with members of far-right groups across Europe, which in turn caused some far-right groups to distance themselves from his actions. The BBC quoted a Norwegian terrorism expert who was aware of Breivik's web postings as suggesting that in the context of his online discussions with others in the far right, 'Breivik did not stand out with a particularly aggressive or violent rhetoric. He was quite mainstream' (BBC News 2011).

Brevik's case also highlighted another feature of the contemporary far right; stopping short of describing himself as a member of the extreme right, he declared his politics as 'Cultural conservatism, or a nationalist/conservative orientation known as the Vienna school of thought. As for the political movement, I would describe it as a national resistance movement, an indigenous-rights movement or even a right-revolutionary movement' (Friedlander 2011). This finds its echoes across Europe as far-right groups reposition themselves as respectable, describing themselves simply as being culturally conservative, and frequently declaring themselves to be the defenders of indigenous rights. The far right appropriates the progressive language of the mainstream it attacks; in some kind of perverse post-political parody, the political mainstream responds to the threat of the far right by hardening its stance on immigration, appropriating, it seems, from the far right. No wonder in the final hearing before his trial, Breivik demanded a medal (Waterfield 2012). Even more curious; in his manifesto Breivik actually denied his own Islamophobia, claiming that he didn't actually *hate* Muslims; he simply loved his country and culture. Denial and Islamophobia? Now *there's* a story …

It is also an important question because, in spite of the hate attacks that take place with increasing frequency, one of the most important ways in which people have sought to deny the existence of Islamophobia is by seeking to reduce it to the banal question of religion. Thus, the argument goes that what is at stake is not the right of minorities to protection against an increasingly prevalent racism, but simply our right to criticise religious beliefs. But I am not sure this will do as a definition for Islamophobia. This logic presupposes a hard distinction between race and religion that might appear superficially compelling but which fails to account for the contingencies of a world in which even religious subjects are racialised, or the interplay between race and religion. This book does not, therefore, engage with questions about any supposed essential opposition between Muslims and secularism, nor with the prospects of post-secularism, nor with questions of religious discrimination. What it deals with is the relationship between Islamophobia and racism. It seems that there is more at stake here, and a more complex picture of displacement and effacement of the political primarily in relation to the apparent impossibility of openly discussing Islamophobia as a primarily racist expression. In part this focus might reflect the fact that I have no academic interest in religion and no personal investment in it, having lost all faith in god and religion at some point over the past decade. More fundamentally than this it reflects the importance of tracing out the emergence of Islamophobia in relation to changing expressions of racial politics, and in recognising that simply to criticise a religion is not necessarily to be Islamophobic.

Telling Tales

Lieutenant Columbo is ambling ever closer to solving the case, and has just observed 'that maybe a real detective doesn't belong in the movies'. Perhaps we can take something from this; perhaps real subjects do not always belong in books either. But unlike Columbo I cannot fall back upon some intuitive positivism or pluck out a curiously apodictic conclusion with which to end my tale. I cannot offer any dramatic flashes of logic to illuminate the scene; there is no great revelation of the true order of things; I have no subjects to grill. Instead I ask only that you remain mindful that this is but a story and, as I seek to tell it through discourse theory, ask that you remember this epistemology 'is not (and should not) be read as another royal road to wisdom. Its usefulness can be judged only as one would judge a piece of literature or cinema. Namely, is the story that it tells compelling?' (Sayyid and Zac 1998: 256). Truly rich tapestries have been woven around Muslim minorities in the West, from ethnographic accounts to media exposés, and from far-right propaganda to mainstream political demands that the unintegrable finally give up whatever beef they hold towards Western values and, well, just *integrate*. Sheehi (2011) and numerous others have explored the various modes of constructing contemporary knowledge about Muslims, so recognising that there is precious little to be added to such a fruitful line of inquiry, and an ever-decreasing number of native informants to be fetishised, I am more concerned with finding the loose thread to see how the picture unravels...

I am really seeking to narrate a story about the stories we tell about Others. Although Islamophobia is a comparatively recent entry to the political lexicon, it has been the object of increasing scholarly interest (cf. Allen 2010; Geaves *et al* 2004; Gottschalk and Greenberg 2008; Sayyid and Vakil 2011). Despite this increasing coverage, none of it has really sought to systematically situate Islamophobia on a wider field of racial politics. My aim in this book is therefore to offer a conceptual account of Islamophobia as a political expression of racism. All stories must start somewhere, but I want to avoid starting at the beginning with some simple linear account. Instead I want to start by considering how the naming and conception of Islamophobia itself unravels. It is therefore helpful to briefly sketch out the conceptual vocabulary through which I seek to elaborate my account of Islamophobia.

The need for a conceptual engagement with Islamophobia is illustrated by the continued debates surrounding the nature of the phenomenon – is it merely religious discrimination, or more properly related to racism? – and even the utility of the term itself. In the context of war on terror in which acts of Islamist terrorism have come increasingly to the forefront of public and political consciousness, there has been a dramatic increase in the level of public awareness about Muslims (and about Islam, although the latter is not a focus for this book). As the question of exactly who Muslims are has become increasingly prominent, we have witnessed countless media investigations and exposés, interventions by think-tanks, and studies funded by states, frequently under the auspices of counter-terrorism work but also framed by wider concerns about integration. All of this has occurred as a supplement to more traditional forms of academic enquiry, in which questions about Muslims and their relationship to the West have been increasingly posed and investigated. It seems that knowledge about Muslims is not a major problem for us in contemporary times.

If there is no shortage of information about Muslims in the public domain, in shorter supply have been attempts to think through conceptually the terms on which we have come to understand the signifier Muslim. This question is at the heart of this book, since the continued debates over how Islamophobia can most fruitfully be understood – whether as a fabrication, as merely a form of religious discrimination, or as an expression of racism – reflect a series of underlying, but frequently unexamined, questions concerning the terms on which Muslim identities are to be grasped. In political practice the question of what does the signifier Muslim take as its object is reflected in contests over the content of the signified, as Islamists on the one hand promote a particular way of understanding what Muslim means and how it can be mobilised in politics to create a counter-secular subject position, while on the other hand Western states have increasingly attempted to promote an understanding of Muslim that is more compatible with liberal secularism, neoliberal accumulation, and democracy by seeking to foster 'moderate' Muslim subject positions. At stake in both academic understanding and in political practice is therefore an underlying question concerning the ways in which the term Muslim is used, and an implicit recognition that this in turn has implications for political practice and for proper understanding of Islamophobia. But such questions are frequently under-explored in the academic literature. Simply to investigate, say, the ways in which the media or states represent Muslims does not necessarily shift us beyond an apodictic understanding of the term; the oft-repeated claim that the media offers a distorted representation of Muslims implies a kernel of truth that can be mined as the ultimate arbiter of correctness or distortion. In other words, the assumption remains that the locus of our attempts to think through Islamophobia lies not in thinking critically through the terms of debate, but rather that it lies in deploying the correct 'facts' about Muslims.

In this book I want to shift away from such an emphasis to explore the ways in which the signifier Muslim is deployed, and to consider how the contests which surround it also reflect struggles over the nature of the social, and how they have the effect of instituting particular subject positions that can be occupied, struggled over, renounced, or transformed through political practice. Such an endeavour requires me to shift away from empiricism and to locate myself within conceptual and methodological approaches to the analysis of discourse. In this I want to begin by suggesting that there is no kernel of truth to which any signifier is innately connected. Take, for example, the signifier 'chair'. If one asks what 'chair' means, the response might be that a chair is something with four legs. But so, too, might a grand piano have four legs. Ah, might come the response, 'but you can sit on a chair'. But one can also sit on horses, which also have four legs. This glib aside is intended to illustrate a fundamental point about the language we use, insofar as our words do not access any innate kernel of truth, but merely direct us to other words. In this, I am not suggesting that there is no reality, as the glib denunciations of post-structuralism so frequently posit. Rather, I want to suggest that there is indeed something called the real that exists beyond the symbolic, but that language gets in the way of our being able to directly access it. Our attempts to insert the real into the symbolic order have the effect of constructing something called reality, which is entirely mediated and constituted by language.

There is no social phenomenon about which we can speak without recourse to language. So, to return to the earlier example, even if we ignore that not every chair has four legs or that not everything that people sit on can be classified as a chair, our arbiter of what might or might not be understood as a chair is not some innate property of chairness, but rather a product of a particular set of conventions, expressed through language, which have provided a particular way of envisaging, understanding, bringing into being, and using, certain artefacts as chairs. This is not a product of some ahistorical essence of chairness, for if it were so, then one would be forced to assume that chairs had existed in some more or less stable form since before the advent of the signifier itself. This book therefore begins from the realisation that there is no way to speak of social phenomenon other than through language, and that there is no language with which to speak of them other than language itself; even empirical claims do not exist outside language and their referents can only be understood and enunciated through language. Richard Rorty has expressed this in a rather more elegant manner by noting that:

> Truth cannot be out there – cannot exist independently of the human mind – because sentences cannot so exist, or be out there. The world is out there, but the descriptions of the world are not. Only descriptions of the world can be true or false. The world on its own-unaided by the describing activities of human beings-cannot ... When the notion of 'descriptions of the world' is moved from the level of criterion-governed sentences within language games to language games as wholes, games which we do not choose between by reference to criteria, the idea that the world describes which descriptions can no longer be given a clear sense. (Rorty 1989: 5)

As such, this book is located within anti-foundationalist theory, an approach that privileges the analysis of discourse and the concept of the political. The term discourse has been used in many different ways within social sciences research, including socio-linguistics and ethnomethodology. As an analytical approach, it is most explicitly associated with critical discourse analysis, a range of approaches associated with the work of Fairclough (1995) and Van Dijk (2008) among others. Influenced by the work of Foucault, critical discourse analysis tends to treat discourse as something more than merely written or spoken languages, and as a subset of social practices. This book is informed not by discourse analysis, but rather by a strand of post-structuralist political theory known as discourse theory. A set of approaches influenced by the works of Jacques Derrida, Jacques Lacan, Julia Kristeva, and Judith Butler, the emergence of theory as a political analytic was informed in particular by the work of Ernesto Laclau and Chantal Mouffe (1985). Discourse theory in this sense does not provide a structured methodology for social and political investigation, but rather it provides an ensemble of analytic tools which can be brought to bear on the analysis of meanings and political practices in a contingent and radically contested social terrain.

Discourse theory posits a broader understanding of discourse than does critical discourse analysis, recognising all meaning bearing practices, customs, beliefs, and activities as reflecting a discursive logic. Discourse theory therefore rejects superficial assumptions concerning a distinction between the discursive and the extra discursive, instead concerning itself with the articulation of linguistic and non-linguistic elements in discourse (Barnard-Wills 2012: 66). The starting point for discourse theory is that the meanings of all social phenomena are bestowed through discourse (Carpentier and De Cleen 2007: 267). This does not validate the facile rejections of anti-foundationalism ('everything is socially constructed'), because discourse theory is not in fact based on the idea that things are constructed through language. Rather, discourse theory recognises that the only ways in which events and entities can be accessed is through the use of language (Sayyid and Zac 1998). Sjölander (2011: 27) notes, to suggest that objects are constituted as objects through discourse is not a question of whether or not entities exist outside language and thought, but rather that the meanings they assume depend on the ways in which they emerge as objects of discourse. Sjölander cites Laclau and Mouffe's (1985: 108) example of earthquakes to support this point, and this is a helpful metaphor for phenomena knowable as earthquakes exist independently of the language we use to describe them. However, different discourses provide different grammars that can be used to narrate them, and these in turn establish conventions that establish the plausibility (or otherwise) or different modes of analysis, explanation, and action. To use an example once taught to me when I was a Master's student, in Norse mythology, earthquakes were said to be caused when the gods trapped Loki and suspended a snake above his head; as Loki's wife Sigyn caught the venom, she spilled a drop, and Loki's resulting painful writhing caused earthquakes (Lindow

2001). To speak of earthquakes in the contemporary world is clearly likely to conjure rather different ways of debating and understanding the same phenomenon. Irrespective of the empirical claims on which hegemonic contemporary explanations for earthquakes might be based, their explanations are contingent upon a range of conventions governing the production of scientific knowledge at a particular point in history, and in turn they constitute the earthquake in particular, historically contingent ways.

For this reason, one of the widely held criticisms of discourse theory is that it erases certainty and reduces a complex world to one of endless relativity. Such criticisms miss the point of discourse theory, which is not concerned with divining an eternal kernel of truth underlying complex social phenomena, but which is rather concerned with the ways in which attempts are made to fix and contest meanings. This is not a question of simple relativism, but rather it is centrally concerned with revealing the politicality of the social. In this it is helpful to note the privileging of the political within contemporary discourse theory. The sedimented practices and relations that comprise the social can be said to be constituted through discourse; that is, they have arisen as a result of hegemonic ways of attaching meaning to them as a basis for organising society (Barnard-Wills 2012: 72). After Laclau and Mouffe (1985), we can understand the political as a moment of institution; a radical rupturing that can take the form either of an attempt to institute new social relations, or as the moment at which the contingency of existing social relations is laid bare. The emphasis within discourse theory on recognising contingency and rejecting essentialism is far from being an anti-political pursuit of groundless relativism. Rather, discourse theory provides an assemblage of conceptual tools with which to step outside the comfort zone of what we take for granted as the true order of things and to instead account for the centrally political nature of the contests that are played out in different ways of accounting for the same social entity or phenomenon.

Let us take, for example, the question of Muslim identities. The question of how Muslim identities can best be understood lies at the heart of debates about the nature of Islamophobia. Following some apodictic logic, some tend to suggest that if Muslims can be categorised as having *essentially* religious identities, then any discrimination that they face must be better understood as religious rather than racial discrimination. In other words, even though it is widely established that modern racial categories have no basis in science, the assumption is that racism can only be traced out in cases where the recipient has an *essential* racial identity. From within the terms of my discourse theoretical approach, I am inclined to approach this problematic rather differently, as will be clear throughout the course of this book. First, the persistence of such debates reveals the ways in which the same group of people come to be organised through discursive categories in different ways at different points in history, as groups previously identified in terms of assumed primordial ethnicity or ascribed phenotype increasingly identify (or are identified) as Muslims. As such, they highlight the contingency and contestedness of the language that we use to make sense of human agents.

Second, in highlighting this contingency, they also draw our attention to the playing out of a racial politics that seems to have come into play, not simply in response to acts of Islamist terrorism and mass murder, but also in response to shifts and tensions within the dominant racial grammar in society. Simply to assume 'they are Muslims' or to attempt to divine whether they are Muslims or members of some other, assumed primordial group, is not an analytical task but a normative one. The analytical task is actually to uncover the politics at stake in the tensions that such questions imply, the ways in which they reveal the contingency of prior namings and racialisation, how this plays out against a wider racial politics, and the different social relations and political practices that are made possible through the different ways in which the category of Muslim is constructed through Islamophobia, as well as in response to the emergence of a phenomenon increasingly organised under its naming as Islamophobia. Discourse theory is a helpful approach to the study of such phenomena precisely because it rejects essentialism. Writing from a background in critical race theory, I am all too aware that essentialism is a central technique of racism (cf. Patel and Tyrer 2011).

At this point it is helpful to briefly sketch out three concepts that are important to discourse theory. Having already noted that discourse can be understood as an assemblage of meaningful activities and practices, it is helpful to note the concept of articulation which is central to discourse theory. First, articulation can be understood as the process through which different discursive elements are combined in attempts to establish meanings by establishing certain relations between signifiers (Laclau and Mouffe 1985). Second, nodal points play an important role in attempts to fix meanings. Because discourse is fundamentally slippery and contested, certain types of signifier are introduced which act as nodal points, or quilting points, around which other signifiers will be arranged. Quilting is a helpful metaphor for this process; the reader can picture a chair with quilted upholstery and consider the buttons as quilting points, with the lines that fold into them being the signifiers that they organise and attempt to fix or fasten. The Gramscian concept of hegemony is helpful in shedding analytical light on the ways in which discourses are quilted around certain nodal points, since the successful establishment of a nodal point in discourse is a hegemonic act designed to stabilise and fix meanings. Third, the concept of subject position is helpful in drawing attention to the ways in which discourse works to open particular types of political possibility. All social agents have identities, but what is often simplistically termed 'multiple identities' – that is, simultaneously being a teacher, a brother, a socialist – are better understood not as being multiple identities, which would imply a somehow fractured subjectivity, but rather as multiple subject positions. Depending on how we are positioned within particular discourses with which we identify or are identified with, we occupy a range of subject positions. Within the hegemonic discourse of family, for example, I might occupy the subject position 'brother' but not other positions. These subject positions open certain possibilities for political practice while foreclosing others, but what they mean is ultimately also contested. For example, when people of Pakistani heritage occupy the subject position of 'Asian', the ways in which they are racialised make it possible to express agency in quite distinct ways in order to resist racism, affecting everything from the type of alliances they can form to the ways in which they can name (as 'racism') the phenomenon they seek to challenge. However, when they adopt a 'Muslim' subject position, either through choice or ascription, the type of alliances they can form might be transformed, and even the naming of the phenomenon they face might be contested (whether it is racism, or Islamophobia).

In sketching out the conceptual terrain of this book in terms of discourse theory, it is helpful to note that the analytical tools from which I draw are associated with the horizon opened by the discourse theoretical approach of Laclau and Mouffe (1985), elsewhere elaborated by Howarth *et al* (2000), Sayyid and Zac (1998), and Torfing (1999) among others. This book also reflects a concern with biopower, and as such it is important to note that there is some congruence between later Foucault and the discourse theory of Laclau and Mouffe, such that Barnard-Wills (2012: 64) suggests that they can be construed as being part of the same analytic. This book is not Foucaultian, but a sensibility informed by Foucault haunts the concerns I address and the ways in which I engage them.

Structure

Since wherever one starts becomes by definition the beginning, by critically opening out Islamophobia on a wider field of contestation, I want to set the scene for the racial politics that follows not only from the phenomenon, but also its naming and conception. At this stage I want to set out five brief observations that I think highlight some of the questions at stake in the racial politics of Islamophobia:

1. The emergence of contemporary Islamophobia appears to relate to a wider move through which racialised subjects have increasingly identified under a common Muslim identity. This is not simply a question of identity politics but has wider implications for the politics of racialisation.
2. The implications of this transnational subject position for racial politics have been reflected in an increasing concern about the mis/recognition of Muslims.
3. The apparent tension between Islamophobia and hegemonic understandings of racism is reflected in its naming.
4. In spite of the tendency to exceptionalise racism, the rise of a popular politics of Islamophobia reveals the extent to which post-racial racism has inflected the mainstream.
5. Debates over Islamophobia do not only reflect questions about racial politics, but also present wider questions that are framed by a condition often termed post-politics.

1. Islamophobia and identity politics

Although the war on terror provided new ways of quilting existing representations of Others, Islamophobia predated 9/11. Its origins can be traced to an identity politics through which racialised subjects sought to express an agency not generally afforded within the racism's biopolitical logic, through the collective assumption of a naming ('Muslim') that disrupted previous namings and racial ascriptions. This is not simply an abstract question, but more of a problem. In liberal regimes, in which participation is contingent upon recognition of a stable identity, the terms on which subjects are recognised have a great impact on the kinds of subject positions they can adopt (e.g. whether racial or religious), and thus the kinds of politics in which they can engage. Of course, if the identities themselves (or the terms on which they have been symbolised) are destabilised, there are obvious implications for a system based on straightforward knowability and unproblematised recognition. That is to say: how do you even know who you think you know any more? In broader terms, it also creates another type of political problem if subjects start renaming themselves in large numbers, since this disrupts conventional knowledge frames, destabilises the play of identities in a racialised social setting, and in doing so, it has the effect of placing the ontology of the social into crisis (Tyrer and Sayyid 2012). The emergence of a Muslim identity politics has thus posed a political question, and the ways in which it has been answered have often conventionally involved some sort of positivist deduction through which we can ascertain whether the identities at state are ontically pure racial subjects or ontically pure religious subjects.

The difficulty we have here is that we live in societies with long histories of embedded racial symbolic systems to such an extent that it can be easy not to notice just how fundamental racial classification is to the organisation of social life. So aside from the fact that there are no ontically pure racial or religious identities in the first place, the attempt to categorise Muslims as ontically pure religious subjects institutes a whole new racial politics, because it involves marking them as non-racial. In societies in which raciality, subjecthood, and recognition are closely bound up these non-racial subjects thus seem somehow incomplete, incorporeal, and absent, because everyone (even white people, the invisible), has a proper raciality. These questions are not peripheral to Islamophobia, but they are central to it. They are central to the expression of Islamophobia, which constructs Muslims as incomplete subjects, and they are central to the very naming and popular conception of Islamophobia as a non-racism.

2. Mis/recognition and racialised subjects

The thing about colour coding the world is that it grossly simplifies things to such an extent one can easily forget that each time we racially recognise other subjects, we are not simply reading racial meanings off their skin, but we are inscribing them onto their very bodies. This is quite a violent way of describing a violent practice that doesn't always seem so because after a couple of hundred years of practice, it has become routinised, normalised, and even commoditised. Within this common sense world, what happens if somebody wants to step outside the logic of race is a political question (cf. Sayyid 2004) because it has the potential to throw the whole system into chaos. At its most banal, it makes it very different to recognise who is who any more. Such situations create anxiety, and where there is anxiety there is always the possibility that mistakes will be made. For example, during the war on terror a new mode of racism emerged under the label of 'mistaken identity'. The canonical form of this new racism involved Sikhs in the West being abused, attacked (and sometimes murdered) by people who apparently mistook them for either Osama bin Laden (yes, really), or just a random Muslim. Such cases are interesting for three reasons. First, they illustrate how easily one can conjure up a phantasmatic Other to overcome all the anxieties that arise from not really knowing who you can trust in a dangerous, political world, or even who is who any more. Second, they illustrate the spillover effect of Islamophobia and its purchase over a wider field of racial politics; in this they underline that Islamophobia is far more fundamental to contemporary racism than many people assume. Third, they highlight an interesting paradox at the heart of Islamophobia's very definition, under which the same act can be defined in very different ways depending on the subjects involved (as non-racism or as racism).

The problem of Muslim mis/recognition also relates to the wider concerns about Muslim integration that have emerged, for there are clear implications for the politics of integration based on traditional understandings of racial politics when confronted with a group that seems to step outside the grammar of race. It is therefore striking that such concerns are presented as new and contemporary, when in fact they have been openly expressed for considerable lengths of time in a range of contexts. For example, in the United Kingdom the trope of the supposed political excess of the inassimilable other became an organising feature of racial politics even earlier than that with the famous 'rivers of blood' speech by Conservative MP Enoch Powell in 1968, which Hewitt (2005: 25) goes still further to suggest it was influenced by debates about immigration in the United States. Moreover, Powell's speech received considerable support – some trade union groups organised marches of support. Nor in France, where Sarkozy thrice described banlieues rioters as *racailles* (*Le Monde* 2005) when Minister of the Interior, has there been a lack of mainstream debate about immigrant assimilability, and its figuring in racial politics saw the rise of the Front National gather pace from the 1980s onwards. In Germany, too, where former chancellor Helmut Schmidt argued that successful multiculturalism requires an authoritarian state (Deaux 2006: 37) and that 'to convert them [Muslims] to democracy will take generations' (Prizel 2008: 35), there had been an increasing focus on integration following Schmidt's election as chancellor in 1980, after which he had proposed the need to integrate existing immigrants while concluding that four million immigrants was enough (Martin 2002: 12). As Paul (2009: 2) notes, even as multiculturalism has been advertised in Germany, it has been accompanied by a proliferation of media headlines proclaiming its failure, and the dual nature of multiculturalism as encompassing a responsibility to integrate was reflected in Berlin's 2007 slogan for integration: '*Vielfalt fördern – Zusammenhalt stärken*' ('Supporting diversity – strengthening cohesion'). Work by Bommes (2010) is helpful in drawing attention to the ways in which social sciences research on immigrants in Germany emerged with a strong focus on integration as a problem, further underlining that it is not only in politics, but also in academic research, that integration has been a long-standing topic for discussion. The contemporary panics about the failures of integration and multiculturalism mask longer disc/continuities which in turn help place Islamophobia in the context of wider racial politics, while also pointing to the ways in which Muslim subject positions appear to interrupt established racial politics.

3. Naming Islamophobia

But Islamophobia is not simply a matter of seeing difference, for it is a most fervid discourse, capable of mobilising a range of passions. In his novel *Atomised* Michel Houellebecq writes that:

This book is principally the story of a man who lived out the greater part of his life in Western Europe, in the latter half of the twentieth century. Though alone for much of his life, he was nonetheless closely in touch with other men. He lived through an age that was miserable and troubled. The country into which he was born was sliding slowly, ineluctably, into the ranks of the less developed countries… (Houellebecq 1999: 3)

I wanted to cite Houellebecq for two reasons. Houellebecq is one of many people who have found themselves accused of causing offence to Muslims, a topic to which this book will shortly turn. In Houellebecq's case, he actually faced trial for criticising Islam and was acquitted. More importantly, the protagonist in Houellebecq's opening passage seems laden with underlying anxieties about the decline of previous certainties. In a wider condition of generalised fear and anxieties, what does it mean to speak of the centrally affective and emotional investments made in Islamophobia? If we are interested in the stories that people are telling about the world around them and their Others, surely we also have to listen to the mood music that sets the scene.

But why stop there? If Islamophobia sporadically erupts from these wider anxieties in violent moments of hate and fear, should we not also consider its emotional and affective investments? If we are to do so, it seems that we also have to address the *–phobia* inscribed in its very naming, and consider what is at stake in this for our understanding of anti-Muslim racism: are emotion and affect really all that irrational, or are they central to a particular political rationality of racism? Accepting that feelings matter does not just help us historicise Islamophobia, it also helps us analytically.

4. Beyond exceptional racism

The Breivik case highlights the links between an international network of hard-right activists mobilising against what they feel is a threat of Islamisation. Islamophobia and the rise of the far right seem intertwined, but how? There must be more to this than simply reflecting the fears of wider populations and governments about extremism. At the same time, it is often possible to see some resemblances between the far right's discourse on Muslims and expressions in the political mainstream, as far-right activists appeal to progressive notions such as rights, and politicians of the centrist neoliberal consensus harden their lines on immigration and integration. One way of looking at this is to suggest that they are all just cynically appropriating each other's lines to keep the plot muddling along without any serious mishaps. But the problem of contemporary racial politics runs deeper than this, and it is helpful to place this muddled politics in the context of a wider condition that has been marked by the displacement under post-politics of the political itself. The problematisation of difference is also part of this process, so understanding how a particular mode of neoliberal politics frames the emergence of particular forms of racial politics is helpful in placing Islamophobia politically and historically.

5. Islamophobia and politics

Muslims are increasingly reminded of their responsibilities to integrate. This is not in itself problematic, because government itself relies upon subjects accepting their position within particular symbolic systems (law, say). In the case of Islamophobia it becomes problematic because Muslim integration is often broached in terms that suggest their very difference itself is the obstacle to their integration. Once you approach problems dealing with particular subjects as not being contingent and political (and therefore, addressable through political practice), but rather being a product of what makes 'them' *them*, it actually becomes very difficult to organise a functional plural democratic society, because the emphasis is no longer framed in terms of contingent problems that can be easily addressed without stereotyping entire groups, but in terms of identities themselves (which are far harder to transform). One way in which we see this problem manifest is in terms of the way that Muslim political identities are framed. This is not peripheral to the problem of Islamophobia, but central to it. If Islamophobia is viewed as a non-racism on the problematic grounds that Muslims are not ontically pure racial subjects, then this in turn institutes particular subject positions that can be occupied in political practice. One manifestation of this been the emergence of a politics of offence through which Muslims are engaged as a culturally different population that apparently threatens 'our' way of life. While debating and criticising religion should not necessarily be seen as Islamophobic, because of its problematic conceptualisation, the politics of offence has been repeatedly appropriated and mobilised (for example, by far-right groups) as a way of targeting minorities without facing accusations of racism. In turn, because this problematic conceptualisation displaces substantive political engagements with the racial politics at stake in Islamophobia, Muslim minorities have often found themselves pursuing a politics of offence in the absence of other political alternatives. This comes down to an underlying question concerning how those represented as lacking or excessive – the abject (Kristeva 1982) – can engage in politics on the very terms that mark their abjection. It also underlines the importance of engendering more imaginative approaches to the question of Muslim politics.

These five points draw attention to some of the central questions and challenges presented by the politics of Islamophobia, and they are explored in the chapters that follow. As I explore these questions I shall draw attention to the ways in which a particular hegemonic discourse that I term Islamophobia has found its expression across multiple dispersed and often seemingly contradictory nodal points to construct Muslims in particular ways. At various points I shall also draw upon metaphors from popular culture. I do this partly as a means of providing illustration for underlying points. I also do it because, as Tyrer and Sayyid (2012) note, popular culture provides resources that can be called upon in order to illustrate or interrogate tensions within hegemonic epistemes. Popular cultural representations of ethnicised and racialised minorities have frequently drawn upon problematic hegemonic ideas about race. This also works in a less obvious manner insofar as the tensions and preoccupations worked through in more banal ways in popular culture often also tell us something about wider cultural and political conditions that can also frame, in more subtle ways, questions concerning the knowability of the social world.

Anyway – enough of the talking...

1

Framing Islamophobia

So, where to begin? Perhaps we should start at the beginning by pointing out that Islamophobia is a form of religious discrimination that emerged most forcefully as a backlash against Muslims in the wake of the terrorist atrocities that occurred on 11 September 2001. Only it didn't. The term was originally coined in the late 1980s (Quraishi 2005: 60). Then again, it had first been used some decades earlier at the start of the twentieth century (Vakil 2011). But wait, for Islamophobia is not a form of religious discrimination at all, but an emblematic expression of contemporary biopolitical racism (Tyrer 2011). Anyway, these conflicting accounts are actually of little consequence, since Islamophobia does not even exist other than as a cynically imagined political device designed to override our right to offend the foolish by critiquing their beliefs (Toynbee 2005). Since these disagreements over Islamophobia are so fundamental to its meaning, we really ought to start over from a different point of departure and begin with a recognition of its contestedness, for perhaps in this we can find the key to unlock the politics at stake in Islamophobia. To do this it is helpful to begin in Britain since this is where such contests first emerged in their current form and have been most visibly played out, and then to broaden our understanding of this field of contest to other fronts.

Although the term Islamophobia has a longer history than is often acknowledged, the publication of the Runnymede Trust's report *Islamophobia: A Challenge for Us All* (Runnymede Trust 1997) revived the term and opened up a new political field by drawing attention to the phenomenon of discrimination against Muslims that seemed to occur in a number of fields and which was increasingly visible in media portrayals. The context in which the report was produced was shaped by two related factors. First, an earlier report on anti-Semitism published by the Trust (Runnymede Trust 1994) had recommended that a similar report on discrimination facing Muslims be produced. This implied an acknowledgement that Islamophobia's form is not unique, but that there are certain parallels with wider expressions of racism with which we are familiar in the West. Second, a significant shift in racial politics in Britain had witnessed the emergence of a Muslim identity politics that appeared to displace traditional modes of identification along the lines of established racial and ethnic signifiers, and this brought into play questions concerning the relating emergence of a form of discrimination that emerged around their naming as Muslims. The report termed this form of discrimination Islamophobia, a naming that had the effect of exceptionalising Islamophobia by disarticulating it from wider expressions of racism with which it seemed to share a family appearance. This move was cemented through the report's definition of Islamophobia as 'unfounded hostility towards Islam' (Runnymede Trust 1997: 4), which combined with the reference to Islam in its coining to open a space for conceiving of Islamophobia as a form of religious, rather than racial, discrimination. This definition was qualified with the recognition that Islamophobia 'refers also to the practical consequences of such hostility in unfair discrimination against Muslim individuals and communities, and to the exclusion of Muslims from mainstream political and social affairs' (Runnymede Trust 1997: 4). This recognition implied that religion was not the only thing at stake in Islamophobia, but that the treatment of human populations was also a factor, and as such it hinted at the possibility that its manifestations mirrored those of racism. But the curious thing about the ensuing debates was the extent to which they mobilised a curious series of narrative devices that had the effect of instituting a quest to isolate the ontically pure form taken by Muslim identities as a means of determining whether Islamophobia could most helpfully be understood as racial or religious. At the heart of these contests was the notion that subjects who are essentially religious experience religious discrimination while those who are essentially racial experience racism, and as they played out they gave way to a wider politics concerned not simply with the terms on which we can construe Islamophobia, but with the pursuit of a politics in which fictive racial certainties became the final arbiter of the political acceptability of enunciations about

Muslims. A more colloquial way of expressing this would be that a wider politics was introduced through the red herring of race.

What? Ham? Are You Crazy?

A synonym occasionally substituted for red herring is MacGuffin. Alfred Hitchcock used MacGuffins to good effect in a number of films including *North By Northwest*, in which Roger Thornhill (played by Cary Grant) finds himself at the sharp end of a manhunt having been mistaken for a man named Kaplan who possesses secret information. Now information, whether secret or otherwise, is always a good thing to have, but in this case it counts for nought, for neither the viewer nor Roger Thornhill ever discover what it is. In any case there is no guarantee that the real keeper of this information even exists. Hitchcock used the term MacGuffin to describe such futile devices, and his explanation of the term involved a conversation between two passengers on a train. One enquired into the nature of a package in the charge of his fellow passenger. The owner replied that it was a MacGuffin, which he defined as a contraption designed for catching lions in Scotland. When the first passenger drew attention to the absence of lions from the Highlands, the owner of the mysterious package replied 'Then that's no MacGuffin' (Cohen 2005: 156). A MacGuffin is thus a pretext or red herring (Insdorf 1994: 43); a device that has a presence in spite of its apparent immateriality, which is crucial in driving the plot forwards, and yet which is at the same time insignificant since it simply does not exist – nor does it matter – outside the economy of the plot it is deployed to press.

The notion of MacGuffin is an interesting metaphor for the politics at stake in how we understand what is meant by Islamophobia. For although it is well established that there is no scientific basis for the racial categories we use, debates about Islamophobia came to entail a quest to trace the existence of this most fluid and contested of social constructions as a means of determining whether or not Islamophobia can be said to exist. Within the terms of this debate, the idea was repeatedly expressed that since Muslim identities are not properly racial, either Islamophobia cannot be accurately described as racism or, worse, it cannot be said to exist at all. Thus, rather than engaging in a substantive analysis of the nature and form of Islamophobia and its positioning within a wider racial politics, the quest to uncover the essential nature of Muslim identities (whether properly racial or not) acted as a device that could drive forward a wider narrative of denial while foreclosing politicisation around experiences of Islamophobia. Race thus took the form of a red herring that could displace particular types of debates and modes of politics and institute others. But in itself there is nothing novel about the suggestion that Muslim identities lack a phenotypical basis. Once we accept that race has no scientific basis but instead refers to the ways in which subjects are constructed as racial, then to suggest that Muslim identities lack this biological racial ground is neither remarkable nor unique among social groups (Patel and Tyrer 2011). Thus: Muslims are not properly racial – but so what? In the style of our lion-hunting rail passenger, we could perhaps retort, 'Then that's no MacGuffin'.

Nevertheless the notion remains that the failure to trace a phenotypal basis for Muslim identities can undercut its recognition. For example, Weller (2006: 303) frames Islamophobia as discrimination on religious grounds and notes that the refocusing of the far right British National Party's racial politics onto Muslims constitutes a 'suspension' of its racist agenda (Weller 2006: 318). This is curious, for all the evidence suggests that its focus on Islamophobia does not displace its racial politics but that it is central to its contemporary articulation. To support his argument Weller cites Islamophobic BNP literature from 2001 issued under the slogan 'Winning for White Oldham: Winning for You' (Weller 2006: 318), but this undermines his position because a politics mobilised around racialised subject positions such as White is clearly organised under the horizon of race. That its Others are rearticulated as Muslim does not dispel its racial intent, but it does open up a new form of racial politics in which the ambiguous nature of Islamophobia (whether racial or religious) presents the opportunity for disavowal and denial of racism. The contests over the nature of Islamophobia and the continued deferral of its recognition as racism thus have the effect of keeping open spaces for the pursuit of racial politics that would otherwise appear politically incorrect, anachronistic, or extreme were traditional signifiers for racial difference to be employed. Across Europe and the United States, parties of the populist far right have made the most of this kind of MacGuffinery about phenotypical race that reduces the very definition of racial politics to a surface effect of the inherent biological difference of the racialised, rather than the contested object of a wider politics. The space opened by this reliance upon notions of the ontically pure racial subject as the determinant of racism has been exploited by the far right with a certain cynically knowing innocence. For example, on a number of occasions in 2008 British National Party activists issued Islamophobic leaflets and then, when their members were arrested, staged demonstrations that would coincide with the release without charge of the activists who, of course, had not committed crimes under UK race law (Patel and Tyrer 2011: 41). In 2006 the party's leader Nick Griffin – a man previously convicted of incitement to racial hatred on account of his holocaust denial – was again tried in court for incitement to racial hatred, this time on account of his Islamophobic rhetoric. Griffin and his co-defendant were, *of course*, cleared on this occasion, and in his defence Griffin made the key point that his views could not be described as racist precisely because they had not attacked a race. In contemporary far right discourse this logic is especially important, for in framing the disavowal of racism it enables political parties to remain within the terms of the law. For example, after the Flemish Vlaams Blok party was subjected to a de facto ban on grounds of discrimination in 2004, its relaunch as Vlaams Belang was accompanied by attempts to formally clean up its act while making the Muslim question even more central to its rhetoric; this was, after all, possible without risking the accusation of racism. In February 2012 Vlaams Belang politician Filip Dewinter initiated a 'women against Islamization' campaign accompanied by a poster in which an attractive young woman (his daughter) posed in bikini and burka, emblazoned – the poster, not the model – with the slogans: 'Vrijheid of islam? Durven kiezen!' [Freedom or Islam? Dare to choose!]. In an interview in *De Standaard* under the headline 'Dochter van Filip Dewinter is een boerkababe' [Filip Dewinter's daughter is a burkababe], An-Sofie Dewinter explained her decision to participate in the campaign on the grounds that 'women are fighting against the Islamization of society. We must dare to choose between freedom and Islam' (De Standaard 2012). This provided a justification of the campaign as simply a legitimate engagement over women's rights pursued through criticism of Islam in the abstract.

But there was more to the campaign than simply a critique of religion, and it also involved Filip Dewinter taking to the streets with two burka-clad women bearing posters emblazoned with the slogan 'Stop immigratie' [Stop immigration]. Indeed, in her interview with *De Standaard*, An-Sofie also claimed that White women are subjected to pressure over their attire by ethnic minority youth, and noted the prospect that they may eventually have to wear a headscarf, shifting the emphasis away from a critique of religion to the threat of Others. The attempt to deny the racist nature of Islamophobia is of utility in extending a particular racial politics without risking the accusation of racism, and in doing so it also centres problematic ideas of phenotypal racial difference, not by labelling Muslims as biologically bounded but by contrasting Muslims against other minorities who are held as such. It thus guarantees the continued hold of race as the basis for organising society and distinguishing between subjects, because it holds phenotypal race as the logical arbiter of whether racism can be said to exist. However, it also constructs Muslims as a lack – as lacking raciality. An important feature of the attempts to deny Islamophobia's racist nature is that they enable the far right to present themselves as defenders of democratic values such as free speech, through the argument that they are not targeting minority populations but simply criticising religion. In fact this putative defence of free speech is not the sole preserve of the populist and far right; Richardson (2004: 128) claims that liberals have used the question of free speech as a 'stock' topic against Muslims. Indeed, when the Runnymede Commission on British Muslims and Islamophobia first published its consultation paper, the *Independent on Sunday* newspaper ran a headline accusing the Runnymede Trust of wanting to be Islamically Correct (Runnymede Trust 1997: 4). Writing in the *Guardian* newspaper in the context of wider political debate about protection against anti-Muslim racism which she opposed, Toynbee (2005) asserted a hardened distinction between race and religion by way of arguing in turn that the notion of Islamophobia is simply a 'nonsense'. In a similar vein Kenan Malik (2005) retreated into similar factual MacGuffinery to argue not only that Muslims are not ontically racial, but moreover that the extent of Islamophobia has been exaggerated both to stifle free speech and consolidate the power of Muslim community leaders. In 2010 the novelist Ian McEwan broadened this, suggesting that to criticise Islam is not racist and that Islamists who promote such agendas are the 'shock-troops for the armchair left' (Adams 2010).

In turn this logic has given way to the emergence of a politics of offence involving contests over the right to offend Muslims. I shall return to this in Chapter 5, though for the time being I am concerned with how this has overshadowed attempts to recognise Islamophobia by reducing it simply to a question of the right to criticise religion. Thus, this politics emerges in the space opened by the contests over the nature of Islamophobia (which are themselves moored to assumptions about the ontic purity of racialised subjects). In this context the Netherlands has proved an important site of struggle over free speech. In 2004 the Dutch film-maker Theo van Gogh released his controversial film *Submission*, based on a script by Ayaan Hirsi Ali that engaged with the problem of violence against women in Muslim societies. Van Gogh's own advocacy for free speech was not unproblematic; some years previously he had been convicted of anti-Semitism. Following his murder at the hands of an Islamist extremist his renown grew, and the influence of the case on debates about Muslims and Islamophobia across Europe cannot be understated. Cherribi (2011) has demonstrated its role in shaping the emergence of Islamophobia beyond the Netherlands to Germany and Austria, arguing that 'neither the [Danish] cartoons [of the prophet Muhammad] nor [Geert] Wilder's *Fitna* would have been possible without the precedent of *Submission*, which raised the provocative spectre of what could be made of the Western free press among Islamic fundamentalists. After *Submission*, 'Europe simply could not leave the topic of the free press and Islam alone' (Cherribi 2010: 209). In the Netherlands Geert Wilders, Leader of the Party for Freedom (PVV), twice went to trial before finally being cleared of hate speech in 2011. Alexandre Caeiro and Frank Peter (2007) discuss a further case where in September 2006 a French teacher named Redeker wrote an article about the 'Islamic threat' that was published in *Le Figaro*. This led to criticism of the newspaper on *Al Jazeera* and its banning in Tunisia and Egypt, while the teacher received death threats that forced him out of his job and home. In the ensuing furore *Le Monde* published a cartoon that 'perhaps best expressed the angst of large sections of French society: in a depressing and sombre modern city populated by menacing women covered in black, a white Frenchman gesticulates anxiously to a friend about to eat a sandwich: "What? Ham? Are you crazy or what?"' (Caeiro and Peter 2007: 26). It is perhaps also worth noting that a *Le Monde* columnist also responded to Redeker's article by stating that 'We would certainly not have published it. Our "Debates" pages are not a place for empty insults but for analysis' (Todorov 2010: 147). In their discussion of the Redeker case Caeiro and Peter note that the attempt to represent the case as the inevitable result of a clash of civilisations silenced the voices of Muslim dissent that had condemned the appalling threats made against the teacher. In this there is an important point to be made, for the contests over Islamophobia that give way to a wider politics of offence have the effect of foreclosing politicisation against Islamophobia while opening an alternative field of racial politics that places the Muslim question at its heart.

This has been a central feature of what we can term Islamophobia, and in this light it is worth noting that there is a movement within the European extreme right that is centrally concerned with meeting this fictive threat to the survival of the population. This is reflected in the language of war used by the terrorist Breivik but also, for instance, in the faux-paramilitary naming of the English Defence League and its organisation, like every self-respecting army, into divisions which march under flags. But it is also reflected in the routine invocation of the trope of threat that is a feature of far right discourse; for instance in 2005 Roberto Calderoli of the Lega Nord declared: 'Let them [Muslims] return to the desert and talk with the camels, or to the jungle and talk with the apes' (Betz 2007: 44). In this, the attack is clearly not against Islam, but against Muslims who are represented as a threatening population and symbolically excluded from the nation. The case of the Lega Nord is instructive, for it demonstrates above all the peculiar purchase of Islamophobia on a wider politics. Through its pursuit of Islamophobia over the past decade the Lega has facilitated wider shifts in its politics, so that just as Geert Wilders was an obscure figure outside the Netherlands until his focus on Muslims shot him to global renown, by supplanting its fierce regionalism with Islamophobic rhetoric, the Lega Nord opened spaces for a new politics with scope for new alignments and a raised profile across Europe, and allowed it to overcome the limits that would otherwise be placed upon its potential political influence by dint of its traditional focus on Padovan cultural survival.

This also involved a further move through which its anti-Muslim focus and expressions of Christian cultural superiority also marked a significant shift from its earlier ambivalence towards the church (Chiantera-Stutte 2005: 120). This shift was reflected when the priest Don Gianni Baget Bozzo urged Umbert Bossi to place the defence of 'our identity against the Islamic invasion' at the heart of Lega Nord policy, as if there had been any doubt in the first place (Betz 2007: 44). Similarly, in 2000 after Cardinal Biffi suggested discrimination against Muslim immigrants in favour of Catholics, Lega Nord politician Sartori made a number of media interventions questioning the willingness of Muslims to integrate and drawing attention to their threat to democracy (Betz 2003: 92n). As Trevisan Semi (2003) has shown, in constructing Muslim immigrants in terms of contagion – even as one of the three plagues threatening humanity (Trevisan Semi 2003: 286) – its representation of Muslims as seemingly inhuman non-subjects resonates with older anti-Semitic metaphors and Nazi representation of Jews (Trevisan Semi 2003: 292). It is difficult to read such instances as a straightforward critique of religion, for they take the form of a coded attack against a human population that is seen as threatening the life and well-being of the nation. Indeed, as Allievi (2002) notes in an Italian context, while Muslims mobilise to seek recognition, this discourse of threat and somehow exceeding national law has fuelled a wider xenophobia. Islamophobia is thus imbricated in a wider racial politics, and it provides a particularly plausible defence against accusations both because of its pliability and because of the continued circulation of discredited ideas about phenotypal racial difference: because Muslim identities cut across traditional phenotypical racial and ethnic distinctions, it has a wide purchase, and the fear of Islamisation mobilised by the far right can cover a range of evils – crime, immigration, assimilation, cultural difference – while naturalising them simply as a critique of abstract religious beliefs and a defence against them. In turn, this opens a new politics with scope for new alignments and attachments. Thus, even in spite of the peculiarities of the case of the Lega Nord, its shift towards Islamophobic rhetoric reflects the wider anti-Muslim turn of the far right across Europe. Similar examples of the threat supposedly posed by Muslim populations are presented wherever Islamophobia emerges and Muslims are attacked as a population constructed as threatening the majority culture. For example, although Switzerland's Muslim population had hitherto been thought of as well-integrated (Seib and Janbek 2011: 112), in a 2009 referendum over 50 per cent voted in favour of a move to ban the erection of new minarets on mosques. The importance of this case lies in the way in which it explicitly conflated the notion of excessive Muslim difference with politicality so central to Islamophobia, for the ban was based on the notion that minarets are political rather than religious symbols (Doe 2011: 167). In this the opposition between the naturalcy of race and the politicality of religion was curiously displaced by a distinction between religion proper and symbols of Islam as political rather than religious, which was necessary to ensure that the ban could not be construed as an attack against religion. But the minaret issue was framed by a wider process of securitisation of immigration in Switzerland which constructed Muslims as potentially threatening to the nation, and which fed into a wider problematisation of minorities. For example, while campaigning for re-election in 2007 the Swiss People's Party (SVP) infamously used a campaigning poster that depicted a black sheep being kicked off the Swiss flag by a white sheep, so that only white sheep remained on the flag (Paterson 2009). During the campaign to ban minarets two years later, the iconic campaigning poster depicted a threatening, darkened figure of a burka-clad woman standing in front of a Swiss national flag that was penetrated by a number of stylised minarets resembling missiles. In this the political threat posed by minarets was conflated with an existential threat to the survival of the nation, and the juxtaposition of a recognisable, if heavily essentialised, Muslim figure served to link the notion of threat posed by Islam with the presence of Muslim populations. The Swiss minarets ban was significant for it represented an attempt to squeeze out of public space and visibility this jarring, alien presence. As such it belongs in the wider context of attacks against multiculturalism, attempts to ban the burka and hijab, all of which are ways of regulating access to public space.

De-Essentialising Muslim Identities

This brief discussion highlights a further difficulty with discussions that have attempted to force the denial of Islamophobia by retreating into phenotypical notions of race. In this I have conflated a range of seemingly contradictory figures, from those who would be viewed as occupying progressive positions, to far right racists and holocaust deniers, with a huge spectrum in between that takes in everyone from satirists to former Muslims. This is clearly problematic; for example, Polly Toynbee and Kenan Malik are on record for their opposition to racism and thus while their critiques of Islamophobia share a family resemblance with those of the far right, they are clearly not attempting to progress the same racial politics. This distinction is important because the tendency towards essentialism in accounts of Islamophobia stretches to the different forms it takes. But while both Toynbee and the far right British National Party have contested the proper existence of Islamophobia through a retreat into problematic racial (un)certainties, Toynbee (2004) has still managed to recognise the increasing levels of attacks against Muslims and argued that the prominence of the notion of Islamophobia has ceded ground to groups such as the British National Party. This muddled position indicates the contestedness of Islamophobia and the need to shift beyond reductive readings of racial politics, and its confusion illustrates the impossibility of countering Islamophobia in the absence of a clear conceptualisation of its centrally racist nature. But this also highlights a further contradiction, for it seems curious that while we are able to trace out distinctions between different kinds of politics in the contests over Islamophobia, within the dominant framing of Islamophobia as a banal question of religious criticism or discrimination rather than racism, it seems difficult to account for Muslim resistance to Islamophobia in anything other than essentialist terms. This is an effect of the reduction of Islamophobia from racism to the criticism of religion. This places practical restrictions upon channels and registers through which those occupying Muslim subject positions can engage in democratic politics, forcing them to mobilise by appropriating notions of offence rather than under the rubric of racism, as I shall discuss in Chapter 5. Another of its effects is to force a conflation between religious criticism and the Islamophobia through which Muslims are subjected to harassment and violence. This mitigates against understanding Islamophobia, but it also prevents us from being able to differentiate between the different political identities that come into play when Muslims challenge Islamophobia, so that we are left to assume a continuity between those who really would mobilise solely over religious offence, and those who would challenge the wider demonisation of Muslim populations. Quraishi (2005: 60) warns that the false homogenisation of Muslims enables some to promote selective interpretations of religion on issues such as free speech. Bassam Tibi (2008: 127) has further claimed that while it is right to challenge Islamophobia, there also 'exists a constructed Islamophobia, often cultivated on purpose by Islamists to create taboos that prohibit free speech about them and their activities'. In other words, there is an Islamophobia and something that is not actually Islamophobia. The essentialist case would posit the latter as a defining form in order to elide or deny the former, and it would do this based on reference to the assumed real nature of race that renders Islamophobia fantastical. The premise of this is the assumption that Muslims themselves seek to collapse the distinction between racism and offence, although such argument is undermined by the fact that the case for Islamophobia as a form of racism rather than religious discrimination has by no means been uniformly expressed by Muslims. For instance, Inayat Bunglawala (2008) of the Muslim Council of Britain has argued that in the context of increasing anti-Muslim hostility, the major challenge is to take all forms of religious discrimination seriously, thus indicating a religious rather than a racial framing for Islamophobia. Thus Bunglawala makes the same conflation. But while this distinction is difficult to draw because the far right in particular attempts to keep it blurred, it needs to be made; after all, the extremist who murdered Theo van Gogh reportedly claimed that he was not motivated by van Gogh's descriptions of Muslims as goat fuckers, but rather by what he saw as his religious duty. In other words, the reduction of Islamophobia to merely religious discrimination plays to the interests of the far right and people like van Gogh's killer, but in doing this it reduces our ability to grasp the racial politics at stake in it, and prevents us from being able to conceive of the objects of Islamophobia as anything other than purely religious subjects.

Thus this conflation does not just conjure the ontically pure racial subject (against whom Muslims, with their apparently inadequate raciality, are contrasted), but it also conjures into view the Muslim as regulated by Islam (whatever that may be). Sabet (2008) has argued that Western social sciences are incapable of dealing properly with Islam because they are unable to grasp the revealed nature of Islam.

I would disagree; in fact, what we witness in this essentialisation of Muslim politics and subjectivities is a result of the incapacity to conceive of Muslims as anything other than ontically pure religious beings; beings who are regulated by culture (religion) but lack the agency to transform what that culture means. Allievi (2002: 91) makes a similar argument in an Italian context, suggesting that 'Muslims are not "in essence" different from others, although their presence poses a problem quantitatively greater than that of other religious minorities. To overcome these barriers, it is necessary that the question of the juridical (and political) treatment of the presence of Muslim minorities be *de-Islamized'*. I agree that this kind of exceptionalism is not helpful for two reasons. First, the inscription of Muslims as ontically pure religious subjects (though not racial) in a world in which all subjects are racialised, marks them as a lack (incompletely racial) in their excess (religion). Second, as this logic manifests in the naming and conception of Islamophobia as a non-racism, it disarticulates Islamophobia from a wider racial politics. The attempt to assert a sweeping rejection of Islamophobia based on the reductive logic that it takes but one form – the cynical claim that religion has been criticised – simultaneously essentialises subjects and constitutes an antipolitical logic that seeks to foreclose the debate and proper contestation of the politics of Islamophobia that has emerged. On this curious point it is helpful to pause and rethink things for a moment. After all, what is racism if it is not also political?

The Political Meaning of Racism

Contests over Islamophobia are thus at the same time contests over the meaning of the label Muslim: does it refer to a phenotypal race, or to an essentially religious group? This presupposes the fixity of identities and the notion that the political meaning of a given discourse can be divined from tracing out the essential identities of its objects. But political practice is centrally concerned with the construction of identities, and the political meaning of racism does not emerge from the skin colour of the racialised, but rather from the ways in which life becomes the object of power, as Hesse (2000) notes. While I do not locate my analysis within a Foucaultian framing, I note the recognition by Viego (2007: 46) in his psychoanalytical account of racialisation that 'Foucault can be read as remarking on the ways in which categories of ethnicity and race are internal to the management and reproduction of biological life'. It is frequently noted that Foucault did not leave an extensive corpus of writing on race. While this is certainly the case, his lectures at the College de France in 1975–1976 (Foucault 2004) clearly establish his conception of the intimate ravelling together of power and racism as central to the political function of racism. Foucault broadly outlines what he sees as the emergence of modern racism in the early nineteenth century through a distortion of earlier notions of race struggle into an understanding of racism as a biological struggle for the survival of the fittest species, in which the various species are understood through the logic of race.

This shift in turn gave way to the emergence of a new mode of racism at the end of the century based on a relation of war (Foucault 2004; Terranova 2007). To Foucault this had two functions: first, through recourse to race, it drew a boundary around the population of the nation as the basis for a distinction 'between what must live and what must die' (Foucault 2004: 254). Second, this went further to establish a relation of war based on the logic that the preservation of the life of the population necessitates the death of the other. In this, Foucault's conception of killing is not concerned with murder, but rather as a wider operation that reflects the wider forms that the death of a subject can take, from differential rates of mortality to political acts which take the form of the stripping of a subject's political value (Foucault 2004: 254). Foucault cites expulsion as an example of killing, so we can read it symbolically in terms of a range of practices that have the effect of constructing the racialised as external and threatening to the population. The relation of war with which Foucault is concerned is not constructed in military terms (we will be conquered), but rather in terms of well-being as a threat to the survival of the species itself (understood in racial terms). Racism thus reduces enemies to a threat of contamination, abnormality, degeneracy, so that the relation of war is rather expressed through the logic that 'the more abnormal individuals are eliminated, the fewer degenerates there will be in the species as a whole, and the more I – as species rather than individual – can live, the stronger I will be … (Foucault 2004: 255). By opening out racism analytically Foucault thus establishes it as a political rationality that enables the operation of power. This forces us to acknowledge that this form of power cannot be reduced to a surface effect of the existence of different phenotypal races, but rather that racism provides a technique through which social problems – Foucault cites madness and criminality as examples (Foucault 2004: 258) – can be constructed in racial terms as though they are somehow hardwired into the deviant, and as though their persistence cannot simply be reduced to a contingent problem that must be overcome in some way, but rather that they pose a threat to the very survival and health of the population itself.

I do not locate my analysis within a strictly Foucaultian framing. One reason for this is that while Foucault's conception of racism opens it out analytically, this is actually to the extent that it also opens the possibility to read virtually any distinction between a threatening and a non-threatening population as racism. This elides the specificity of racism and its colonial roots. For this reason, it is helpful to supplement Foucault's conception of racism with Hesse's conception of race as notes the emergence of race as 'a governing practice to distinguish between "whiteness/Europeanness" and "non-Europeanness/nonwhiteness" in terms of regulations, affinities, spaces, and discourses in modernity's colonies' (Hesse 2011: 164). Foucault is, however, helpful in drawing attention to the fact that the world is inhabited by countless multiplicities of beings who appear to possess an innumerable array of different features in almost infinite combinations, but nature is not a stable basis for politics (Lemke 2011: 4) and cannot therefore provide an incontestable basis for the institution and organisation of the social. For this reason particular forms of politics come into play that take life (and its limit) as their object (Swiffen 2011: 63), and takes the form of the administration of life and enjoyment (Zizek 2006: 310). While we might exist with distinctive physical features – for example, skin colour – these are not reducible to race, but rather the knowledge systems that (re)produce race take as their object the constitution of subjects and populations. Once we acknowledge the political meaning of racism, we are thus also forced to accept that any attempt to determine a phenotypal essence among its objects is problematic. Thus, when Muslims are constructed as lacking proper raciality (as they are through the rejections of Islamophobia's racism), this cannot be read as an absence of racism, but rather as a condition of its operation, so that in racialised social settings in which raciality is conflated with proper subjecthood for the racially and ethnically marked, on the one hand those who apparently lack raciality present a political problem (how can they be constituted as a bounded population) and on the other hand they can be constructed as somehow being incomplete subjects or limit figures (Tyrer 2011). Within this logic, Muslims are thus simultaneously a lack or an incompleteness, and yet they are also an excess that has somehow exceeded their taming and drawing forth as members of a racial population.

And yet the perversity of this impossible logic lies in the fact that we can speak of Muslims as a distinct population, no matter how difficult to recognise they might seem to be. Precisely because we can recognise them as a population, we can understand that they are as racial as any other group. Of course, some have moved beyond the attempt to draw a hardened distinction between race and religion, for example by considering Muslims as 'quasi-ethnic' (Meer 2008), or considering the 'ethnicization' of Islam (Tibi 2010). But within the terms of a political reading of racism, these distinctions are not particularly helpful, for ethnicity is in any case framed within the logics of race. As Hall notes, the more important ethnicity appears to be, 'the more its characteristics are represented as relatively fixed, inherent within a group, transmitted from generation to generation, not just by culture and education, but by biological inheritance' (Hall 2000: 223). Because race and ethnicity work through an equivalence between the cultural and the biological (Hall 2000: 223), they can better be understood within the terms of the political nature of racism itself.

Agency and the Racialised

The struggles over what is meant by Islamophobia thus take the form of attempts to fix the meaning of Muslims, whether racial or religious, natural or political. The denial of Islamophobia's racism in turn naturalises its racial politics based on the attempt to represent Muslims in terms of incomplete raciality. But the problematisation of Muslims as non-racial is difficult to sustain when one recognises that race is not read from subjects, but rather it is ascribed through political practices. It is therefore important to note that two other problems emerge from the repeated invocation of the racial red herring. First, the notion that Muslims are incompletely racialised is, of course, nonsense. Even if we ignore the ways in which Muslims are racialised as a bounded population group, it is difficult to sustain the argument that Muslims are not racialised for all social subjects in a racialised society are racialised in some way even if some racialised subject positions (such as Whiteness) are understood in terms of invisibility. From Pakistanis in Bradford to Somalis in the Netherlands or Moroccans in Spain and Italy (to paint a reductive and very broad brush sketch), even taking into account the presence of convert Muslims, we are dealing with populations who are already symbolised as racial subjects. The notion of the inadequate raciality of Muslims ignores this, unless we take it for granted that Islamophobia is better understood as a form of racism against people on account of some underlying primordial raciality.

For example, Adriano Purgato has acknowledged that Islamophobia seems to disturb classical racial inscriptions, arguing that the 'point of no return' in the shift from the 'Marocchinofobia' of the last century to the Islamophobia of today can be fairly precisely dated to 9/11, after which attention shifted from ethnicity to religion, so that the north African or Arab has in turn become Muslim (Purgato 2006: 69). Although the relationship between Islamophobia and wider forms of racism is a point I shall return to in Chapter 3, Purgato's point is helpful insofar as it involves an implicit recognition of the role of racism in shaping how racialised subjects are perceived and subjectified. But the agency of the racialised to transform the terms on which their identities are symbolised is equally important. Curiously, this agency is omitted from the contests over the nature of Islamophobia, which posit that Muslims are able to choose their identity (by dint of choosing their faith) unlike the 'properly' racialised who have no choice in the matter. For example, in Britain in 2005 the Labour Member of Parliament Robert Marshall-Andrews drew upon the notion to express his reservations towards protection from religious hatred:

> The difficulty is that there is a profound difference between race and gender and religion. Our race and our gender are what we are and should be protected. Our religion is what we choose to believe. It is a system of beliefs, fundamentally and quite properly held. It seems to many here and out there that there is, in truth, very little distinction between one's religion and one's politics. (Hansard 2005)

The same argument was rehearsed by Kenan Malik (2005), who noted that it was in this lack of agency among the racialised that 'the fundamental difference between race and religion' can be located. The repeated allusions to Muslim choice are important because they underline the ways in which Muslim difference, located in its supposedly incomplete raciality, is read in popular narratives as a political excess rather than a natural phenotype. But this questioning of choice misunderstands race by reducing it solely to biological inheritance, eliding the crucial question of racist ascription. Tariq Modood (2005) and Nasar Meer (2008) have questioned the wider point by noting that individuals born into particular structural positions and social environments might not necessarily have completely unfettered choice in their religious affiliation. Whether one terms it socialisation or enculturation, it is easy to see how this is so. But while this problematises the notion that religion entails completely free choice, it fails to address the underlying argument which shores up race, because it also elides the agency of the racialised. Individuals might not have power to select the biological features with which they are born, or even to predetermine the nature of the dominant cultural influences (including religion) into which they are introduced, but they do have significant power to unsettle and challenge the namings through which they become racial. Even within the terms of traditional ideas about scientific race, misrecognitions and misascriptions occur, and indeed the prospect of this made practices such as 'passing' a possibility as one mode of resisting racial ascription.

But a more common practice among racialised minorities has been to resist by interrupting racial namings and ascriptions through rearticulation. The attempt to reduce racism to a handful of biological features while eliding the agency of the racialised reduces racialisation to the surface effects of an undirectional exercise of power. But all namings and collective identities are forced through political practice and the exercise of power (Sayyid 2004), and their political nature centrally assumes that we must recognise the ways in which namings are contested, and how this contestation in turn transforms both the labels and what they are held to mean. For example, labels such as 'negro' were applied in the context of a world system organised around a colonial slave economy managed from the West, and the naming of particular subjects as 'negro' displaced prior collective namings with the effect of concealing the histories that had produced them. But terms such as 'negro' were in turn transformed and ultimately displaced through political struggles by the populations they named, as a result of which a new range of namings emerged (cf. Omi and Winant 1994). The term for this process is rearticulation, and it works by combining previously existing discursive elements in new ways, so that new meanings can be constructed as the basis for creating new political subjectivities. Elaborating on the ways in which rearticulation is reflected in racial politics, Omi and Winant (1994) make the point that race is best understood as an 'unstable equilibrium' constantly subject to contestation and responses aiming to recentre it and create the effect of stabilisation. Its contestation involves questioning 'the meaning of race and the nature of racial identity (e.g., "blackness," "Chicanismo," "minority" status; or for that matter, "majority" status, "whiteness"), while state initiatives seek to reinforce or transform the "unstable equilibrium" of racial politics in response to movement demands' (Omi and Winant 1994: 89). This is a helpful analogy for the process through which Muslim identity politics has forged a new Muslim political subjectivity that has had the effects of transforming the wider field of racial politics. One can look at most social circumstances and see quite clearly that in spite of past historical encounters with Muslims, the existing racial vernacular in Europe and the United States has been dominated by terms assumed to have a biological hold, or failing that, by secular ethnic labels. Such terms tended to differ from context to context, and they reflected the different migration histories and experiences of colonialism, so that one society's Asian minorities could be another's sub-continental South Asians, or the South-East Asians of another society, who in turn could be the Far Easterners in another context. The groups today named as Muslims were historically organised under a range of different formal and informal namings, from the *beurs* of France to the Bangladeshis of East London. However, the emergence of a Muslim identity politics unsettled these namings by supplanting them with the primacy of identification as Muslim. The process through which this has occurred has not been even, but it is striking that during the period in which Islamophobia has most strikingly increased in range and ferocity, the trend among minorities to identify as Muslim has increased.

The Vanishing Point of Race

The search for phenotypal raciality as a means of determining the nature of racism is, of course, a red herring, for race is socially constructed. And yet it is something more than a red herring, for as we have seen, it enables the curious racialisation of Muslims – those 'goat fuckers', as Theo van Gogh described them on television (Pieterse 2007: 181) – as incompletely racial, and in this as an excess, a presence which reminds us of our powerlessness and vulnerability as they interrupt our ability to experience the nation as complete and closed, to understand race as fixed and bounded, and to interrupt our rights, even as across Europe they are securitised by states, attacked by the far right, and the nature of the racism they face – a perfect form of what Goldberg (2009) terms as racism without race – goes denied. No, race is more than just a red herring. So, too, is the MacGuffin. Mlado Dolar (1992: 45–46) notes that the logic of the MacGuffin as a vanishing point can be better understood as the object of desire, or an infinite metonymy in which the focus is signification but the content of the signified is strangely irrelevant. In this we can see how race works as an endless metonymy that collapses and vanishes as it passes to other significations (Blackness…) that introduce the racially marked body as the object of desire. The scandal of the apparently incomplete raciality of Muslims is thus the possible loss of the object of desire: the subject that is racialised, orientalised, eroticised through racist in/ascriptions. Thus the figure of a young white Flemish woman in a bikini and burka simultaneously reintroduces an eroticised orientalist aesthetic underpinned by an investment in the corporeality of Whiteness and ascribed raciality while rendering invisible and absent the troubling figure of the Muslim who threatens to interrupt these processes of racialised desire formation. Such anxieties produce racial visibility as a remainder that guarantees the integrity of the racial signifier, which is to point out that the scandal of the inadequate raciality of Muslims is reworked through this discourse as a means of keeping open the possibility of the properly racially marked subject. We thus see emerging from the red herring of race the problematic notions of visibility, anxiety and phobia that are bound up with Islamophobia. And it is to these notions that I turn in Chapters 2 and 3.

2

Now you see me: fantasy and misrecognition

Questions about visibility loom large in discussions about Muslims (cf. Jonker and Amiraux 2006; Peter 2011) and there is a mode of Islamophobia that appears to oscillate between suspending Muslims in invisibility and inflating their difference as a hypervisibility. For example, the populist and far right campaigns about Islamisation frequently deploy the burka as a shorthand for the Muslim presence, so that all but the most contested and problematised forms of Muslim difference are rendered invisible. The question of Muslim visibility is therefore not unproblematic, and it has given way to a manifestation of Islamophobia that appears to entail cases of mistaken identity. The most obvious manifestation of this has been an increase in hate attacks against non-Muslim minorities – particularly Sikhs – who appear to have been mistaken for Muslims, although it also takes other forms and has included cases of Muslims being mistaken for Islamist extremists and arrested. In this chapter I am concerned with these problematic visibilities because they do not occur in spite of the wider racial politics at stake in the contests over Islamophobia, but they appear to be emerging in its wake.

The question of what happens when one subject is radically misread and mistaken for another is a recurrent theme in the popular culture of modern disciplinary societies. For example, such questions emerged as a recurrent theme in Hitchcock's films, and were explored in *Saboteur* (1942), *Spellbound* (1945), and *I Confess* (1953) as well as in *North by Northwest*. One of Hitchcock's most interesting explorations of the effects of misrecognition was in *The Wrong Man* (1956), which drew upon the real-life case of a nightclub musician mistakenly charged

41

with a violent theft. In the film, Manny Balestrero is mistaken for the felon *almost by chance* – or so it seems – and Henry Fonda's portrayal of a man haunted by an arbitrary twist of fate plays out questions of power and agency; as Godard noted, the innocent bass player appeared passive and almost inert throughout (Ishii-Gonzáles 2004: 144*n*). This treatment of the Balestrero case seems a helpful metaphor for the problem of mistaken identities that has emerged as an Islamophobic possibility. But it is also helpful in drawing attention to the limits of the apodictic, empiricist logics of difference that have underpinned the quest for ontic racial purity as an arbiter of whether or not racism is racism. Balestrero's innocence is finally established by chance when the real perpetrator is apprehended and confesses to his crime. In other words, an epistemological investment in empiricism is at stake in the case, so that the substitution of the wrong man for the materiality of the real villain permits closure and corrects the earlier error. But where does it leave us if the figure for whom the object of mistaken identity racism does not empirically exist?

The Void Without

Before we exemplify mistaken identities racism, it is helpful to draw attention to its grounding in the debates over the materiality of Muslims. This is reflected in two ways: first, in the problem of recognising subjects who appear to be incompletely racial and second, in the assumption that if Muslims are not properly racial then the appeal to Islamophobia is itself based on a fundamental misrecognition (the misrecognition of Muslims for a phenotypal race). If we take the argument seriously that Muslims lack raciality, then it must follow logically that when we look at a Muslim, we do not *see* a Muslim, but rather we see an ontic fullness that betrays the Muslim lack: we see a properly racial subject – a Bangladeshi, a Somali, an Arab ... But a Muslim? As a being that, within the terms of dominant framings of the racial imaginary, exists only through choice, faith and imagining to interrupt the ideal of ascribed racial subjectivisation, Muslims must therefore only constitute a political illusion; beings who cannot be seen as such. This presents us with a reminder of who Muslims should really be, and of the solidity of race, so all that is real must inevitably vanish into air ...

Thomas Deltombe's study of Islamophobia in the French media offers one illustration of this difficulty. Noting the construction of the 'invisible enemy' that disturbs us all the more because of its ability to take advantage of globalisation, as well as the wider trope of the double life of the apparently integrated terrorist other, Deltombe (2007: 269) reminds us of the ways in which the problem of recognising threatening Muslims have played out. But this difficulty is not only a question of the problem of recognising the threat, because it is underpinned by a more fundamental problem of recognising Muslims (whether threatening or not) generally. The founding problem of Muslim visibility is that raciality is not just the principle coordinate for complete subjecthood in racialised social settings, but also that it dictates our understanding of the materiality of bodies. We can say that race is symbolic; it provides us with a way of organising the innumerable forms that life takes into bodies, species and populations in ways that suppress certain modalities of bodily difference and emphasise others, as a means of organising them under a limiting rubric that is historically contingent. Race is therefore not static, so in different contexts it operates to name and render visible different groups in different ways. One way of looking at this in relation to the question of Islamophobia is by noting that it has never simply been a question of difference, but of how a seemingly inconceivable array of differences can be organised to create a viable basis on which populations can be administered. As such the question is not simply one of how raciality can be read from the surfaces of racialised subjects, but rather how it is inscribed, and phenotypal characteristics such as skin pigmentation and bodily features have been central to the marking and problematisation of the bodies of the racialised (Jackson 2006).

Although the hollowness of racism's scientific claims is well established, the cultural racisms which emerge in the wake of this debunking do not displace modern ideas of phenotypal race but supplement them, so that the idea of a hardwired difference between groups is elaborated through notions of binding, monolithic culture – strange habits, smelly food, alien clothing. Culture does not displace biology because as Hall (2000) notes, it is constructed as though it is biologised. Race thinking thus reduces the agency of the racialised and denudes them of proper being; as recipients of inherited traits, whether phenotypal or cultural, they are also passive bearers of them.

In Fanonian terms, racialised selfhood can be read as a libidinal lack in being (Marriott 2005: 160), so that the logics of modern colonial racism construct the raced Other as a black skin, or mask, with a void within. Even the hyperinflation of racialised difference – for example, the figure of the hypermasculine Black male – has the effect of transforming the Other into a giant void. In contrast to this, Islamophobia is marked by the perverse racialisation of Muslims as inadequately racialised (Tyrer 2011). This apparently incomplete raciality interrupts and unsettles such bodily inscriptions because Muslim corporeality seems more troubling as a consequence of their apparently incomplete raciality. The putatively inadequate raciality of Muslims implies a certain incorporeality (Tyrer and Sayyid 2012), so that in contrast to the representation of the colonial raced subject as an amplified or inflated black surface containing a void within, the proposition is reversed in Islamophobic discourse, as Muslims are represented through the logics of a phenotypal absence/void without, and a hyperinflated difference within.

For this reason, it is worth noting that the emphasis on visibility in writings on Muslims also frequently manifests in the representation of Muslims as somehow ghostly, fantastical, or phantasmatic (Tyrer and Sayyid 2012). For example, Daulatzai (2007: 135) has argued that Muslims are racialised as phantasmatic, excessive, and perverse. Vincent Geisser (2003: 82) has referred to the fantasmatic vision of others as underpinning what he terms 'un fantasme conspiratif: l'islamisation du monde et des banlieues françaises'. I am interested in the split role of the fantasmatic as a fantasy projection and the phantasmatic as spectral. The problem of incorporeality thus gives way to a mode of Islamophobia in which Muslims are conjured as ghostly, and as such this opens a wider politics concerned with dealing with the ghostly. For example, Anna Maria Rivera (2005: 33–4) has noted that 'il fantasma di una Francia islamizzata' – the fantasy of an Islamised France – in which gender equality and secularism were figured as being undermined by Muslims, could be organised under appeals to Republican values and successfully mobilise public support in France for a headscarf ban. In this it is interesting to witness how in the apparent absence of a proper racial corporeality (even in its presence, for we are all racialised), forms of clothing loom large in imaginings of Islam, and the burka has emerged as a particularly important front. In

April 2010 a law was passed in Belgium to ban the wearing of the burka in public, while a similar ban was introduced in France a year later. Moves towards similar legislation have occurred in the Netherlands, and in February 2011 Hesse became the first state in Germany to introduce a burka ban for public sector workers. In Italy a draft law to ban the burka was approved by a parliamentary commission in August 2011. But the politicisation around the burka has appropriated it from debates about women's rights and transformed it into a major point of engagement over the Muslim question more broadly. Thus it is also important to note that the burka is worn by very few women in Europe; figures suggested by Moors (2011: 157) indicate that it is worn by about 0.003 per cent of the population of the Netherlands, while in the wake of moves towards banning the burka in Italy Izzedin Elzir, head of the Union of Islamic Communities in Italy, remarked that he had only seen ten women wearing the burka throughout his two decades living in the country (Faris 2011). It is reported that only thirty women in Belgium wear the burka (BBC News 2010) in spite of which, as I noted in Chapter 1, the Vlaams Belang has made the burka an important feature of its anti-immigration and anti-Muslim politics. Unsurprisingly, given the position of vestments as a site for the inscription of Muslim lack in excess, Donnell notes advice issued by the Muslim Women's League in America that warned:

> In the current climate of escalated religiously-motivated violence since the terrible attacks of September 11, Muslim women in hijab (headscarf) are particularly vulnerable because, for many years, western media and literature have consistently portrayed covered women as the predominant image of Islam. As a result, Muslim women in headscarves and other Muslim-style clothing are often the first and easiest targets of hate violence. Donnell (2003: 123)

Although this refers largely to the hijab rather than the burka, it is nevertheless a helpful illustration because of the ways in which the hijab and burka tend to be conflated and mistaken for one another in popular discussions about Muslims. The warning issued by the Muslim Women's League also illustrates the ways in which women and their clothing have been given a particular prominence in the politics of Islamophobia, so that the contests over the burka cannot simply be read as mobilisations over women's rights as they are appropriated in wider anti-immigrant and anti-Muslim racial politics. The burka plays an important role in this because the figure of the burka wearing women becomes a symbol of what Muslims will make us become, as An-Sofie Dewinter indicated in her interview with *De Standaard* (2012). What made her appearance in a burka-bikini ensemble was precisely the flesh on show; the contrast between the corporeality of the proper racial subject and the void without of the Other. This logic of the phantasmatic threat has emerged as an organising principle of Islamophobia and its hold is remarkably resilient. For example, on 22 July 2011 news of a terrorist attack in Norway began filtering through. Anders Behring Breivik murdered over seventy people in total, including sixty-nine young people attending a youth camp on Utoya island, whom he shot in a calculating murderous rampage. Breivik's motives were well documented in his online postings and in a lengthy manifesto that he also published on the internet. Breivik may have been more extreme than most on the extreme right in his actions, but he was nevertheless commended by some including Mario Borghezio, a Member of the European Parliament who had previously praised the indicted war criminal Ratko Mladic as a patriot. Borghezio was suspended from the Lega Nord as a result of his outburst, and as the apparent links between Breivik and other members of the European far right grew, others swiftly moved to condemn his atrocity and play down any substantive links. However, even if Breivik's methods stood out (though they were far from being the only far right terrorist incident in the West) his racial politics cannot be understood outside the context of the Islamophobic discourse across the West that has constructed the fantasy of a Muslim conspiracy to Islamise the West, and which appropriates certain symbols as means of giving an incorporeal materiality to this ghostly threat and rendering it hypervisible. Discussing the links between Breivik's own views and those across the far right, Liz Fekete has highlighted the importance of signs of Muslim visibility such as minarets, veils and mosques as signs of politicality, and she proceeds to argue that:

> By linking any sign of being Muslim to a homogeneous and repressive force that is said to be global Islam, the extreme Right portrays Islam as a political and criminal ideology that, in the

name of security, must be cordoned off from the body politic. Geert Wilders and his supporters argue that there is an Islamic essence, at odds with modernity, at the heart of which lies the Qur'an. As all Muslims believe that the Qur'an is the literal word of God and will not accept that the Qur'an is open to human interpretation in order to apply it in different times and places, all Muslims are fundamentalists. The only good Muslim is an ex-Muslim, according to this way of thinking (Fekete 2012: 35).

Breivik's expressions of hate thus only make sense within the wider context of Islamophobia as one of the nodal points through which Islamophobic discourse is expressed. The question of Muslim visibility is crucial to this project because of the ways in which the hyper-inflation of non-bodily signs, the Muslim threat is symbolised precisely as one that is not of flesh and blood, but rather this threat is spectral, and one that can spring up anywhere, but which we only notice (too late) through the appearance of traces of its haunting: through mosques, minarets, and burkas. Within this discourse the lack of the Muslim subject – its non-racial excess – is counterpointed against the bodily flesh of Europe; of An-Sofie Dewinter bravely defending us against the incorporeal Muslim threat, of Anders Behring Breivik highlighting the bodies ravaged by this presence as he asks 'how many thousands of Europeans must die, how many hundreds of European women must be raped, millions robbed and bullied' (Fekete 2012: 34).

Thus it is precisely because of its relative scarcity that the burka is central to the imagining of Muslim hauntings, because as a primary mode for visualising the Muslim presence it renders other Muslims invisible, suddenly, shockingly conjuring into view the fantasmatic being who threatens us. The burka itself becomes fantasmatic, so that in its deployment on posters campaigning for the minaret ban in Switzerland it loomed like a threatening black ghost – and its blackness is significant – that haunts the nation, interrupting its closure and threatening to tear it apart. This was effective precisely because it works to perversely materialise the incorporeal, erasing the supposed ontic purity that we should instead be able to see. In this erasure, the burka comes to work as a void without which conceals the surplus within, so that the invocation of burka in racial politics operates as another mode of representing the supposedly incomplete raciality of Muslims which, in contrast to the colonial trope of the bodily substance lacking a soul, is instead manifested as a void without and a soul within, where the soul is figured as an excess; a political surplus (choice) that lacks the corporeal substance to transform it into a proper subject. In this the fantasmatic nature of the burka also comes into vision as a way of guaranteeing the integrity of the racial signifier through its very transgression.

The burka is also important for another reason indicated by the alternative mobilisation of burka as a problem of security, for in displacing and masking traditional corporeal inscriptions (brown skin …), it also makes it difficult to recognise whether subjects really are who they purport to be. A twist to this logic was provided by Le Pen who felt the ban on hijab a bad thing since at least hijab allows us to properly recognise Muslims (Fekete 2012: 35).

Honour Among Thieves?

The problem of Muslim incorporeality thus also gives rise to a problem of recognition. This is important in a general sense since incorporation into liberal regimes is contingent upon recognition, so the terms on which we can recognise subjects determines their access to democratic institutions and their relationship to civil society is instituted around the kind of subject positions they are recognised as occupying. As such the problem of how we recognise Muslims (whether as ontically pure racial or ontically pure religious subjects) shapes the possibilities for democratic interactions and frames the issues to be considered in Chapter 5. At this point it is interesting the ways in which the problem of recognising these sometimes fantasmatic creatures finds its expression across a wider field of racial politics, not only because doing so can help us to understand the political rationality of Islamophobia as it is brought to bear on Muslims, but also as its purchase over other groups is increased as a result of seemingly mistaken identifications through which other minorities are targeted as though they are Muslims.

Perhaps the most interesting form of this phenomenon has become knowable under the rubric of 'mistaken identity' racism. The canonical form of this has involved attacks against Sikhs in particular. Within hours of the 9/11 atrocities reports of hostility against Sikhs began circulating in the United States. Early accounts included reports of uncomfortable experiences in public spaces, difficult encounters with law enforcement officers, and racial harassment. The grim extent of the latter problem has been has been highlighted by the Sikh American Legal Defence and Education Fund (SALDEF), which has recorded no fewer than 700 hate crimes against Sikhs in the United States in the years following the 9/11 atrocities (Nagra 2011). In the wake of the 7 July 2005 terrorist atrocities in London, attacks against non-Muslims also increased, with a Sikh gurdwara in Kent firebombed the same day, and a further five gurdwara attacks and two serious assaults against Sikhs occurring within a short space of time (Nagarajah 2005). Other cases involved verbal abuse and assaults, many of which targeted the turban, resulting in some Sikh men feeling under pressure to attempt suppressing such markers of difference by removing their turbans and cutting their hair (BBC 2004; Gohil and Sidhu 2008; Page 2006). The problems faced by non-Muslim members of ethnicised minority groups have not been restricted to street-level attacks and abuse by racists, but have also involved state interventions such as stop and search (Pantazis and Pemberton 2009: 649), humiliating searches of turbans performed by airport security (Neiyar 2011), and other miscarriages such as the arrest of a turbaned Sikh man as a terrorist on a US train on 12 September 2001.

The first interesting feature of such incidents is that they have frequently been organised under the sign backlash. This is problematic since it essentialises them as part of a teleology of racist politics. A parallel for this would be that of a chess game, in which two protagonists each have clearly defined and immutable identities and engage in a sequence of distinguishable moves and counter-moves that lead us through the encounter. But politics does not work through such simple linear logic, and racism is no different in this respect for the identities of its protagonists are not fixed and immutable, but struggled over, renounced, and rearticulated as racism racialises its objects and is itself resisted (Patel and Tyrer 2011). Besides, the moves themselves do not follow a straightforward trajectory, and in engagements in which even what constitutes a move is contested – for example, the ways in which racism can be disavowed by targeting groups who appear to lack complete raciality – a move can take numerous forms which may not follow sequentially or even be localisable to a prior manoeuvre or terrain. It is problematic to term these hate crimes as a backlash for this inscription essentialises the characters involved – by forging a similarity between the 9/11 terrorists and the victims of subsequent hate crimes – and dehistoricises the incidents, valorising whatever claims racists might make to justify their actions. This restricts our analysis by effectively severing the episodes from the wider context of racial politics. Racist antagonisms are the products of a wider racial politics, and they can simmer in apparent equilibrium and under informal negotiation on an ongoing basis, punctuated by sporadic outbursts in the context of specific stimuli to take a variety of forms from 'race riots' to shifting patterns of racist victimology. The notion of backlash introduces a sense of honour among thieves; a sort of informal racial protocol that establishes the violence as a collective punishment against the racialised for the horrors inflicted by the few. The notion of a backlash also attempts to fix racist incidents as a proxy mode through which the war on terror is waged, establishing false continuities and simple linearities, and in turn disarticulating Islamophobia from its own histories.

The second key feature of these crimes is the dominance of the mistaken identity frame. In this respect Sikhs have been particularly targeted, and the hold of the mistaken identity framing for anti-Sikh hate crimes has been increasingly considered in media coverage and in documentaries such as Amanda Gesine's *Mistaken Identity: Sikhs in America* (2003) and Puneet Issar's *I am Singh* (2011). But if the notion of backlash is problematic, then the mistaken identity frame is no less so. As Puar (2007: 187) notes, 'The "mistaken for" itself is not a mistake, insofar as it is the very point. The claim to have made a mistake functions as an alibi, a foil, for the prominence of resemblance, indicating that the Sikh is a fine replacement (one other is as good as another other) or a substitution (the Other is undifferentiated and needs to remain so)'. In other words, we cannot guarantee that it is a mistake at all, and to suppose that racism neatly compartmentalises its objects in hermetic categories goes against all that we know concerning the fluid, messy, contested nature of the social construction of race. An illustration of this can be found in the case of a Sacramento cab driver named Harbhajan Singh who was violently assaulted on 28 November 2010 by attackers yelling 'Osama bin Laden' (SALDEF 2010) in a rallying cry that has been widely employed (cf. Jayadev 2003). Even granting the observation that only racism's incompetence matches its cruelty (Deleuze and Guattari 2004: 198), it would take a remarkable degree of ineptness for racists to so regularly conclude that the mass murderer was not hiding in Pakistan at all, but that he was rather improbably disguised as a law abiding American and employed in the heartland. Clearly, racist expressions cannot be read literally; when racist assaults are played out to yells of 'Osama bin Laden' this might not be because an especially challenged racist genuinely believed they had found the murderous beast, but rather because 'Osama bin Laden' is deployed in such contexts as a marker for radical alterity. There are also other effects of inserting the Other into the symbolic chain in this way, for not only does it introduce an element of justification into racism (responding to the existential threat said to be posed by Muslims) but it also introduces the Other as a non-subject; a cipher or even a pure caricature rather than the rights bearing subject and citizen that she actually is.

If it is unconvincing to read such assaults as entailing a genuine mistake, then it is no more credible to suggest that while the victim was not misrecognised for bin Laden, she was, at least, misrecognised for a Muslim, or even that the attacker cared? To draw a parallel, I recall a conversation in which a British Asian acquaintance mentioned having been called the n-word in Liverpool city centre in broad daylight. Should we therefore suppose that this was also a case of mistaken identity – or was the n-word used simply as a signifier for racial difference? The sorry-didn't-realise-it-was-you logic of the mistaken identity framing ignores the cynical instrumentalism of racism, it assumes that racists truly care which Other they target, and by forcing a literal reading of a racial signifier as moored to a stable ontic referent it constricts our understanding of racisms in context while guaranteeing the existence of the real Other against whom the attack should have taken place. The logic of mistaken identity also works in another way. Who is the ideal victim, the absent Muslim who haunts the incident without ever being present? In its own perverse way the logic of mistaken identity reveals to us something of the rationality of racism, for in this proliferation of Others the interval between the ideal victim (the absent Muslim Other for whom the true Other was mistaken) and the founding fantasy Other of the racial attack (the dangerous Other) is closed. Thus, through her very absence the absent Muslim becomes the racist's fantasy through this logic. And the focus on 'mistaken identity' now requires us to conceive that there are not just two agents in play in the encounter (the racist and the Other), but also a third, the absent Muslim, the one who is not the Other but the Other of the Other; the invisible power structure, the one who pulls the strings and caused all this disharmony in the first place, and whose existence in part assures us of the coherence and hold of the symbolic order (Zizek 1999: 362) that constructed in the first place the terrifying fantasy of race.

Beyond Fantasy

Racism is intersubjective and in this we can say that it always targets the Other, for the Other is always present, always inserted into the symbolic order by dint of being the object of racism. Alterity is always exterior; the Other is the always Other. The mistaken identity framing for racist attacks against Sikhs also forces a second question: for whom was s/he mistaken? In the case of Islamophobia, the answer can only be that s/he was mistaken for the absent Muslim. But the absent Muslim, that incorporeal phantasm which haunts the imaginary and interrupts attempts at symbolisation, maintains a spectral presence, haunting yet never really there (Tyrer and Sayyid 2012). We cannot say with certainty that the real object of the attack exists, for she has not manifested. The absent Muslim thus exists only insofar as we can say she has been prefigured in the racist fantasy and must really be *out there*. The absent Muslim is thus, it seems, a fantasy. Here things become even more confusing, for there is also another fantasy in play: the fantasy Muslim that the racist confused for the fantasy absent Muslim. Racism, in other words, is not an empirically bounded pursuit. It is structured around certain fundamental fantasies and manifests in a proliferation of other fantasies.

So here's a question: if one cannot expect to change a racist's mind by presenting empirical evidence that racialised subjects are 'not like that' (Myers 2003: 104–5), then is it credible to suppose that a racist would even care whether he targeted the correct Other or simply some other Other? Just what are we trying to say here about the principled and empirical nature of racism? Thus the rubric of mistaken identity also conjures the fantasy object of Islamophobia – the absent non-subject – and is contingent on our belief that this fantasm really exists, and that the symbolic order that conjured it really is coherent. The fantasy form that Islamophobia takes is such that when Muslims are mistaken for threatening others, then under the same framing we would also have to consider them as victims of mistaken identity. But this cuts to the heart of the politics of Islamophobia, which is not understood as racism on the grounds of the apparently incomplete phenotypal raciality of Muslims. In this we can observe that the notion of Islamophobia as not racism thus also conjures its own fantasy, that of the ontically pure racial subject. We are thus left with a paradox: in the presence of Muslims we have the absence of racism, but in the absence of Muslims we have the presence of a form that can be characterised as racism. In other words the denial of Islamophobia's racism displaces analysis of its form or political rationality through the sole emphasis upon the fantasy of the racially complete subject. This case also illustrates another paradox at the heart of the politics of Islamophobia in that while incidents targeting non-Muslims are characterised as cases of mistaken identity, those involving Muslims are not. Thus not only is race the arbiter of how we understand racism, but it is also the locus for our attempts at recognition; mistaken identity is not read at the level of individual subjects but rather at the level of the racial category alone, so the rubric is necessarily essentialist.

It is important in this context to note that the past decade has witnessed a surprising range of manifestations of mistaken identity involving Muslims. Patel and Tyrer (2011) cite a number of instances of mistaken identities cases including the arrests of Maher Arar, Lotfi Raissi, and Hicham Yezza. An innocent Canadian businessman, Arar was detained on a stopover at Kennedy International Airport and subjected to extraordinary rendition to Syria where he was tortured. After over 300 days in prison, Arar was finally repatriated to Canada, where a Commission of inquiry into the incident reported that he had not posed any threat to Canadian national security. Despite this, he remains on a US terrorism watch list and was thus unable to enter the United States even to attend a *Time* magazine event that recognised him as an influential person. For his part Lotfi Raissi found infamy as the first major arrest connected with 9/11, when at the behest of the FBI, British police arrested him in a counter-terrorism raid on his London home in the early hours of the morning. An Algerian airline pilot, Raissi was accused of involvement in the 9/11 plot, although this was not the case. Hicham Yezza, a postgraduate student at the University of Nottingham, was caught downloading terrorism documents from the US Department of Justice website for academic purposes and was arrested on 14 May 2008 on the charge of 'commission, preparation or instigation of an act of terrorism' under the Terrorism Act 2000. Shortly afterwards a second student, Rizwan Sabir, was also arrested in connection with the incident on the same charge. Both were released six days later, although attempts were made to deport Yezza, who instead ended up serving five months of a nine-month sentence for visa irregularities. These have not been isolated cases, as cases such as the 2006 Forest Gate counter-terrorism raid demonstrate. On 2 June 2006 an anti-terror raid was carried out on a house in east London which resulted in the arrest of two innocent men, one of whom was shot by the police. According to some subsequent claims the raid had been launched on the basis of evidence provided by a prisoner convicted of dishonesty offences. In another case four actors returning from the Berlin premiere of Michael Winterbottom's (2006) docu-drama *The Road To Guantanamo* were reportedly detained by police for questioning. One of the actors, Riz Ahmed, later released a satirical song inspired by the incident, *Post 9/11 Blues*, which was banned from UK airplay.

We can also broaden our understanding of cases of mistaken identity involving Muslims by considering the use of profiling practices employed in the war on terror that had the effect of criminalising many innocent people. In this we can thus pause for a moment and consider if a profile, whether enforced by the state through a routine stop-frisk operation or privatised through individual citizens' attempts to inform on suspicious neighbours, also constitutes another fantasy, for even if its operation is based upon the most sophisticated scholarship, and even though we face a very real threat from Islamist terrorism, the subject of a profile is not an empirically real individual who is out there, but an aggregation of what that subject might appear like *if* s/he really exists. In practice the operation of profiling has thus been shown to throw up countless cases of mistaken identity. For example, post-9/11 policing practices in the United States conflated law enforcement with immigration enforcement and drew in a range of profiling related practices both formally (such as airline watch lists, police stops and searches) and informally (reporting the dubious neighbour) (Meeropol 2005). The combined result of these was that 96,000 tip-offs were received by security services in the wake of the 9/11 atrocity, and before long 1,200 had been arrested and questioned, of whom 762 were placed on the INS Custody List as believed to have been involved in 9/11 or of undetermined involvement; held in secret conditions, not one detainee was in fact linked to 9/11 (Murray 2004: 31). Elia (2006: 157) states the collateral damage in stark terms, noting that 'thousands of Arab American men were rounded up, arrested, deported, or otherwise disappeared'. In total up to 2,000 people were detained, and in a lengthy passage Mathur (2006) provides some insight into its effects on innocent people. Noting that profiling practices extended beyond straightforward policing to financial profiling that prevented people from wiring money to overseas relatives, Mathur recounts the arrest sweeps that impacted upon communities in the wake of 9/11:

law enforcement officials began picking up South Asian and Middle Eastern men off the streets, from their homes and from their workplaces. Arrests were made on the basis of tips, reports of 'suspicious activity', which apparently consisted of having a South Asian or Middle Eastern appearance. These reports came largely from neighbours, disgruntled colleagues, employees, ex-girlfriends or landlords. Most of the arrests took place between 2 and 6am and the 'midnight knock' came to be dreaded. Men were taken away from their homes in handcuffs, while their wives and children were held off at gunpoint. An attorney who lives in downtown Jersey City, just across the Hudson river from Manhattan, witnessed one of these raids in her own neighbourhood:

"It was a few days after September 11th. I was on my way home and found my block was closed off by SWAT teams and surrounded by police and emergency vehicles. A number of Arab and Middle Eastern families lived in one building. As I watched, men were led out and separated from their families. Women in headscarves carrying babies and holding children were lined up against the wall. The kids were crying. Helicopters hovered above flashing red, white and blue lights. A huge crowd of neighbours, representing in its make-up the diversity of the neighbourhood, watched and cheered, chanting 'U-S-A! U-SA!'" (Mathur 2006: 34–5)

The use of profiling was not restricted to the United States. For example, in Germany a *rasterfahndung* [dragnet] was set up in 2001 to trawl data for potential terrorist suspects based not on their concrete existence as terrorists but rather on an aggregate profile constructed on the basis of factors such as age, gender, and place of origin. In total over 8,000,000 people were profiled before the practice was ruled unconstitutional in 2003. In Britain section 44(1) and 44(2) of the Terrorism Act (2000) allowed use of blanket stop and search powers in particular areas for renewable periods of time up to 28 days each, and the huge increase in Asians searched was not only a result of the discretion of individual officers but the result of a determined effort to focus law enforcement on particular ethnic groups (Moeckli 2007: 661). Moeckli (2007: 663) also cites Lord Scott's justification of Section 44 stop and search powers to the House of Commons Home Affairs Committee on the grounds that such activities 'might require some degree of stereotyping in the selection of the persons to be stopped and searched and arguably, therefore, some degree of discrimination'. In 2009 Lord Carlile, the UK government's independent reviewer of anti-terror legislation, noted the lack of evidence that Section 44 searches could prevent a terrorist atrocity, and that 'while arrests for other crime have followed searches under the section, none of the many thousands of searches has ever resulted in a conviction for a terrorism offence. Its utility has been questioned publicly and privately by senior Metropolitan police staff with wide experience of terrorism policing' (Travis 2009). Carlile also noted that there was no shortage of anecdotal evidence suggesting that police forces were increasing their stops and searches more generally in order to balance the books and make official data look less skewed towards members of certain ethnic and racial groups (Travis 2009). Despite this he remained supportive of retaining Section 44 powers, although they were ruled unlawful by the European Court in January 2010 following a case brought by anti-arms trade campaigners.

Given the failure of racial profiling practices to crack the problem of Islamist terrorism but its curious success in targeting the innocent, some have suggested that its main attraction lies in its promise to protect us against threatening Others (Patel and Tyrer 2011: 11). Curiously none of this is accounted for within the mistaken identity framing. But it is not only profiling practices that conjure a fantasy, and not only cases of mistaken identity involving innocents that display this logic.

In June 2011 three Muslim men were sentenced to 25 years each for participating in a terrorist plot against synagogues in the United States. Judge Colleen McMahon quite rightly concluded that the men were engaged in a horrifying plan and that they deserved to be punished, but rather less predictably she described the entire plot as a 'fantasy' (Weiser 2011), and concluded that the defendants were not terrorists but 'thugs for hire, pure and simple'. McMahon concluded, moreover, that 'there would never have been any case if the government had not made one up ... no one except the government instigated, planned and brought [the plot] to fruition' (Greenberg 2011). The case had resulted from a sting operation involving a controversial informant claimed by the defence to have scoured mosques looking for easy targets before recruiting them to a plan for which he also supplied the money, supplies, and knowledge (Glaberson 2010). During the case the judge described one of the defendants as 'utterly inept' and suggested that 'only the government could have made a "terrorist" out of Mr. Cromitie, whose buffoonery is positively Shakespearean in its scope' (Weiser 2011). I do not wish to rehearse the seemingly complex and troubled biographies of the convicted men for this might detract from the fact that they were clearly in the process of undertaking an act of horrifying violence. But the case is important in one respect: it illustrates what can happen when states cultivate fantasy for their own ends, not only in carrying out sweeps for likely possible suspects but actively recruiting them to carry out terrorist atrocities being planned by its own employees. Of course, further examples abound – Archer and Bawdon (2010) devote an entire book to the case of a British deadly poison plot involving Muslims that never was.

Beyond Mistaken Identities

> a letter always arrives at its destination.
>
> (Lacan 1972: 72)

The limits of the mistaken identities framing can be traced to its logic, which presupposes the existence of another ontically pure subject for whom the wrong person has been mistaken. Edgar Allen Poe's story *The Purloined Letter* provides us with a number of alternative approaches to this problematic. Poe's story centres on the theft of a letter by a Minister, whose possession of it grants him the power to blackmail the Queen. The police are asked to retrieve the letter because the Queen is unable to do so without compromising herself, although their quest proves circuitous and not unproblematic. One possible reading of this is provided by Schlag (1998: 3), who notes Detective Dupin's conclusion that the police were unable to find the letter because although they had employed an exaggerated set of principles for searching, as they were using inappropriate principles, their search would thus be fruitless. This is a useful metaphor for the problem of other intersubjective relations, such as racial attacks. The failure to analyse the form of the phenomenon, instead focusing upon the nature of the identities at stake in the attack ignores how racism in fact subjectifies and thus forecloses our ability to grasp analytically either the identities at stake or the nature of the incident. Another reading of the case is provided by Lacan, whose analysis draws our attention to the ways in which the subjects involved in the encounter enter into an intersubjective relation based on difference that is made possible by the letter's positioning in relation to them. In Lacan's reading the letter operates as a pure signifier which is repeatedly displaced, so the issue at stake is not the meanings of the identities of the individuals nor the meaning of the letter, but rather the effects of the letter upon the different characters that produces meanings. In this, Lacan's reading reveals traces of the power brought to bear in subjectivity itself (Stavrakakis 1999). This is a more useful way to understand the ways in which racisms produce certain effects and meanings, so that just as the different subjects who come into contact with the letter in Lacan's reading take on certain qualities, the same is also true in the case of Islamophobic violence. This opens the way to understanding more broadly how it is that the political rationality of Islamophobia comes to have a wider purchase over subjects other than just Muslims, enabling it to emerge as a defining form of racism.

But the political utility of this defining form of contemporary racism relates also to its deniability, to the ways in which it can be exceptionalised as a non-racism that only affects a limited group, and its disavowals consolidated through justifications that make reference to incompetence rather than intent. In the face of this there is a sense in which we seem powerless to do anything about Islamophobia, and in this an alternative reading is also helpful. Zizek

(2005) has argued that Poe's story reveals to us the impotent gaze: that of the Queen who is impotent to act on the theft of the letter without incriminating herself. But the big Other – the ignorant King who represents authority – is also impotent to act (Zizek 2005: 74). This thus introduces the notion of passive, impotent observation to something that does not pose a threat to our well-being, yet which cannot straightforwardly be symbolised, which cannot be represented (Zizek 2005: 74). In this there is a further parallel to the seemingly unstoppable rise of Islamophobia, as it targets the absent Muslim even when it takes Muslims as its objects; that invisible non-subject whose presence is symbolised through lack and absence, sporadically summoned into terrifying moments of hyperreal visibility as a void lacking proper corporeal form which manifests in burkas, minarets, and violence, but never in the form taken by complete subjects. This is not to suggest that Muslims do not pose threats and problems, for recent history demonstrates that the danger of Islamist extremism is very real, although this recognition is underpinned by an acknowl-edgement that violence is not innate or peculiar to Muslims, but that it surfaces across all social groups, always presenting wider political questions. However, it is to recognise that the dream of ontic purity is imbricated in racial fantasies as it conjures forth its own nightmarish visions of lack and excess that organise fields of knowledge and visibilities in ways that foreclose our ability to conceive of Muslims as real subjects. The wider reluctance to rethink how we can symbolise this presence thus has implications for a far wider field including democratic practice. But the fantasmatic visions that are so central to Islamophobia are but one mode of its operation. I think it is time also that we consider some of its other modalities, by considering its centrally visceral form to consider what is at stake in the emotions and affects of Islamophobia – you could say I have a feeling …

3

Once more, with feeling: Islamophobia and racial politics

Certain conjurings seem to burst through into our world in moments of shocking hyperreality as though from another dimension. One way of putting it is to suggest that they leave us lost for words, struggling to integrate them into the symbolic. But to consider them simply as a fantasy seems lacking, for at the same time they manifest as terrifying. If fantasy is the handmaid of Islamophobia then its power to mobilise seems contingent on its visceral nature. It is therefore helpful to turn to the question of affect and emotion since it seems that to disentangle Islamophobia from this wider play can help us grasp the importance and usefulness of its distinctive affective naming, and that it can also help us to further historicise its emergence. To do this I first want to turn to another case of mistaken identity because I have left unremarked the possibility of innocents being mistaken for real Muslims. Of particular interest to me is the case of Jean Charles de Menezes, a Brazilian electrician shot dead in July 2005 by British counter-terrorism officers who had mistaken him for an Islamist terrorist named Hussain Osman. There is something at play in this case that can help us understand the epistemic conditions under which certain anxieties and fear come into play in a world in which we see both a Muslim identity politics that seems difficult to symbolise and a real threat from Islamist terrorism.

Two Minutes Between Stops

Zizek (2002: 45) has argued that the 9/11 atrocities had traumatic effects. In this the attacks burst through the symbolic fabric but could not properly be symbolised. As Salecl (1998: 178) notes, 'memory primarily has to do with the non-remembering of trauma, the real around which the subject centres his or her very being. When we tell our stories, it is at the point at which we touch the real that our words fail'. Thus, because the traumatic event has not been symbolised, it defies straightforward narration, as though 'the "event" of the trauma never took place' (Shepherdson 2008: 92). Jacques Rancière (2010) has challenged this, suggesting that 9/11 cannot be read as marking a rupture in the symbolic order. In other words, the attacks cannot be read as traumatic within the terms of the discussion here. Rancière (2010: 98) argues that the events of 9/11 did not throw into question the ability to incorporate the attack into a recognisable symbolic frame, and moreover that it merely 'brought to light the new dominant form of symbolizing the Same and the Other that has been imposed under the conditions of the new world (dis)order' (Rancière 2010: 104). Thus, because the atrocity could be incorporated into an existing symbolic frame, it could not be read as indicating a rupture through which the real exceeds the capacity for symbolisation. This reading is not helpful because it reduces the idea of a rupture in the symbolic order to something that cannot under any circumstances be symbolised. The task that faces us when confronted by the radicalised deficiency of the symbolic is to introduce a symbolic dimension that will make the trauma thinkable, allow us to work through its effects and integrate it into memory. After 9/11 this occurred through the discourse of the war on terror which enabled the events to be made sense of within a new framing that simultaneously drew on recognisable symbols (our military power; democracy; war ...) while recognising the differences of the new context in a world in which 'everything changed' after 9/11 (the idea that this was not a traditional war, even when waged against states such as Iraq). The discourse of the war on terror emerged to retroactively integrate the attacks into the symbolic field, to offset the effects of its traumatic rupturing by a real that seemed so difficult to make sense of. Thus, even in spite of the real psychological traumas rendered by the countless terrorist attacks since then, these incidents could all be immediately symbolised through the discourse of the war on terror. The success of this operation is such that nine years, ten months and eleven days later, when news filtered through of Anders Breivik's terrorist attacks my immediate, knee-jerk response was simply to assume that they, too were the work of Islamist terrorists. It provided us with a way of making sense of moments that could otherwise have manifested as a traumatic bursting through of the symbolic by the real. But this discourse itself exacerbated underlying anxieties. I am interested in exploring this question, but before I do, I also have to recognise that the anxieties people have faced throughout the encounter with terrorism have not only been produced by our leaders and politicians, but also by terrorists themselves. To acknowledge this I want to turn to a case from the war on terror that helps to show something of the affective and emotional stakes at play in the face of the terrorist threat *and* state responses, and to consider how these might also draw our attention to an underlying anxiety, heightened during the war on terror, of how to symbolise these seemingly non-racial subjects.

On 7 July 2005, Islamist terrorists launched an attack of horrifying violence on London's transport system, causing the murder of over fifty innocents in addition to the beasts who were responsible for the indiscriminate slaughter. A fortnight later further failed terrorist attacks in the capital set into chain a desperate manhunt for four terrorists linked to a flat in Tulse Hill that was placed under police surveillance. On 22 July 2005 it seemed that the hunt for one of the perpetrators, Hussain Osman, had reached its climax in a shooting on board an underground train at Stockwell Station. It soon transpired that things had gone very tragically awry, and that police had instead shot and killed an innocent Brazilian electrician named Jean Charles de Menezes. I want to note that I am not levelling accusations of Islamophobia or racism against those whose accounts of the event I shall draw upon. Rather, I am interested in how played out in these retrospective accounts are retroactive fixings and unfixings of racial knowability. The Menezes case has received surprisingly little academic coverage, and much of the emphasis has been upon power, in which the emphasis in Squires and Kennison (2010) on organisational and procedural questions such as command and control remains something of an exception. Gillborn (2008) frames the case in a wider racial context which leads him to draw attention to the links between the shooting of Menezes and the reported 600 per cent increase in reported cases of 'religious hate crime' that followed the 7/7 atrocity (Gillborn 2008: 24), a move which enables him to suggest the predictability of such trends and incidents when approached from within a Critical Race Theory paradigm. O'Driscoll (2008) employs an explicitly biopolitical frame, though this leaves open the most pressing questions about race and recognition that occur in the case. Although race is mentioned in Vaughan-Williams (2009), here the emphasis is upon biopolitical practices at stake as they relate to his conceptualisation of temporal and spatial bordering practices. In this account, spatial bordering practices are framed by regulation of life and mortality through sovereign acts in urban space, while temporal bordering is set out through reference to the 'lightning strike' of sovereign decision. Since this strikes down with shock and awe, seemingly without warning, it centres upon a reading of the affects at stake in the case, although the question of how this relates to racial misrecognition is not within the scope of his focus.

Race surfaces rather briefly in Moeckli's conjecture that it might be credible to wonder about its role in the misrecognition of Menezes for Osman (Moeckli 2007: 667), though this is not really explored. Garner (2007: 13) asserts rather more boldly that Menezes would probably not have been shot had he been blonde haired and blue eyed, and that 'the point of this is to demonstrate that being or not being white can be a matter of life and death'. On one level this simple truism appears helpful, but although I want to temper my criticism of this reading by noting that the focus of Garner's book is on Whiteness, it still fails to get to grips with the racial politics at stake in the misrecognition of Menezes by eliding the question of being or not being Muslim that was central. This cannot be reduced simply to a broader White/non-White framing in a policing operation in which the search was for a terrorist who was Muslim, and in a wider context in which Muslim identities seem to interrupt straightforward racial recognition, as we have seen. Patel and Tyrer (2011) also offer a short discussion of the case, but here we see a constriction of the question of visibility which elides the fantasmatic conjurings of dangerous others, and the reading of affect offered in this case is reduced solely to the 'affective richness' of the readings of Menezes and the assertion of their centrality to the racial misrecognitions that occurred throughout the case (Patel and Tyrer 2011: 152).

As such, while Patel and Tyrer draw attention to the ways in which this challenges what is supposed to be meant by the systematic operation of race, on the basis of recognising that race is slippery and unstable so its systematicity must act through racial fixings that give the impression of stability (Patel and Tyrer 2011: 153), their account does not properly theorise the possible interplay between affect, visibility, and racism. Joseph Pugliese's account stands as the original, and probably the most sophisticated, academic treatment of the incident. Pugliese immediately draws attention to the fantastic, noting that after its initial reporting of the shooting, the *Sydney Morning Herald* swiftly changed its headline to: 'A bomb suspect? In the end it was a police fantasy' (Pugliese 2006: 1). This allows Pugliese to consider the fantasy played out in the initial 'eyewitness' accounts presented to the news media. In these, early eyewitnesses recounted having watched as an Asian man dressed suspiciously for the weather with a bulky jacket from which, in one account, protruded wires, fled police and leapt over the ticket barrier at Stockwell Station. The fantastical nature of these accounts was also illustrated when the QC for London's Metropolitan Police told the 2008 Inquest that 'You cannot use the eyewitness evidence to constitute what happened, because if you did, you would have people firing into the carriage from outside, you would have Arabs firing into the roof of the carriage, and many other actions and words spoken that cannot have happened or cannot have been said at the time before the shooting' (cited in Patel and Tyrer 2011: 153). This recognition of the fantastical at stake in the case is organised by Pugliese's recognition that fantasy comes to gain the appearance of reality through the 'violent exercise of power' (Pugliese 2006: 4). The helpfulness of this is more widely illustrated by the ways in which Islamophobic fears of Muslims appropriate particular tropes – we have seen the example of the far right's appropriation from progressive political discourse on women's rights and their rearticulation in anti-Muslim racism – that enables the fantasmatic figure of the burka-clad woman to appear as a particular reality of Muslimness in spite of her existence as a small minority within a minority. This enables Pugliese to suggest that the Brazilian Menezes was thus resignified as (South) Asian through a corporeal inscription contingent upon the systemacity of what Pugliese terms a racialised regime of visuality that finds its expression through racial profiling practices.

Pugliese's account opens the way for reading racialised profiling in terms of the primacy of the visual, and thus the ways in which particular fantasies are conjured as subjects are rendered (hyper)visible through racial inscriptions. By drawing attention to early eyewitness accounts he foregrounds how these processes are not restricted to state practice, but are privatised and dispersed among ordinary citizens based on the hold of race. Menezes was fundamentally misrecognised for a Muslim, in other words for a figure that is particularly disruptive to the racialised regime Pugliese discusses. Eyewitness accounts presented to the Independent Police Complaints Commission investigations into the events of the day (2007a, 2007b) and the Stockwell Inquest (2008a, 2008b) complicate this, although none of these were available when Pugliese's piece was written. These are riven through with a plethora of other racial misidentifications; Patel and Tyrer (2011) draw attention to a host of misrecognitions that occurred between Menezes' departure from his flat and his shooting: 'IC1' [white] (IPCC 2007a: 57), 'light skinned' North African (*ibid.*), Mongolian eyes (*ibid.*), Asian with a bulky jacket (IPCC 2007a: 64); the scale of the misrecognitions is such that one almost loses track of whom is being mistaken for whom, so we read in a particularly harrowing recollection from a passenger (Stockwell Inquest 2008b: 64) of her terror as a man with 'light', 'olive' and 'mixed race' colouring with a 'dark brown or black' beard, who appears to be a 'tall Asian male' (Stockwell Inquest 2008a: 65) with a rucksack behaves in ways that ultimately causes her to flee the train, to the sound of gunfire behind her on the train. The passenger was neither the terrorist nor Menezes, but a police officer, while another officer in the same carriage also describes noticing the clothing of an 'olive skinned' man in the carriage (Stockwell Inquest 2008a: 2), who in turn seems to have been another officer; further forward the train driver ran out into the darkness of the tunnel when he saw on his in-cab CCTV screen that 'fanatics' seemed to have taken over the train; these too were officers in plain clothes or, in the driver's words, 'in mufti' (Stockwell Inquest 2008b: 3).

What makes the various misidentifications throughout the affair so striking is that they are couched in such a wide range of racial signifiers. Here, the eyewitness accounts are so striking precisely because they were not couched in a language of Islamophobia; had they been so, the sense of misidentification would have been far less jarring. Instead of people being misidentified for Asians, north Africans, people with traditional phenotypal markers of difference, each of which appears to compound the problem of identifying the incorporeal raced subject, there would only have been one fundamental misidentification repeated throughout, rather than the range that occurred, in which each of the misidentified subjects would simply have been mistaken for a Muslim. Islamophobia emerges as a way of finding a language to speak of a presence that is difficult to place within a conventional racial grammar. While Pugliese's account is helpful in introducing the notion of the fantasmatic that is missing from other accounts, but that what stands out is a certain symbolic deficiency; an ontological problem in which the presence of Muslims introduces an excess that appears to resist proper symbolisation, and that this has certain spillover effects to that not only is it difficult to racially place Muslims with any certainty, but it also proves difficult to correctly place non-Muslims from a range of ascribed racialised subject positions with any degree of accuracy. Thus, a more fundamental fantasy is being transmitted through the encounter, which is a society in which race retains its systemacity and subjects can be accurately placed and categorised racially. The problem of Muslim knowability manifests through a particular set of symbolic difficulties. Islamophobia makes it possible to deal with these, and it does so precisely by introducing a language predicated upon covering up the split in the symbolic fabric of race by reinserting an implied notion of the coherence of the racial signifier through its contrast with the non-raciality of Muslims. One possible way of dealing with these difficulties is through fantasy, so the fantasmatic excess that accompanies Islamophobia cannot be understood solely on the level of visuality as Pugliese implies, but it also has to be understood through the question of affect. Fantasy is not the only possible response to the anxieties presented by the ways in which Muslims seem to present a symbolic crisis, and to explore this I want to turn now to the question of Islamophobia's naming as a phobia. Doing this can help us historicise Islamophobia and better understand its relationship to a wider field of politics, but it is also helpful in order to understand the emotion and affect implied in its naming.

Fear as a Bad Adviser

How quickly the apparently solidly laid foundation of one's existence could crumble

Patrick Süskind, *The Pigeon*

While recognition of Islamophobia has been a fraught and drawn out political process, even among its staunchest advocates the term has seemed problematic and at best provisional. Despite this, it has been widely translated (Vakil 2011); for example, one need only consider interventions such as Vincent Geisser's (2003) *La Nouvelle Islamophobie* to recognise the term's purchase beyond the anglophone world. This spread appears rather remarkable given the debates that have surrounded it. Chapter 1 sketched out some of these by focusing upon the question of raciality, but the inscription of phobia means that it is helpful to return to the contests over its definition. Considered literally, the term implies two things: first, that Islam is its object, and second, that its form is fear. If it is unhelpful to conceive Islamophobia as being centrally concerned with religion, it is nonetheless helpful to rehearse a further point in support of this argument before turning to the question of fear. The words we use are not simple reflections of an underlying and unproblematic reality. The naming of Islamophobia to centre religion is curious because centuries of debates over religion in the West have bequeathed a well-developed lexicon for various categories of religious criticism or rejection, ranging from blasphemy and sacrilege to impiousness and profanity (and let us not forget more banal notions such as critique). On the other hand, its elision of racism is unsurprising, because we also have far shorter histories of recognising or discussing racism in meaningful ways (and longer histories of denial), as a consequence of which we have relatively few helpful terms for racism. Racism does what it says on the proverbial tin, and at a stretch, we also have terms such as xenophobia. Islamophobia exists in a tension: its specific naming disarticulates it from a wider racial politics, and yet at the same time we are left with the problem that it needs to be named in order to historicise and conceptualise it, especially given that, even in spite of its wider effects, it is unusually precise among racisms in targeting a particular group. Monica Massari's (2006) *Islamofobia: La paura e l'Islam* is helpful in this respect, insofar as Massari opens her discussion of Islamophobia's definition with a consideration of the Runnymede Trust's (1997) conception, but this does not prevent her from concluding that Islamophobia is a form of racism that articulates elements such as religion, nation, and race, frequently organising them in terms of culture and cultural difference (Massari 2006: 65). This leads Massari to conclude that this neoracism operates as a form of racism without race (Massari 2006: 81), a point that resonates with Tyrer and Sayyid (2012), who draw upon Goldberg's conception of racial neoliberalism as entailing the pursuit of precisely such a racism without race (Goldberg 2009). In conceptualising Islamophobia as a form of racism, Massari observes that much of the hostility that has occurred across Europe has been directed less at things related to Islam, but more towards people perceived as being Muslim, regardless of whether or not they actually are (Massari 2006: 81). I find her conceptualisation helpful, and it brings us to the second part of Islamophobia's naming.

In this respect a further problem with the Runnymede Trust's (1997) definition of Islamophobia can be found in its double inscription of affect and irrational fear. This conflation and confusion has been repeatedly rehearsed in succeeding discussions. One of its effects is to supplement the notion that Islamophobia is about religion rather than racism, so that its racism can be disavowed through the claim to rationality. For example, Toynbee's (2005) reading of Islamophobia merely as a device to prevent critique of religion, and entitled 'My right to offend a fool' could be read as an illustration of this logic. Thus, hostility to the notion of Islamophobia as racism emerges as a triumph of rationality. Indeed, even the supporters of the extreme right justify their anti-Muslim politics as being a perfectly rational fear, and in this context in which Islamophobia is rationalised through disavowal, it emerges as a defence not only of democracy but also of reason. As a consequence, Islamophobia in turn is often viewed as courageous (Todorov 2010: 8). This problem of defining Islamophobia points to a misunderstanding of racism and to a misunderstanding of the role of affect in political practice. To Jasmine Zine, Islamophobia can only actually be understood 'as part of a rational system of Western social, economic, political and cultural power' (Zine 2006: 35). As Andrew Shryock (2010: 10) notes, any emphasis on Islamophobia's supposed irrationality fails to grasp its causes, forms, and effects. In other words, if emotion is not to be understood as irrational, then perhaps there is something in the *phobic* structure of this phenomenon that can enhance our understanding of its political rationality and enable us to grasp the specificity of its focus on Muslims without either disarticulating it from a wider field of racial politics on the one hand or rendering Muslims invisible on the other. Before we can explore the phobic metaphor for anti-Muslim racism, it is helpful to consider the relevance of affect and emotion to political practices. This is important, for although questions about Muslims tend to be explored in terms such as the relationship between religion and politics, what is left underexplored is the question about the relationship between emotion and politics. This question has a particular relevance at a time in which we speak of 'fear', 'terror', and '-phobia', but also because in the context of the wider liberal problem in dealing with emotion and affect, as Mouffe (2005) has highlighted, the far right has increasingly mobilised through a very affective politics. Before proceeding further, it is helpful to set out a distinction between affect and emotion, which are often treated as somehow overlapping yet somehow different and complementary. Whereas the former can seem possessed of a certain energy, tension, or intensity that might be experienced bodily but is not symbolised, the latter is symbolised even as it is experienced bodily, so that another way of expressing the distinction relates to 'the border between the real and the symbolic' (Shepherdson 2008: 83). We can immediately grasp from this distinction one political use of affect and emotion insofar as theoretically at least, it would seem that the ability to produce or mobilise certain affective responses in subjects could induce people to behave in particular ways. For example, if my employers were to play the excruciating sound of fingernails being scraped down a chalkboard each time I leave my desk, the indescribable bodily responses this would induce in me would likely ensure certain responses on my part (work harder or flee). On the other hand, since emotion always retains a particular symbolic link, it helps organise our relationships to our bodies in particular ways. Thus the ability to employ emotion and affect in politics can be of use in organising bodies and regulating life.

There is an implicit investment in affect within Foucault's conception of governmentality, in which the success of panopticism is to some degree reliant upon the anxiety of the governed leading to self-surveillance. Subsequent works have placed an increasing emphasis upon the relationships between affect, emotion, and power. This literature has also been influenced by the attention paid to bodies, emotions, and affects in feminism and queer theory, and frequently draws upon phenomenology in order to situate biopolitics in a flexibilised, post-Fordist context in which the original functions of the traditional disciplinary institutions are seen as having somehow come into crisis (cf. Tyrer 2011). To Tie (2004: 169), once we accept that the distinction between power and domination is predicated upon the awareness of subjects, then it is also important to recognise that these states of awareness might not only be discursive, but that they can also be achieved through affect and its organisation through discourse as emotion. Sara Ahmed (2004a) has considered the operation of economies of affect, which Richard and Rudnyckyj (2009: 59) suggest is dependent upon an understanding of their operation as domains in which subjects are produced through the creation of continuities between state and self in much the same way as the family (or other Foucaultian economies). Literature on an intensification and radical dispersal of the operation of power has emerged in the wake of Deleuze's re-reading of Foucault (Deleuze 1992), in which a shift from discipline, predicated upon enclosure in disciplinary institutions, to control, based on immanence and the problematisation of clear distinctions between inside and outside, so that rather than passing through a particular sequence of disciplinary institutions, individuals are constantly acted upon through modulating forms of control (Topal 2011; Lazzarato 2006).

Imbricated in this is a recognition of the increasing role of affect, so that the shift from discipline to control is seen as being played out through a move from discipline based on the discursive constitution of subjects to control based on information and the direct accessing of bodies through technologies of affect and at-a-distance control (Clough 2003; Lazzarato 2006; Terranova 2007). Such interventions tend to situate contemporary political uses of affect in the context of wider shifts in the organisation of capital accumulation (e.g. Fordism to post-Fordism; informationalisation, and so on), and as it plays out amid an intensification of power, and they note that it occurs through a range of ways. For example, Puar's (2007) analysis sets out how this policing of somatic intensities comes into play in a range of questions such as suspect profiling and cases of mistaken identity. This broad and varying literature on affect helps us to historicise the emergence of contemporary Islamophobia in the context of wider shifts and trans-formations and an intensification of biopolitics. But it still remains to consider how Islamophobia emerges in a wider context of affect, and whether its emergence takes a form that can usefully be characterised as phobic. To achieve this it is first helpful to retreat from the concept of phobia into a less specific modality of fear. Shryock (2010: 9) has noted that 'the insidious nature of Islamophobia is not located in fear alone, or in hate; nor is it found in the designation of enemies as such, since a society or group can define its enemies, or be defined as enemies, for entirely legitimate reasons. One can, for instance, consider al-Qaeda an enemy, fear their policies, and hate the violence they espouse without being an Islamophobe'. One cannot understand Islamophobia simply through recourse to the notion of a fear of Muslims. This again excep-tionalises Islamophobia and disarticulates it from a wider politics of emotion and affect, so that we are left dealing with a symptom alone: the named fear of Muslims (or, of Islam as its problematic naming indicates). For example, Muslims may present certain fears and anxieties that do not reflect their actual capacities (or otherwise) to harm us; in this we can see them as symptoms of a wider problem during the war on terror. They might also present certain anxieties because of the ways in which they interrupt symbolic authority of race, but this is again a symptom of the impossibility of a society organised around the stable hold of such problematic signifiers. But we cannot understand a problem only through its symptom. As Svendsen (2008: 111) notes: 'Political fear does not arise in a vacuum – it is created and maintained. Its function is to promote various political practices'.

Within the literature on fear some emphasis has been placed on the formative role of media reporting about crime and security which, under the rubric of risk, heightened a general sense of anxiety and insecurity which has subsequently been consolidated and entrenched as a mode of neoliberal governance (Altheide 2006). Seemingly every area of human life has been securitised, from sexual health to the food we eat, from the risk of contagion to our online behaviour, from the architecture of cities with all the surveillance technologies this entails to the securitisation of clothing and bodies. Daily we learn that cigarettes, alcohol, sex, cycling without a helmet, saturated fats, polyunsaturated fats, winter, antibiotic resistance, others, and even ideas can kill. These are not the only sources of anxiety, whether about jobs, finances, body image or our ability to keep up with the latest technology and desirable goods, so even if the security industrial complex were to be dismantled it would prove impossible to place the mischievous genie back into the bottle for anxiety has been rendered diffuse, privatised in the most intimate of ways, and impossible to pin down or localise. Svendsen (2008: 46–7) describes this as a condition of 'generalised fear as a mood rather than a specific emotion'. Like a mood it seems enveloping, and in turn its pervasive nature creates the sense that events are changing too quickly, 'things are falling apart, that they no longer make sense' (Erickson 2010: 2), and that events somehow lie beyond our gift; as a result of which it is bound up with popular calls for increased control (Altheide 2006: 16). The ubiquity of this anxiety is the basis of its hold. Such a condition can perhaps be more helpfully understood as ambience (Papastergiadis 2006), since it operates on the basis of its saturation and yet its unremarkability; through anxiety, fear is no longer a condition of extreme threat but rather an everyday condition of insecurity in neoliberal societies. Of course, these are not the only sources of anxiety; we live beneath horizons of security measured and disseminated by states, financial institutions, private corporations, always colour coded so that whether our anti-virus software is out of date or the threat to national security has elevated, the message cannot easily go unnoticed or lost as simply another toxic turd dodged amid the shit storm of information that fertilises anxiety as it spews continuously from all parts of the societally-organised anxiety machine. Adriano Purgato (2006: 7) has argued that phobias – and in this he also considers Islamophobia – have become a twenty-first-century obsession in the context of the information and media age with its constant streaming of images.

Ambient anxiety has been produced on an industrial scale and this is especially visible in the case of the security-industrial complex that has become staggering in its size (cf. Priest and Arkin 2011) as well as its effects. If Islamophobia emerges in the context of anxieties, then the discourse of securitisation that has become a dominant paradigm for dealing with global political problems has two implications. First, there is the question of what securitisation means in relation to political problems. Here, Buzan, Waever and de Wilde (1998: 29) note that to securitise an issue does not simply entail treating it as a political problem, for despite the appearance of a hyper-politicisation, it actually entails removing an issue from normal politics so that 'in another sense it is opposed to politicization'. The contemporary discourse of securitisation is, in this light, a manifestation of post-political logic, and the articulation of Islamophobia with security in turn frames the post-political nature of contemporary Islamophobia. Second, the generalisation of security has the effect of Monahan (2010: 19) has the effect of privatising security, producing 'a new kind of citizen, the insecurity subject' (Monahan 2010: 19). This privatisation of security is itself framed by the neoliberal logics of post-political Islamophobia. Just as the naming of anti-Muslim racism as Islamophobia implies that it is privatised, so too is the securitisation which has fuelled the spread of Islamophobia privatised.

But the production of anxiety is routinised and dispersed across the social; for instance, Katz (2007: 352) has written of the hold of a banalised conception of terrorism in structuring urban space as a way to solidify a 'porous nation' (Katz 2007: 355). This can be witnessed in a range of ways, from the increased use of surveillance technologies in the name of waging the war on terror, to the increased use of stop and search practices, and from the design of city centre retail developments so as to be most resilient in the event of a terrorist atrocity to, in a current case, proposals to site surface to air missiles in residential blocks to defend London against terrorist attacks during the 2012 Olympic Games. Such practices do not only respond to anxiety, but they cultivate it; Todorov has noted, for example, that processes associated with globalisation have created a series of anxieties, but citing responses to questions about integration and national identity that these invoke, he suggests that 'the nature of the reactions to this change does not strike us as likely to quieten the anxieties it has aroused' (Todorov 2010: 210). This observation is helpful because it draws our attention to a particular series of anxieties that have emerged around race and culture as difference and its management have been securitised, a risk attendant upon processes of national and regional securitisation (cf. d'Appollonia and Reich 2010). This has given way to a wider set of claims concerning the supposed excess of alterity that needs to be managed (Grillo 2007). In this sense, even ignoring the threat posed by militant Islamism, 'ordinary' common or garden Muslims seem to radicalise the condition of contemporary anxiety because of their inadequate realisation as a political surplus that exceeds symbolisation in racial terms, and which interrupts the closure of the nation. This fear of excessive difference is a fantasy, for difference is always exterior and has always existed in many forms, but it refers to a deficiency, not to the fact that there *is* too much difference but rather that this difference appears to overwhelm us because it is incompletely tamed. Untamed difference is a symbolic problem, a difficulty that emerges when the categories by which we organise the world appear incapable of con(s)t(r)aining all that difference, and it is at the same time an ontological problem that most forcefully reminds us not only of the impossibility of the closure of the nation but the inadequacy of its symbolic basis. Not only do others not appear in their place, but as a result of this, our own sense of self identity is threatened; we too seem to be dissolving. So the far right mobilises around anxieties that our identity is eroding and that 'the indigenous' [Whites] have been subjected to 'ethnic cleansing' and eradicated from our cities, so that 'we' are under threat.

So, we live in anxious times. Still, anxiety is not phobia – so what is?

And They Walk Among Us: Muslims as Phobic Objects

Zizek (1997: 79) notes that 'the subject "is" only through its confrontation with the enigma of *Che vuoi?* ("What do you want?")'. Fantasy covers this problem and the anxieties that are attendant upon it by covering the space that is left, providing a way of acting out desire that could almost appear scripted. Thus the fantasies that we see in the apparent absence of Muslim can be understood as a working through of the question of what the Other wants in absence (and in the context of the ontological difficulty presented by dealing symbolically with the Other). Another way of dealing with anxiety is through a primarily defensive response, and this we can see as a problem of proximity, of what happens when the Other encroaches too much. Here it is therefore helpful to introduce a further distinction, between anxiety and phobia as a defence. Phobias take countless forms; for example, following a terrifying childhood encounter with a steam train, the American writer Ellery Leonard developed agoraphobia, a phobia of water (despite being a good swimmer), and a phobia of trains; his autobiography *The Locomotive-God* explored this and recounted a debilitating adult encounter with a passing locomotive in 1911.

In seminar IV Lacan offers an account of phobia based on a reading of Freud's famous Little Hans case. The young Hans had developed a phobia of horses, which in Lacan's reading had arisen as a response to the boy's traumatic experience of his own body which had led him to mistake his own bodily sensations for his mother's desire. As such, the trauma also concerned his own mortality, for this mistaken association would have left no space for Hans, who would have been reducible simply to being the object of his mother's desire (Van Haute 2002: 115). The phobia had been developed as a protection against this anxiety, so that the horse enabled a symbolic reordering that simultaneously served to keep the anxiety at a distance and making it manageable by introducing an element that enables symbolisation. In this, Hook and Neill (2008) note that the object of the phobia operates rather like an empty signifier, since it lacks a fixed meaning but can be introduced to protect against a range of disturbing anxieties. The object of the phobia is thus not the problem, but serves a symbolic function because anxiety, figured in terms of loss, can be worked through by attaching it to a specific object. Phobias can enable a wider condition of anxiety or trauma to become nameable, and through this symbolisation, to be dealt with pragmatically (held at a distance) or worked through in some way. In this there is a distinction between fantasy and anxiety. In this, the structure of phobia has some promise as a metaphor for this racist discourse that seems to take Muslims as its objects.

As Muslim difference has been problematised as excessive, across the West attempts have been made to tame or erase that difference, through the logics of integration that tell us this difference has gone too far. What is problematised is not *per se* the behaviour of the Other, but rather that the infractions of some others can be generalised as a condition of Otherness. As such the Other's assumed infractions can be explained through her/his excessive difference from us. This phobic response thus emerges in the wake of the anxiety over the closure of the nation (and of our identity). This introduces a tension into contemporary discourse on integration through which states have emphasised distance – measured culturally, socially, geographically – as a cause of ethnic conflict in the West. For example, Trevor Phillips, Chair at that time of the Commission for Racial Equality, argued that some parts of the country were turning into 'black holes into which no-one goes without fear and trepidation, and from which no-one escapes undamaged ... If we allow this to continue, we could end up in 2048 ... in a New Orleans-style Britain of passively co-existing ethnic and religious communities, eyeing each other uneasily over the fences of our differences' (BBC 2005). But the idea that racism is born through distance ignores its emergence in proximity. As Zizek notes, the form of contemporary racism is of hatred against the neighbour. Diken and Laustsen describe in stark terms the logic of asylum seeker dispersal practices, describing refugee camps as 'perfect materializations of a "fear of touching"' (Diken and Laustsen 2005: 87); racism works by attempting to increase social distance precisely because it is felt in proximity. This mode of racism precisely reflects in contemporary concerns about bordering practices which are seen to have failed and left 'us' overrun, awash with difference that can no longer be contained by physical borders or symbolic boundaries of race.

Islamophobia does not simply emerge around distance, but also in proximity – the fear of the Other who cannot easily be recognised because of the disruption to our systems for racial classification, systems which also traditionally work to impose distance between the self and the Other. In this, phobia is a helpful metaphor because it emerges through the potential for proximity. Once we accept that Islamophobia emerges through proximity, we therefore also have to question some fundamental assumptions, such as the idea that the objects of this phobia have patently failed to integrate. In this we can see that if the conduct of Others is problematic, then this can be read as a political problem (how they can be induced to obey laws or informal conventions), but that in Islamophobic discourse this is reinscribed as a cultural problem; it is not a function of their difference, but their proximity; for integration is not a problem when 'they' are overseas, but only arises in a postcolonial context when 'they' are among us.

Massari (2006) notes that Islamophobia primarily targets Muslims, but in making this argument she notes that it does not target, for instance, places of worship. This is helpful in the sense that Islamophobia *does* target places of worship, as we can see from the attacks against mosques and gurdwaras that occurred, for example, after the terrorist atrocities that hit London on 7 July 2005. For example, in December 2011 two white men, one of whom was a serving soldier and supporter of the English Defence League who had joined Facebook groups with names such as 'Nuke all mosques', were convicted of arson and each sentenced to ten years in prison after attempting to blow up a Staffordshire mosque by feeding a gas pipe into it and starting a fire. In other cases, members of the English Defence League have repeatedly mobilised around their own putative 'fear' to organise marches against mosques. Attacks of various forms have occurred against mosques across Europe, and mosque building has met forms of opposition that vary in their creativity – and each time the justification is this named fear. In Cologne lengthy debates over the plans for its Central Mosque were couched in social terms and supported by the organised right, but did not prevent the project from progressing; in Lodi, near Milano, Lega Nord protesters claimed in October 2000 that a pig's urine had been spread on the site of a proposed mosque (Allievi 2005: 53). The targeting of places of worship is not new, but this does not mean that Islamophobia is centrally about religion rather than race.

The best-known mobilisation against a mosque has occurred in response to proposals over the Park51 mosque and cultural centre project in Manhattan, the so-called 'Ground Zero' mosque. It actually transpires that the development will not take place at the site of the 9/11 atrocities, but two blocks away and in a site already in use as a prayer facility (Blumenthal and Mowjood 2009). It therefore seems hardly helpful to view this as an insensitive affront to the Ground Zero memorial site. Despite claims by the project's backers that it would operate as a multi-use space designed to improve interfaith and intercommunal dialogue, combining a prayer space with cultural facilities including a cinema, the most vociferous opposition to the project has conflated Islam and Muslims in general with the Islamist extremists responsible for the earlier terrorist attacks. As such, the opposition has invoked wider fears about Muslims, claiming the project would represent a victory for Islamist extremism. For example, according to Logan (2011: 124) the then leader of the Tea Party Express, Mark Williams – a man who Logan notes has also described President Obama as 'racist-in-chief', an 'Indonesian Muslim', and a 'welfare thug' – responded to protests over the 9/11 mosque project by describing Muslims as savages who worship a monkey god. In other quarters the links were made directly or implicitly, and became almost conspiratorial after Obama announced on 13 August 2010 that the developers were within their rights to develop the centre on land that is in their private ownership. Even when expressed in more sophisticated terms the responses frequently mobilise fear to a level that is almost conspiratorial. Newt Gingrich was reported in *Time* magazine as accusing Obama of 'pandering to radical Islam' (Ratnesar 2010), while Dinesh D'Souza (2010: 203) has argued that the project needs to be understood in the context of traditions of triumphal Islamic architectural commemoration of victories over enemies, and thus 'the radical Muslims would like the Ground Zero mosque built so it can stand as an enduring symbol of resistance to American power, and President Obama evidently agrees with them'. Such claims reflect a wider context in which Obama has been repeatedly located outside the fantasy of the nation (cf. Wright 2011), whether by repeatedly questioning his citizenship (Logan 2011: 122), or through the smear that he is a secret Muslim plotting to undermine the United States from within. Reflecting the continued hold of these narratives about the President, in late 2011 a *Newsweek* survey reportedly found that a majority of Republican party supporters polled believed President Obama to be in support of the global imposition of Shariah law and militant Islamist objectives (Serwer 2010). The conflation of Obama with Islamist extremism is clearly problematic; in its most vicious expressions at the hands of sections of the grass-roots right, it reflects a radicalisation of Islamophobia: the problem of a Black man who not only walks among us but who is sufficiently integrated in the system to have become *President*.

In fact, the problematisation of places of worship is not new. Nevertheless, this does not mean that Islamophobia is centrally about religion rather than race, and in this we reach the point at which Massari is also correct – for the targeting of places of worship is *not* primarily an attack against religion, against some abstract set of ideas. To cite a banal example, in the 1960s Charles De Gaulle suggested that his village, Colombey les Deux Églises would have to be renamed Colombey les Deux Mosquées if Algerian immigration continued. In this we have the mosque figured as a reflection of the central problem of all racisms, which is shared by Islamophobia: not that there are too many of 'them', but simply that there are too many of them in proximity (i.e. in 'my' country). This reflects the logic of all racisms; indeed, one can see a certain strand within some neo-Nazi thought which seeks to deny its own racism by claiming to support the existence of the Other, so long as the Other is held at arm's length. This is why even Breivik was able to claim that he was not motivated by hate towards Muslims, but by love towards his own people; a position that resonates with Sara Ahmed's (2004: 25) reading of a passage from the Aryan Nations Website.

We see in this emotion as a political rationality, and Ahmed writes that it figures the racist in particular ways, identifying the racist in terms of love, rights and a connection with place, and the Other as threatening in proximity (Ahmed 2004: 26). Breivik's massacre and his declaration at one point not to hate Muslims reflect this attempt to spatialise racism in particular ways and to couch it in terms of love and rights in the context of his anger and unarticulated hatred that 'they' now walk among us, and that 'our' Europe is being transformed into Eurabia. In other words, there is a wider symbolic problem at play; even the neo-Nazis who proclaim to support the existence of Others at arm's length do so out of the fear of contamination and contagion; that 'we' will become like 'them' and the 'White' race will no longer exist. This is one manifestation of what Hesse (1997) describes as a postcolonial problem – a shift from the overseas deployment of the racial frontier which kept us (and them) all homogenous to its domestic deployment. This operates as long as its symbolic authority is not challenged, but as we have seen, Muslims interrupt traditional racial ascriptions, and each attempt to figure them as ontically pure religious subjects only increases the anxieties attendant upon their symbolic challenge, by inscribing them as *not* racial.

Within the logics of racism this is not an abstract problem but a fundamental difficulty, because it challenges the possibility of finding a solution through recourse to race. Like the Muslim, the mosque thus becomes the named object of a particular mode of emotion, a particular form of fear. Still, we might again ask: what does the mosque stand for? For what is it, but a building? In this we see it stands for something else; the collapse of certainties and the portent of any easy distinction between 'us' and 'them' also collapsing in on itself – a loss of symbolic authority. The mosque thus figures as a marker of their presence and the threat they pose. But in Islamophobic discourse it also operates in other ways for still, the mosque is just a building when all is said and done. The mosque as a building is only threatening insofar as it is a receptacle for the real threat – not the threat posed by some abstract set of beliefs and ideas, but the threat posed by the Others who embody them, and symbolised through racial logics, the Muslim figures as an incomplete subject, the void without and the excess within. Like the burka, the mosque as an object of a particular named fear comes to mark a presence that is difficult to mark or recognise. It becomes a proxy for the Muslim; it becomes a void without (the building) and an excess within (Muslims). Even as the mosque comes to signify a mode of integrating – that the Other has moved from guest worker, temporary migrant, peripheral figure, to being embedded in our space – it comes to act as a proxy body, not only as a receptacle for the abject, the fantasmatic, and all our worst fears and anxieties, but also on terms which we can say are a doubling of the representation of Muslim bodies, as a void without and an excess within.

Irony and Racism

In this there is a parallel for Islamophobia, which emerges beneath an affectively laden sign to take particularly visceral forms in the flux of ambient anxiety and the symbolic failures that underlie hate and fear, tolerance and terror. This twin investment in a particular affect and in the naming of a particular phobic object is particularly interesting in the context of a discourse that disavows its racist nature by disavowing its hatreds as justifiable fears about the Muslim threat and by rendering invisible its victims. In anxious times, the symbolic problem posed by the Muslim question heightens anxieties and gives rise to its own uncertainties concerning the possibility for a society that is organised and integrated through the symbolic authority vested in race. Fantasy offers one way of offsetting these anxieties, but the emergence of a phobic form represents another way of dealing with them.

What, then, is in a name? Islamophobia is an obviously problematic naming. It institutes problematic modes of mobilising in support of anti-Muslim racism and ineffective modes of response to its racist nature. In its inscription of Muslim absence lies an ironic resonance with the wider figuring of Muslim absences. It also privatises and banalises anti-Muslim racism. However, the use of the phobia metaphor is not entirely unsustainable, and its naming historicises Islamophobia at a particular point in history where particular anxieties and forms of political practice are taking root. The naming re-establishes its relationship with other forms of racism by drawing attention to phobia as a metaphor for one mode of Islamophobia that problematises difference in proximity as a means of dealing with certain anxieties. In this I am not suggesting that Islamophobia is reducible to this particular mode, but rather that by using phobia simply as a metaphor we can grasp its political rationality and historicise it within a particular political context in which anxieties, affects, and emotions are mobilised in particular ways through (bio)political practices.

4

Post-politics and Islamophobia

I f the rise of Islamophobia has been thoroughly resistible, as Poynting and Mason (2007) note, it has at the same time seemed somehow inevitable. Racial politics are often marked by periods of simmering tension with sporadic outbursts following trigger events which act as catalysts for eruptions of hate, so even in spite of the difficulties attendant upon reducing Islamophobia simply to a post-9/11 backlash, we still have to acknowledge that the subsequent growth of Islamophobia has been impacted by the major events of recent years, including both terrorist attacks and the them/us language of the war on terror. But the toxic combination of intensified modes of biopolitics as control, politics mobilised around a range of affects including the anxiety noted in Chapter 3, and the failure of popular reductions of Islamophobia that deny its racist (rather than religious) form have converged upon the Muslim question. Still, this does not fully explain why the problem of difference should have come to the fore and become so central to Islamophobia. To understand this has some bearing on the wider political field that has proved fertile ground for Islamophobia, but it can also help us to understand why, if Islamophobia was so resistible, so many seemed so impotent to prevent it. To illustrate this it is helpful to begin with a brief consideration of the problematisation of multiculturalism and Muslim integration before moving to consider the symptomatic rise of far-right Islamophobia.

Politics and Difference

Before progressing further it is important to outline a distinction between politics and the political, and to sketch out the ways in which they relate to a broader context in which difference has been increasingly problematised. In drawing this distinction I find a helpful metaphor in the Coen brothers' 2007 film *No Country for Old Men,* in which the lives of three men clash as a deadly manhunt and a caper for loot intersect. The plot is straightforward: working class man finds fate-changing amount of dough, and gets chased by psychopath while ageing lawman pursues both. The latter, Sheriff Tom Bell, reflects with melancholy on a lost order as the film opens: 'I was sheriff of this county when I was twenty-five years old ... My grandfather was a lawman; father too [...] The crime you see now, It's hard to even take its measure. It's not that I'm afraid of it. I always knew you had to be willing to die ... But I don't want to push my chips forward and go out and meeting something I don't understand. A man would have to put his soul at hazard. He'd have to say, "Okay, I'll be a part of this world".' Bell seems unable to prevent the violence of Chigurh the psychopath as though this new form of crime somehow causes the failure of the regulatory system itself, and the only way to deal with it is through the logics of Chigurh. It is helpful to read the film as a metaphor for different approaches to the problem of politics and political practice. At the start of the film Llewelyn Moss stumbles upon the loot that starts it all, and decides to hang onto it because he knows it can transform his fate.

In this there is a parallel with the political itself. Here, the political can be understood as the moment at which the contingency on which the social is instituted is rendered visible and alternative social relations are instituted (Glynos and Howarth 2007: 113). The political is thus centrally concerned with the principles and power that structure the social and it is centrally concerned with contests over the earthly fates of subjects – over whether subjects should accept their allotted fate or transform it. In contrast to this, politics is a regulatory framework that seeks to tame the antagonisms of the political, and Sheriff Tom Bell reflects a traditional regulatory mechanism for protecting the established order by domesticating antagonisms. Chigurh, however, illustrates the processes through which, when traditional attempts to domesticate antagonisms by channelling them into politics fail, space is opened for the emergence of an alternative politics predicated on violence (whether material or symbolic). In this, we can see a metaphor for the broader, sometimes violent, emergence of the extreme right, which seems to step out from a wider context of traditional politics, expressing hardened antagonisms between nationals and Others, and which takes us all by surprise each time this happens. We can most fruitfully understand the implications of these eruptions by placing them in a wider political context.

Our understanding of the regulatory functions of politics is complicated by their condensation around a vision of post-politics, which takes a number of forms, but is broadly characterised by the displacement or suppression of meaningful political encounters, and has been associated with the rise of the notion that traditional right/ left ideological divisions in Western politics have been transcended. Central to this displacement is the centring of a technocratic managerial politics which reduces politics itself to 'competent administration' (Zizek 2009: 268) and in which expert knowledges are increasingly drawn upon as a means of avoiding substantive political encounters in the service of advancing a neoliberal consensus politics (Mouffe 2005). Zizek (1999: 189–90) has traced a series of disavowals of the political that emerge: *arche politics* (attempt to close social space and follow communitarian logic), *para-politics* (which attempt to render politics depoliticised through regulation and competition), *meta-politics* (in which politics occurs as a 'shadow-theatre' to play out another set of issues), and *ultra-politics* (which takes the form of a relation of war). Racism as an ultra-politics emerges in the context of post-politics – as Zizek (1999) has argued, and this chapter considers how this is the case. This takes us away from the problematic exceptionalisation of far-right racism to the margins (cf. Patel and Tyrer 2011) – elsewhere effected through his exceptionalisation even by his far-right brothers-in-arms – and places it into a wider neoliberal terrain of politics itself.

Recognising the ways in which post-politics displaces the moment of the political, causing it to erupt in other forms, or reflecting in more violent suppressions of politics is helpful if we are to build upon our framing for Islamophobia. For example, Chantal Mouffe's problema-tisation of post-politics is especially interesting because it establishes a relationship between post-politics and the rise of the populist and far right across Europe. Mouffe's position is articulated around a number of concerns, but draws attention to the problems that can be created when, rather than mobilising political passions towards democratic ends, mainstream democratic politics simply displaces them from public expression. To Mouffe, the danger of post-politics and the weakening or absence of democratic political struggles resides in the risk of creating a void space that can be exploited by the extreme right as a result of the weakening of traditional political frontiers (Mouffe 1993: 5–6). Developing this argument, Mouffe has suggested that:

> [A]s a consequence of the blurring of the frontiers between left and right and the absence of an agonistic debate among democratic parties, a confrontation between different political projects, voters did not have the possibility of identifying with a differentiated range of democratic political identities. This created a void that was likely to be occupied by other forms of identifications which could become problematic for the working of the democratic system. (Mouffe 2005: 69)

The relevance of Mouffe's position is reflected in the rise of the Islamophobic far right on a political terrain dominated by a managerialised politics and the compression of the political spectrum around a centre-right neoliberal consensus politics. One can thus point to the rise of groups such as the English Defence League in the context of perceptions of increased disenfranchisement or disengagement (Goodwin 2011: 4) that have enabled its anti-establishment politics to take root (Jackson 2011: 15). Thus, in Mouffe's (2005) argument, the seeming compression of the political spectrum takes the form of a constriction of the range of democratic political identities, and the resulting vacuum is exploited by far-right groups which rearticulate traditional political identities such as 'working class'. Mouffe cites the rise of the Belgian Vlaams Belang and the Austrian FPÖ to illustrate her argument, but the basic analysis can be applied across the West, with far-right parties adopting an anti-establishment position while claiming to represent 'the ordinary man'. Such politics have further weakened the traditional left/right division complicated rearticulations of race/class and political responses to these. For example, the 2005 election manifesto of the British National Party simultaneously signalled hostility to socialism and support for strong Trade Unions and the socialist ideal of worker ownership of the means of production. Far-right parties across the West have rearticulated mainstream political metaphors such as social conservatism; thus, as Damian

Tambini has shown, the Lega Nord has employed ambiguous slogans (Tambini 2001: 112) and variously positioned itself as ethno-nationalist, anti-immigration, left-wing, centrist, and part of a right-wing coalition government (Tambini 2001: xiii), even though it is more generally labelled extreme right and has also sought to appropriate symbols associated with fascism (Gold 2003: 109).

Similarly, by the end of the 1970s the Austrian FPÖ appeared to have severed itself from its association with fascism and was even admitted to the Liberal International (Art 2011: 119). From this we can suggest that the rise of the far right is framed by a series of post-political displacements, but three features stand out: first, the rise of the far right has occurred in the wake of a further displacement, through which politicisation over racism is displaced by the logics of state multiculturalisms and diversity management regimes. Second, the far right itself appears to take on post-political tenor by radicalising this weakening of prior boundaries, and thus it takes on the surface appearance of a post-political movement. Third, the far right itself takes on the surface appearance of a post-political movement.

Displacing the Political

Mouffe's (2005: 70) account helpfully outlines the ways in which far-right discourse has successfully replaced the traditional, weakened left/right distinction with a frontier between the people/ the establishment. This helpfully sets out one set of displacements framing the growth of the Islamophobic far right in recent years, but it ignores another. Despite her references to xenophobia, Mouffe does not mention Islamophobia, which has been central to its appeal. To understand this we first have to contextualise our reading of the far right with a consideration of the displacements at stake in the contests over state and civil multiculturalisms. At the outset it is important to note that multiculturalism has various meanings, and that I distinguish between multiculturalism as a horizon (cf. Hesse 2000), multiculturalism as an empirical 'fact', and multiculturalism as a loosely articulated institutional ensemble which has taken a range of forms in different local and national contexts (and been completely avoided in others).

The contemporary politics of multiculturalism have been widely written about from a range of perspectives (cf. Fleras 2009; Fortier

2008; Hesse 2000; Hewitt 2005; Lentin and Titley 2011; Pitcher 2009) and do not need rehearsing, save to sketch out the broad link between its critique and the politics of Islamophobia. For example, in February 2011 French President Nicolas Sarkozy claimed 'in all our democracies' multiculturalism had failed as a result of the preoccupation with maintaining the identities of immigrants at the expense of host countries (*Le Figaro* 2011). In October 2010, German Chancellor Angela Merkel had also delivered a speech in which she claimed that multicuturalism had 'utterly failed', again rehearsing a very similar argument (BBC News 2010). In February 2011 David Cameron, Prime Minister of Britain also spoke out:

> Under the doctrine of state multiculturalism, we have encouraged different cultures to live separate lives, apart from each other and the mainstream. We have failed to provide a vision of society to which they feel they want to belong. We have even tolerated these segregated communities behaving in ways that run counter to our values. So when a white person holds objectionable views – racism, for example – we rightly condemn them. But when equally unacceptable views or practices have come from someone who isn't white, we've been too cautious, frankly even fearful, to stand up to them. The failure of some to confront the horrors of forced marriage the practice where some young girls are bullied and sometimes taken abroad to marry someone they don't want to is a case in point. This hands-off tolerance has only served to reinforce the sense that not enough is shared. All this leaves some young Muslims feeling rootless. And the search for something to belong to and believe in can lead them to this extremist ideology. (Cameron 2011)

These reflected a wider attack against multiculturalism also played out in the media. As Lentin and Titley (2011: 34) note, the critique was radicalised by equating multiculturalism with Muslims and thus by extension positing it as an underlying cause of militant Islamism and terrorism. An interesting feature of the recent critiques of multiculturalism is that as they have played out in public discourse they have lacked any defined institutional object. This has made the critique exceptionally pliable so that a strangely unified chord has struck up across varying locales and political contexts, in countries such as France and Germany that have been historically resistant to multiculturalism, as well as in countries such as Britain with longer histories of varying forms of institutional multiculturalism. In the absence of any specific institutional object of the critique, multiculturalism is defined loosely and through implication as a system of governance. The crisis of multiculturalism is thus read as a regulatory failure through which differences at play under the multicultural horizon have been left unfettered, the results of which are an increasing difficulty in maintaining the cohesion of the nation. What is thus held to be at stake is the assumed failure of an established framework for politics to keep the political at bay. In this we cut to the heart of Islamophobia: the authority and political utility of a particular symbolic system.

This critique of multiculturalism in turn gave way to the insistence that integration has failed as a result of its putative failures, a notion that reflects both the phobia of difference and the problematisation of 'excessive alterity' of Others (cf. Grillo 2007) – as though it is ever possible to have an Other who is not held in alterity. The first observation worth noting is that, as with the critique of multiculturalism, this line finds very similar expression across widely varying contexts. But Western states have different traditions for integration, from France where the Republican ideal and the principle of *laïcité* traditionally disavowed public expressions of ethnic or religious particularity to privatise difference and have informed the problematisation of recognition of difference (Stychin 2003: 53–5), to Britain where difference is explicitly or implicitly organised around distinctions between majority and ethnic minority populations (Mason 2003: 11), to Germany, where Ausländerpolitik traditionally displaced the concept of ethnic minorities, and even to Italy, where debates on minorities have historically been structured around the limited triangle of competing custodial assistential, and promotional strategies (further complicated by regionalism) that construct immigrants as threatening, an underclass needing assistance, and bearers of rights (Koff 2008: 40). There are equally many different models for integrating Muslims in religious terms (cf. Pace 2004). It is rather curious that in spite of this wide variety of institutional frameworks for dealing with integration, contemporary Islamophobia works through the notion that Muslims somehow exceed the capacity of established regulatory frameworks and are inassimilable.

Critiques of integration are often couched in terms of its own impossibility, through the assertion that nobody dare speak of the failure of integration for fear of being branded as racist. I want to ignore the obvious but banal point that debates about integrating minorities have long histories in the West and that failures are routinely cited in public discourse. Instead I want to note that this claim itself implies the real problem of post-politics – the displacement of substantive political encounters – but that its expression is through a post-political register that has the effect of foreclosing countervailing arguments through the inference that if any occur, then they must simply be vexatious appeals to racism. It also seems that something else is at stake in the critique, and that this trope is clearly about taboos; the desire to speak the secret at the heart of the post-racial society without having to face the feelings of the Other, to speak without censure or accusation of racism (even though Islamophobia is popularly misconceived as non-racism). It is thus also about broaching the desire of the Other without having to face the anxieties attendant upon the question of what the Other wants from me; the desire for the Other to fall into my strong White arms and dissolve into me and the fantasy that even if this were to happen it would not also dissolve my own subjectivity. The problem of the desire for perfect integration is, however, that the Other is always in exteriority, and that without an Other against whose difference my own identity is constituted, my own identity threatens to dissolve.

Still, that thing people dare not discuss looms large in contemporary discussions and it expresses the logic of the surplus of the Other that takes the form of a politicality that threatens the closure of the nation, and that this is culturally bound. For instance, Angela Merkel's speech criticising the failure of multiculturalism coincided with a deepening of the debate about Muslim inassimilability in Germany that in 2010 had also seen Thilo Sarrazin, a then member of the Deutsche Bundesbank Executive Board publish a book entitled *Deutschland Schafft Sich Ab*, the title of which expresses perfectly the notion of Germany as having eroded itself, though Sarrazin's argument was not that this had happened as a result of the perfect integration of the Other against whom our identities are constructed, but rather as a case in point of her inassimilability. Despite some criticism the book sold over one million copies and the widespread support it received effectively opened the space for Merkel's intervention. Following a subsequent intervention about Jews, Sarrazin was criticised as anti-Semitic. A subsequent essay in *Der Spiegel* by Peter Schneider (2010) is also interesting. Framing his discussion with a consideration of the problem of history, Schneider argued that an 'unholy alliance' between the conservatives and the left had emerged around a denial that integration and immigration are a problem, and that it was the shadow of racism and the subsequent cries of 'never again' that underwrote this failure to deal with the issue, so that to Schneider, any attempt to make immigrants learn German would be rejected. The interesting feature of this is that it is a trope shared by the extreme right. Schneider was clearly aware that racists might take succour from the words of Sarrazin, but attempted to force a distinction, asking rhetorically whether we can seriously (mis) characterise all those who would agree with Sarrazin as racist.

At this point it is helpful to note that it is not in itself racist to talk about integration. In political and social terms, at its most basic level integration is likely to involve the willingness of subjects to obey laws and in/formal social conventions. In this we can say that integration presents a political problem, namely how one can deal with human subjects and all the contingent behaviour that this problem might entail. But the debates about integration are couched in cultural terms, through reference to ossified notions of cultural difference posited as the real obstacle to integration. This is problematic because it imagines away the possibility of ever arriving at a political response to the problem of integration, since by fixing cultural difference as the problem, then the assumption must be that so long as that difference exists, so too will lawlessness and all the other basic measures by which we might consider individuals and groups to be well (or poorly) integrated. This is the impossibility at the heart of the postcolonial question, and it highlights a problem with race insofar as the simple domestic refiguration of a vocabulary that defined Others at a distance now creates a further problem in that Others are now defined as such within the nation. Thus we witness the emergence of a perfect post-political expression, which displaces the fundamental political questions in favour of the assertion that 'their' behaviour is regulated totally by 'their' difference. But in this a further displacement of the political is effected through two discursive operations: the inscription of 'us' as the real victims of multiculturalism and the symbolic closure of multiculturalism as a legitimate channel through which racialised minorities can mobilise displaces the possibility for mobilisation against racism. In Cameron's speech on multiculturalism this was consolidated through an interesting move in which he implied White racism to be under control while recognising Islamophobia. The coherence of this is only sustained by the contrast between racism *qua* racism and Islamophobia as it is popularly misconceived as a non-racism.

Thus, the problematic naming of Islamophobia resurfaces in the context of a political displacement that overlays the weakening of left/right boundary with which Mouffe's (2005) analysis is concerned. This displacement is further complicated by the question of exactly what is meant by multiculturalism. Within the terms of the critique we are left to assume that its patronage of difference marks it as a heterophilia. But where multiculturalism or its diversity management cognates have emerged as regulatory systems, they have taken the form of institutional frameworks designed to transform the political into politics. They have sought to do this in two ways: first, by establishing institutional frameworks and ground rules through which minorities can interact with the state and civil society; second, by fetishing and commodifying difference in ways that play to the differences among the racialised as a stratagem for undercutting the possibility of a univer-salisable political subject position for the racialised. The fetishisation of difference is not what antiracism is, and in many different contexts it has emerged as a hegemonic way of displacing politicisation over racism through culturalisation and its commodification. It is not even necessary to cite the example of the use of this as a strategy of colonial governance, or a means through which African resistance to apartheid was managed through the attempt to subjectivise the majority as being members of tribes rather than 'Black'. This is one of the processes by which the British state responded to racialised moral panics about Black criminality and to unrest in inner cities during the early 1980s, when it began promoting a state multiculturalism to work against grass-roots mobilisation around a rearticulation of political Blackness based on shared histories of racism that had been influenced by the US Black Power movement. Even if we take seriously the idea that this state multiculturalism, parodied through the popular 'steel bands, saris and samosas' refrain, has cherished difference, then its heterophilia is perhaps more akin to a delusional teenage limerence strictly controlled under the watchful parental eye, for it has been marked by fantasies of difference and associated with surveillance.

In this context the notion that multiculturalism has failed is revealing of underlying anxieties about the impossible fantasy of a nation without diversity, anxieties that are heightened by the presence of a population that cannot be easily integrated into the racial vernacular through which integration as a nation will be symbolised, realised. But it is also revealing of a sense that politics itself has failed; our prior displacements of the possibility of anti-racist politics were insufficient. Thus in this imagining we see emerging not even a para-politics, for what is at stake is not the more tight regulation of minorities, but rather a closure of multicultural institutional space that takes in this respect some of the characteristics of an *arche* politics, through the call for a closed community in which social space is closed around a monolithic national identity. And yet from this vision, and in the wake of this very attempt to problematise antiracist mobilisation by the excessive politicality of racialised subjects, we also see the eruptions of para-politics in the form of far-right groups that draw from precisely the logic that multiculturalism has failed, difference is excessive, and the nation is impossible because of the presence of the Other – that same Other against whom our nation is closed in the first place.

Prophets of Doom

One reason for the importance of Islamophobia to the rise of the far right is that it has also provided a universalisable politics through which it can overcome its natural particularity. Far-right politics is naturally particularised through its exceptionalisation as racist and extremist, and in other cases through the ways in which the nativism of the extreme right has often involved the construction of them/us boundaries against others within the symbolic space of the nation. For example, Lega Nord discourse initially tended to construct Padano identities in terms of Calvinism as distinct from southern Italian identities, so that while it still drew upon notions of Catholic family values (Huysseune 2006: 186), it constructed an opposition between the Calvinistic, hard-working north it represented, the south, and Rome in terms of Catholic backwardness (Tambini 2001: 113). This clearly limited the ability of the Lega to increase its influence, but although the Lega remains a distinctly northern project, its increasing rearticulation of a politics of Islamophobia from around 1999 onwards enabled it to overcome its fierce regional particularism on the basis of a recognisable and more universalisable politics. This also complicated the relationship between the Lega Nord and Catholicism, resulting in increasing references to Catholic values and increasing links with members of the Catholic clergy. Similar points can be made in relation to all far-right parties which, if not particularised by regionalism, could certainly be seen as particularised by dint of their exceptionalisation as extreme and racist.

Islamophobia is universalisable precisely because of the investments made at the centre in the problematisation of Muslim difference. As a result, the far right has mobilised through the rearticulation of recognisable mainstream narratives of the failure of integration and multiculturalism articulated in the popular media and by politicians. This has also proven important in another respect, for as Mouffe (2005: 73) has pointed out, in the absence of a strong left/right boundary around which engagements with the far right can be triangulated, the post-political response to the rise of the far right tended to be expressed through moral registers, positing the 'bad', anti-democratic 'extremists' (them) against the good democrats (us). The problematisation of Muslims as a political surplus threatening to the closure of the nation and, if not irreconcilable within democracy, certainly threatening to its health as a result of its excess demands and difference, provided the extreme right with further scope for appropriation. By rearticulating progressive political metaphors – democracy, rights, freedom of speech – far-right groups have sought to overcome their exceptionalisation as extremist and anti-democratic, and in so doing have attempted to refigure Islamophobia as a fundamentally progressive cause in defence against Islamisation.

Northern Europe has been an important crucible in which this rearticulation has occurred. It is important to note that the appropriation of progressive political metaphors has only constituted part of a wider project that is clearly unreconstructed in most respects. For example, in 2001 Ib Krog Hansen of the Danish People's Party asked rhetorically: 'To say that all Muslims should be thrown out of Denmark? That's harsh, because there are some actual human beings among them, too. But how are we supposed to sort them?' (Andersen

2010). Nevertheless, Islamophobic discourse, even on the far right, has been increasingly rearticulated as progressive, so a contrast between the backwards practices of inassimilable Muslims who threaten to Islamise the West, and the progressive politics of those who oppose them. This has even been reflected in repeated comparisons between Islam and Nazism by the far right. In itself any comparison between abstract systems of ideas seems not particularly problematic, but within Islamophobic discourse this acts as a way of problematising Muslim bodies as the bearer of those ideas. Thus the threat to the West is understood through Islamisation, and through claimed practices such as the removal of non-Islamic symbols, the adoption of Islamic traditions in non-Islamic societies, and immigration through which Muslims become majorities in particular residential areas. Within this discourse, Islamisation operates as a floating signifier that enables its invocation to cover a wide range of social practices involving Muslims that go well beyond the formally avowed criticism of Islam, and that in turn allow the discussion of Muslim populations as a proxy for the threat of Islamisation to basic rights and freedoms. This enables the denial of social problems and discrimination facing Muslims and Islamophobia to be rearticulated as a defence of rights and freedoms – a thoroughly progressive matter. For example, the combination of racism with indignation at the barbarity (implying a concern with progressive issues such as gender rights) can be seen in the following claim by Danish People's Party leader Pia Kjærsgaard:

> The largest part of the present groups of immigrants originates from the third world and is primarily Muslims, which do not present any motivation in becoming part of Danish civilisation. On the contrary, these people arrive with their luggage packed with something quite different. They arrive with the most intense hatred against all that is Western, against all that is Danish and all that is Christian. They arrive with their luggage packed with male chauvinism, ritual slaughtering, female circumcision, and female repressive clothes and traditions, which belong in the darkest Middle Ages. And, above all, many arrive with their luggage filled with religious fanaticism, know-all attitude, and arrogance. (Hervik 2011: 219)

The attempt to rearticulate progressive metaphors with Islamophobia can also be seen in the politics of the late Pim Fortuyn. As a result of the location of his politics within the wider Dutch liberal tradition as well as of his advocacy for gay rights, Pim Fortuyn, leader of Lijst Pim Fortuyn until his murder in 2002 by a green activist, was able to straightforwardly position his politics as progressive in spite of criticisms that it was, variously, nationalist, racist, and extremist. In fact, Fortuyn remained famously resistant to such comparisons, and reportedly threw the BBC's John Simpson out of his apartment when, following a televised interview, the journalist touched upon the comparisons between Fortuyn and Jean-Marie Le Pen (Cherribi 2010: 134). Fortuyn's rhetoric rearticulated anti-immigrant and anti-Muslim politics as belonging within this liberal tradition, and thus as progressive, even when he was rejecting the idea that Dutch subjects born in the Antilles should enjoy the same rights as Dutch-born citizens. Fortuyn's politics thus came to centre on the notion that immigrants pose threats to Dutch tolerance, and in turn that the 'backwardness' of Muslims and the criminality of immigrant youth posed a threat to the majority, drawing upon what Rydgren and van Holsteyn (2005: 49) term 'inverted racism' (that is, the notion that the majority, not the racialised minority, are racism's true victims).

As Betz (2007: 42) notes, as the far-right parties across Europe came increasingly to focus on Islamophobia after 9/11, they promoted themselves not as the far right but 'as genuine defenders of secularism, democracy, and Western values in general'. Thus, whether one considers the rhetoric of the British National Party, English Defence League, Lega Nord, Danish People's Party, Vlaams Belang, or any other populist or far right group or party in Europe, their politics is frequently couched in terms of rights, democratic ideals, and progressive values such as tolerance, free speech, and rights (especially women's rights). In the case of Pim Fortuyn, this enabled him to capitalise by launching an attack against immigrants and Muslims that was couched in terms of tolerance rather than the explicit intolerance, fascism or ethno-nationalism of the traditional far right. One effect of this was that Fortuyn was able to distance himself from the taint of association with Nazism or the traditional extreme right, despite the support some on the extreme right offered him (Klandermans and Mayer 2006: 23). The extent to which he provided the model for the wider far right can be witnessed in an ironic reverse taking place; where Fortuyn angrily rejected comparison with Jean-Marie Le Pen, his daughter, current Front National President Mariane Le Pen, adopted a similar strategy in an interview with Dutch radio by distancing herself from PVV leader Geert Wilders, arguing that unlike Wilders she does not promote 'hate' or wage 'war' on Islam, but simply seeks to defend France from Islamisation. Lijst Fortuyn could not survive after their murder of Fortuyn, but while this reduced it to something of a 'flash party' (Art 2011), as Gillingham (2003: 382) has noted, the influence of his politics was manifested in a mainstream shift from what was perceived as political correctness towards an emphasis on the immigrant problem, facilitated also by the media diet of stories about crime and social problems that had also facilitated the rise of Fortuyn (Cherribi 2010: 134). One of Fortuyn's legacies was thus an important role in the introduction of anti-immigrant and anti-Muslim politics to the mainstream, and the opening of the far right to a progressive language, in defence of tolerance.

The case of film maker Theo Van Gogh played a crucial role in cementing the Netherlands as a crucible for this respectable anti-Muslim racism, in turn influencing the politicisation of the Muslim question in Austria, Germany, and Denmark, as noted in Chapter 1. It was further fuelled by a wider preoccupation with other signs and symbols of Muslim visibility such as hijab (van Driel 2004: ix), and these had the effect of cementing the rearticulation of anti-Muslim racism through the appropriation of progressive political metaphors, and the reconfiguration of Islamophobia as a necessary defence of freedom of expression, secularism, and the rights of women in the face of others whose failure to integrate represented a de facto Islamisation of the West. The success of this rearticulation has been signalled by the emergence of PVV leader Geert Wilders who, as already noted, has been seen as a relatively obscure figure prior to his mobilisation around a politics of Islamophobia. But though more extreme than Fortuyn, Wilders' politics draw from the familiar themes of a defence of the progressive against the threat posed by the alien and backwards, excessively different Muslim presence and the wider cultures of human rights that he sees as imbricated in Islamisation. A speech delivered by Wilders to the Danish Free Press Society in June 2009 illustrates the complexities of his position. In the speech Wilders celebrated the defeat of what he termed 'socialists' in a number of European contexts, noting that:

> It's good news because socialists are the most inveterate cultural relativists in Europe. They regard the Islamic culture of backwardness and violence as equal to our Western culture of freedom, democracy and human rights. In fact, it is the socialists who are responsible for mass immigration, Islamization and general decay of our cities and societies. It are [sic] the socialists who are responsible for the fact that cities such as Rotterdam, Marseille and Malmö seem to be situated in Eurabia rather than in Europe. And they are even proud of it [...] The only moral standard they still seem to apply is the question whether or not it is approved by Muslims. Everything Muslims disapprove, they disapprove too. (Wilders 2009)

This has been a central theme in far-right mobilisation; for example, as Hans-Georg Betz (2005: 147) has noted, central to the rise of the extreme right (certainly in Austria, Switzerland and northern Italy) has been its emphasis on democracy. While this emphasis in far-right discourse has of course been configured around criticisms of the 'corrupt' and 'self-serving' 'elites', it has been increasingly anchored by Islamophobia and the putative threat of Islamisation. This notion of Muslim incompatibility with Western culture is organised in far-right discourse across the West around the notion that the presence of Muslims is incompatible with democracy, and it also witnesses the championing by the (traditionally anti-Semitic) far right of Israel as the only democracy in the Middle East.

Post-Politics, Post-Fascism?

A further illustration of the extent to which the rise of the far right has been framed by post-politics can be found in the way in which the parties of the far right in themselves end up as a weak parody of post-politics in which they formally renounce fascist heritage (where this existed within particular parties), appropriate from mainstream progressive political discourse, and even renounce formally their racist politics. This is perhaps best reflected in the attempts of the far right to demonstrate the limits of accusations of racism. Of course there are limits to this: just as the SVP's minaret campaign was preceded by its infamous black sheep poster two years earlier, its recent campaigning literature has also included a two-page leaflet headed with the following text:

KEINE EINBÜRGERUNG VON VERBRECHERN UND
SOZIALHILFEEMPFÄNGERN!
Klare Forderungen an Einbürgerungswillige!
Stopp der Verschleuderung des Schweizer Passes!
Keine Einbürgerung von Verbrechern, Sozialhilfeabhängigen und
Asylsuchenden! (SVP 2011)

Using highly emotive language the leaflet purported to campaign on race neutral grounds, railing against the squandering of the Swiss passport and the naturalisation of criminals, welfare dependents and asylum seekers, although the associated imagery moors it to a clear racial politics: the front page depicts a caricatured Black man sitting in a hammock with a huge, smoking appendage (a spliff? a cigar?) hanging from enormous, caricatured lips, wearing sunglasses, shorts and sandals, and clutching a Swiss passport while money rains down on him. The second page of the leaflet depicts a similarly caricatured huge Black man holding up a smaller, shaking, white man (clad in a red cap emblazoned with the Swiss flag) at gunpoint.

But just as the mainstream attack on multiculturalism and the formal disavowal of racism have been framed by the logic of post-politics, so too is the far right's denial of racism. Thus, we see the increasing trend among the far right not only to deny its extreme right ideological bases, but also its racism. This has increasingly involved attempts by far-right groups to even claim support among members of minority groups, a tactic used by France's Front National (Karpf 2012) and the British National Party. Even the Lega Nord can point to such support after the biological sister of Mario Balotelli, a leading international footballer who experienced shocking racism in Italy, has declared that she would vote Lega Nord (while noting that she does not actually have voting rights despite having lived in Italy since the age of 12) (Marchetti 2011).

The attempts by the far right to deny its racism frequently operate as a weak parody of liberal tokenism, through reference to token support from small numbers of Black and minority ethnic people to underline the impression that they are not racist. Some parties of the far right have more recently attempted to gain support from some sections of Jewish communities, and although the Vlaams Belang (Moreau 2012) and the Front National (Zaretsky 2011) stand as examples in this respect, elsewhere there have been appropriations of the Star of David on banners in far-right street demonstrations and even in some cases the establishment of tiny Jewish groups within populist right-wing movements. But do such moves necessarily demonstrate that the far right has moved beyond its racial politics or traditional anti-Semitism? While some far-right groups laud Israeli democracy, the attempts to mobilise Jewish support by far-right groups increasingly appear to draw on a heavily caricatured and essentialist representation of Israel as though it is a homogenous and racially pure state. In this there is a parallel with the anti-Semitism of the left, the most obvious example being attempts to institute academic boycotts of Israel, a move that ignores the huge variation of opinion within Israel and writes out oppositional voices. In December 2010 the leaders of the Vlaams Belang, Germany's Die Freiheit [Freedom] party, Austria's Freiheitliche Partei Österreichs [Freedom Party of Austria] (FPÖ) and Sverigedemokraterna (Sweden Democrats) travelled to Israel where they met settlers on the West Bank and released a 'Jerusalem Declaration' attacking cultural relativism and affirming their Islamophobia around references to liberty, rights and the Enlightenment (Moreau 2012: 122). The far right's ostensibly new-found respect for Israel revolves in part on a celebration of its democracy, but it cannot stand as a rejection of anti-Semitism because in common with left-wing anti-Semitism it configures its references to Jewishness around an extra-European territoriality, so we can note that the point at which the far right becomes comfortable in proclaiming that it is not anti-Semitic is within a context in which it can locate Jewish identities as being outside Europe through the cynical deployment of a caricatured vision of Israel. The far right's essentialist readings of Israeli democracy write out Arab Israelis and its continued internal democratic debates about what Israeli democracy means, instead essentialising Israel in terms of implied racial purity and war with Arabs. There is, then, a parallel between the far right's essentialisation of Israel and the anti-Semitism among Islamists and parts of the left. In this the far right's position rearticulates wider anti-Semitic tropes, and with a curious parallel to the post-political Islamophobia that constructs Muslim alterity in terms of politicality, also frames Jewishness as politicality. More significantly, this move elides the lengthy histories of Jewish opposition to racism and the far right. Thus we witness such paradoxes as the case of the FPÖ leader Heinz-Christian Strache – a man who reportedly wants the ban on Nazi symbols lifted (Mullender 2008) – who reportedly attended the Yad Vashem Holocaust memorial clad in a skullcap identifying him as a member of a right-wing student group (Mayr 2011). Indeed, in January 2012 Strache took far-right appropriations one stage further when Vienna's annual Korporierten-Fest ball attracting far-right groups was greeted with anti-fascist protests, prompting him to declare that the disorders outside the ball resembled the Nazi Kristallnacht – 'Das war wie die Reichskristallnacht' – before declaring 'Wir sind die neuen Juden' [we – the far right – are the new Jews] (*Weiner Zeitung* 2012) in an outburst that trivialised and appropriated the Holocaust, representing white Europeans as the victims of its racism, while showing the limits of the far right's post-political pastiche of outward political correctness and tokenism. Jean-Marie Le Pen, Honorary Chairman of France's Front National, responded with a pun that ambiguously referred to Dominique Strauss-Kahn while implying an underlying anti-Semitism (through its erasure of a Jewish name, disarticulated from the European cultural legacy of Johann Strauss, declaring the ball to have been reminiscent of nineteenth-century Vienna: 'c'est Strauss, sans Kahn' [it's Strauss, without Kahn] (*Nouvelle République* 2012).

Reframing Islamophobia and Post-Politics

Islamophobia has enabled far-right parties to overcome other limits on its influence. In part this is because of the near ubiquity of the discourse of ineradicable Muslim difference, which rearticulated in a more radical form by the far right has provided a means of getting beyond its difficult particularity through appeals to a more widely familiar theme. But the problematic naming of Islamophobia as religious criticism, as well as a broader critique of structures through which minorities can politicise for rights, have led to a displacement through which it is difficult to substantively mobilise against its racial politics. As such the far right is able to express its racial politics through an Islamophobic register without facing the taint of racism. But Islamophobia has also provided a further filip to the far right by providing a register through which racial politics can be expressed without the taint of racism (because Islamophobia's racist nature is still routinely denied). At the same time, because mainstream narratives problematise Muslims as democracy's other (cf. Norton 2011), their appropriation has provided the far right with other grounds for universalisation, enabling it to overcome its own marginalisation as anti-democratic and rearticulating its racial politics as a frontier between democrats and anti-democratic Muslims.

One of the ironies of the far right has been its curious capacity to cause embarrassment to the political mainstream by highlighting the similarities between the immigration politics of the mainstream, and those at the extremes of the political spectrum as Betz (2003: 88–9) observes. But the appropriative politics of the far right also forces a further question of which is the greater post-political pastiche – the far-right party appropriating from the mainstream to win support or the mainstream party that annually rehearses the line that it must appropriate the far right's more authoritarian line on immigration and integration to defeat it and win back support from the populist right (cf. Grayson 2011). Thus we can say that post-politics opens space for the cynical rearticular of mainstream metaphors in the service of populist anti-establishment xenophobia, but also that it transforms politics in the mainstream, so that the void left by the evacuation of the political frontier in neoliberal politics can also be filled by cynical rearticulations of xenophobic and racist politics. In this we are again forced to historicise Islamophobia, not by pointing simply to its seeming emergence in response to the excesses of the anti-Semites, homophobes, and terrorist supporters, but rather through its framing by a particular mode of regulating life and mortality through post-political means. Hence the paradox that at the very time we thought we had arrived at a world beyond the possibility of hardened ideological antagonism, we witness violent eruptions such as the emergence of the far right.

5

Democrat, moderate, Other

Islamophobia, then, can be understood as a postcolonial problem insofar as it emerges in the wake of the presence of postcolonial populations that provoke a symbolic crisis to the logics of modernity's racial grammar, and in so doing present a series of questions for the governance of populations under racial logics. It can also be understood as a post-political problem. This dimension of Islamophobia is revealed in the emergence of far-right Islamophobia, although it is also manifested in the logics of Islamophobia in a more fundamental way. Post-politics can be understood as a series of attempts to displace or suppress the political (Mouffe 2005). Since the political is centrally concerned with the possibility of antagonism (Laclau and Mouffe 1985), which is itself predicated upon making a prior distinction between self and Other (or 'we' and 'they'). Islamophobia is post-political in two senses.

First, within the discourse on integration there is a continued investment in the idea that our Others possess an excess of alterity (Grillo 2007) which threatens the wider polity and needs to be tamed and domesticated through integration. Implicit to this position is the idea that difference is not problematic simply because it is different, but rather because it poses a threat. In other words, the discourse on integration proceeds from an implicit diagnosis of the problem of difference as being centrally political, and its attempts to domesticate and tame difference can therefore be read as another mode through which post-political displacements of the political are addressed.

Second, this is post-political because the framing of difference as political within debates on integration has tended to posit that where members of racialised and ethnicised minorities display behaviour that might be considered problematic, this is not a result of the normal contingencies that shape the conduct of human subjects, but is a condition of their very difference itself. In other words, debates on integration themselves displace any consideration of the contingent political nature of complex social problems by privileging assumptions about cultural atavism which fix the emergence of such problems as an inevitable consequence of the presence of difference. The difficulty with such explanations is that by invoking problematic political behaviour as rooted in difference, they make it impossible to conceive of properly political interventions or solutions to social problems involving ethnicised and racialised minorities in a complex world. This problematic poses fundamental questions about the sorts of political interventions that can be envisaged to facilitate the democratic incorporation of Muslims in political practice. In this chapter I am interested in considering the types of subject position from which Muslims can enter into political encounters that can be constituted through the discourse of Islamophobia. To do this it is helpful to consider two different aspects of this question. First, I am interested in the ways in which, within the terms of a discourse that has problematised Muslims in general (rather than just extremists) as excessive, whether the emphasis on 'moderate' Muslim subject positions offers meaningful possibilities for incorporating Muslims into a healthy range of democratic political encounters. Second, it is also instructive to consider another dimension of Islamophobia. Since debates about Islamophobia frequently misconstrue it by reducing it to the relatively simple matter of religious offence, this poses interesting questions concerning what type of subject positions are opened by this investment in offence. A consideration of this question can shed analytical light on the ways in which post-politics frames Muslim political encounters in the West, and to consider whether or not approaches to the political integration of Muslims that are couched in post-political terms are capable of instituting meaningful modes of democratic agency among Muslims – or conversely, whether they are in themselves, part of a problem.

Abjection and Politics

The thing about *film noir* is this: you dive headlong into an abyss of impenetrable darkness; a kind of camp monochrome chiaroscuro with glinting symbolic conundrums foaming up on the high key lighting. And then it all ends in anticlimax. Ninety minutes of simmering sexual tension (let's call it political), then just as she dives headlong into his strong white arms and dissolves, the film ends. It has to end there, because after all that surfing on the waves of a desire that renders men strangely impotent to resist the wiles of a ballsy femme fatale – *noir* is heavily gendered – once she dissolves, so will he, and then they have to go back to being Bogey or Lorre, Bergman or Trevor, *whoever*, because the character we believed in has been trodden into the carpet with the stale popcorn. This is why in the best *noir*, something is always held back (why he turns her over to the cops in *The Maltese Falcon*), and the political question, the tension between self and Other remains open. Because all identities are constituted through difference you cannot simply erase the difference of the Other because if you do, you know that you are going to take yourself with it. This is why when debates about integration are not couched in terms of contingent political problems but as an inevitable result of cultural difference, they are so problematic. On the one hand, we need our Others because we constitute our own identities through the difference between them and us. But on the other hand, as long as we are able to see them as Other, there are no prospects for viewing them as integrated, or as integrable. The terms on which Muslims are fixed as an alien presence draw upon sedimented ways of representing racial difference. The dominant response to the Muslim question has been to position Muslims as ontically religious rather than ontically racial, but this has two effects. First, in social contexts historically organised on the basis of race, it marks Muslims as incomplete subjects as a result of their apparently inadequate raciality. Second, in doing so, it institutes particular types of subject positions that such beings can occupy through political practice.

Another way of expressing this is to suggest that Muslims are represented in Islamophobic discourse as abject. Kristeva's concept of abjection is helpful in this respect, as a reference to the subject that is radically excluded and yet 'draws me toward the place where meaning collapses' (Kristeva 1982: 2). Young (1990) relates abjection to race, drawing attention to the ways in which the separation between self and Other is felt as a nameless lack that necessitates the restoration of borders through symbolic violences against the abject. This draws us back to the inadequate symbolisation of Muslims as incompletely realised/racialised (and thus incomplete) subjects; beings constructed as strangely incoporeal; haunting beings who are not *really* there; beings seemingly capable of provoking fear and revulsion, and of heightening wider anxieties. But how can subjects constituted in these terms engage in politics? Judith Butler (1990: 143–4) asks a similar question in relation to gender politics, and notes that the epistemological frames through which we narrate the world are not unimportant, but actually inscribe certain ways of marking selves and Others that in turn make certain forms of agency possible. 'The body', writes Butler, 'is not a "being," but a variable boundary, a surface whose permeability is politically regulated, a signifying practice within a cultural field of gender hierarchy' (Butler 1990: 139). But signifying practices occur in a cultural field of racial knowledges when, even in supposedly post-racial times, the residues, those superstitions of discounted and discredited notions of phenotypal heredity, still have resonance and are rearticulated in new ways, forming the basis for the ways in which recognition of minorities takes place. The ways in which we signify Muslims are beholden to the assumption that they can be straightfor-wardly classified as an ontically pure 'religious' group, and this inscribes their abjection and the impossibility for recognition or incorporation other than as purely religious groups. I want to suggest that this fundamental difficulty, which reinscribes stable raciality as it discounts it for Muslims, lies at the heart of Islamophobia, but that it also creates particular difficulties in envisioning and constituting Muslim political identities in any terms other than religion. In other words, if we locate ourselves for a moment within the language of integration to read its central problematic against the grain, the vocabulary that is used actually makes it impossible for Muslims to integrate.

For example, the limited nature of our vocabulary for Muslim political identities is striking and perhaps rather disturbing. Within the terms of Islamophobic discourse there is just the obvious label (extremist), which is why one so frequently hears on the hard right the claim that there is no such thing as a moderate Muslim. Academic works, of course offer far more sophisticated typologies; for instance, Mandaville (2009: 499) identifies four major strains within the socio-political outlook of Muslims in Britain: liberal-pluralists (who believe in compatibility and assimilation), communal-pluralists (who believe in the distinctiveness of their identities but recognise points of commonality); communitarians and radicals, neither of which need explaining. Of course, within Mandaville's typology, there are numerous ways of incorporating a broad range of political identities, and Mandaville's work more widely is marked by a clear recognition of Muslim political diversity (cf. Mandaville 2009). However, this kind of typological exercise still reads as rather constraining, and there remains a striking tendency to speak of Muslim political identities through narrow categories rather than through the more inflected and variegated political lexicon with which we speak of non-Muslims.

Within the current configuration of debates it seems almost impossible to speak of Muslims as, say, environmentalists, democrats, progressives, conservatives, socialists, pacifists, welfare activists, LGBT campaigners ... Clearly, such subjects exist, and I am also aware that the vocabulary for progressive democratic politics that I use is drawn from a particular European liberal grammar and that it might therefore seem Eurocentric. This is deliberate, because the ideal that implicitly underlies the discourse on integration is precisely that Muslims should ideally start adopting such subject positions in order to become embedded within the liberal-democratic political architecture of the West. But the imaginative paucity of the language that dominates public discussions about Muslims is such that even if this were to occur, there is no guarantee that we would be able to recognise or express it. This is not just a problem of the descriptive or analytical terms we use, but also a political one, because the same limited vocabulary that prevents us from being able to speak of such subjects also makes it difficult to constitute them as subject positions.

We can take as an example of this the problems that can occur when Muslims attempt to adopt subject positions that do not actually fit into the essentialist framings necessitated by the reliance of an ontic race/ ontic religion distinction. For instance, a hijab-wearing socialist named Asmaa Abdol-Hamid stood for the socialist Unity List [Enhedslisten] in the 2007 Danish election (cf. Lentin and Titley 2011). During the campaign her Muslimness was repeatedly problematised, particularly through references to her hijab, and attempts were made to remove her candidacy. One member of the right wing Danish People's Party declaring her to be in need of 'psychiatric treatment' (Andreassen 2011: 166). Fatima El-Tayeb (2011) has drawn attention to the circulation of assumptions that Abdol-Hamid must necessarily have expressed a politics at odds with the progressive aims of the Enhedslisten, and this has led her to consider the emergence of a 'progressive Islamophobia' (El-Tayeb 2011: 116). In other words, even when she was expressing a politics couched in appeals to progressive liberal democratic metaphors, her characterisation fell back upon the idea that as an ontically pure religious subject, she must somehow have an identity that cannot be reconciled within democratic politics itself. Something similar is also visible in the attempts to smear Barack Obama as a secret Muslim in a context marked by attempts to locate Obama outside the nation through the 'birther' conspiracy theory that has even seen elected Republicans either openly or implicitly questioning the President's citizenship or through attempts to introduce bills relating to the question of presidential citizenship (Logan 2011: 122). The 'secret Muslim' conspiracy locates Obama as a limit figure; inside and yet outside the symbolic boundaries of Americanness, and threatening to democracy itself. Acknowledging the vicious racism experienced by the Obama family, Wright (2011: xv) has also drawn attention to the sale of 'Obama Waffles' at a Values Voter summit for Republican supporters in 2009, with the cartons emblazoned with a cartoon of Obama wearing a Muslim headscarf and the legend 'Point towards Mecca for tastier waffles' (Wright 2011: 28). In this example we can see how even fatuous allegations of Muslimness can come into play based around the assumption that Muslim identities threaten democracy. Gottschalk and Greenberg (2008: 144) also note that 'even American Muslims who successfully enter mainstream U.S. life often attract negative media attention aroused by Islamophobia'.

There are, of course, many instances of Muslims who have adopted a range of political subject positions; for example, the British anti-war Respect Party successfully mobilised Muslim support and has featured a prominent Muslim senior member in the shape of Salma Yaqoob, and across the West a considerable number of Muslims have been elected to represent diverse constituencies. Nevertheless, the problem remains that as Islamophobia is mobilised around the increasing appropriation of progressive political metaphors to counter the green menace, it is difficult to imagine Muslim politics in terms of a diverse range of viable political identities, and this is because of the limited range of subject positions that are opened through their labelling as ontically pure religious subjects. This problematic takes us to the more recent emergence of the moderate Muslim label, and it is worth considering whether this takes us beyond the impasse we have entered. The wider policy framing in which the moderate label emerged presents our first difficulty in considering its helpfulness in opening out our understanding of Muslim identities. In 2003 the US National Security Council budgeted US$1.3 billion to reform Islam (Mahmood 2006). In the United Kingdom, attempts to promote moderacy were introduced under the auspices of the Prevent counter-terrorism programme alongside other aims such as the disruption of extremism. Under the terms of the programme, promoting moderacy is seen as a means of promoting and supporting moderate voices within Muslim communities and enhancing Muslim capacity to resist radicalisation. Figures for the overall programme make incredible reading: in November 2007 £240 million was set aside to finance Prevent work, plus an extra 2,000 police and support staff and training for neighbourhood officers (Hellyer 2009). The scale of the overall Prevent programme is staggering: Kundnani (2009) notes that Prevent also operates through the Department for Children, Schools and Families; the Department for Business, Innovation and Skills; the Department for Culture, Media and Sport; the Department for Children and Local Government; and the Foreign and Commonwealth Office, additionally being delivered on the ground through school, colleges, universities, Youth Justice Board and Youth Offending Teams, with the Department for Communities and Local Government also establishing a Preventing Violent Extremism Pathfinder Fund in 2007.

These origins have thus led some to approach the construction of the moderate label as an expression of disciplinary power (Naber 2008), and they create their own problem: is the moderate label a viable political identity in its own right, or does it inscribe Muslims as problematic, and incapable of articulating a meaningful democratic politics without this prefix? Naber (2008: 3) has drawn upon Mamdani's notion of 'good Muslim'/'bad Muslim' as disciplinary categories, noting that US policies such as the PATRIOT ACT as well as state investigations operate through the logic of good/bad Muslim as a means of targeting non-citizens as 'potential terrorists'. This locates the label of 'good' or 'moderate' within a wider apparatus of state power that thus might not be better suited to policing practice than the opening out of meaningful democratic encounters or viable subject positions from which Muslims can engage in them. This complicates our understanding of the promotion of the moderate label insofar as it must be understood through its inscriptions of power and its relationship with the construction of the label 'extremism'. As a floating signifer, moderacy only makes sense through its opposition to extremism, so each has the effect of inscribing the other (Tyrer 2011). Thus, while the moderate label might have some polemical use, and some value in forcing subjects to make an alignment one way or the other during the war on terror, the label itself is of limited value in more complex forms of political practice. This is because 'moderate' does not provide a repertoire of meanings capable of sustaining the emergence of a healthy range of viable political identities. It may well subsume a broader range of political identities, but it remains a marker of difference that does not actually seek to rearticulate what 'Muslim' means as a political category within public discourse (or political practice among Muslims), but rather it too easily comes to operate as a boundary between good and bad.

In this, moderate can also entail problematic inscriptions of alterity; Tyrer (2011) cites the example of a newspaper interview in which the former mayor of London Ken Livingstone defended engaging with Yusuf al Qaradawi (Hari 2008), in which he defended the theologian's credentials for moderacy in spite of his recorded anti-Semitism and homophobia. The justification of Qaradawi's moderacy was based on a reductive reading in which his homophobia was offset against the fact that Qaradawi had 'said nobody should physically attack homosexuals' (Hari 2008), a response so absurd and problematic on Livingstone's part as to require no elaboration. In the interview Livingstone further noted that Qaradawi was a progressive in a faith that is 'actually where we were seven hundred years ago' (Hari 2008). This temporalises Muslim difference in terms of degrees of alterity in which those most like 'us' are also closest temporally. This illustrates the ways in which the label 'moderate Muslim' also inscribes a sense of muted alterity, in which there is a parallel with the conception of racism extended by Deleuze and Guattari (2004: 197–8) as 'degrees of deviance' from Whiteness. This is a helpful illustration of the ways in which Others are represented not only through a straightforward Othering, but through a cascading series of oppositions which complicates our understanding of the process through which Others are symbolised. However, a more helpful reading of the logic of the moderate signifer is offered by Shryock (2008). Noting the inscriptions of 'good' and 'bad' subjects central to this practice, Shryock suggests that the problem of Muslim integration, when couched in terms of Muslims having to choose American or Muslim identities, also involves a particular liminal inscription through which they also have to denounce the violent and 'engage in these corrective, penitential rites of citizenship even (or especially) when one has no connection to "bad" Arabs or "bad" Islam. Only *after* these rites of belonging have been performed does minoritized citizenship (racialized, ethnic, exemplary, provisional, or exceptional) become possible' (Shryock 2008: 107–8). This draws attention to a central difficulty with the label moderate: since moderacy inscribes extremism through their relationship of difference, far from removing its hold it provides a language for speaking about Muslim political identities that is only possible under the horizon of religious extremism.

This has serious implications for the ways in which we can approach the question of integration and democratic politics both through the ways in which it fails to transform problematic and exclusionary stereotypes about Muslims in everyday speech and in its failure to open out a meaningful array of Muslim political identities that might have nothing to do with extremism. While the term might have utility in deradicalising the radical or in forcing a them/us alignment in broad terms, it is not a helpful basis for political practice because its logic implies a performative border work. For example, in 2011 Baroness Warsi, a Muslim member of the British House of Lords delivered a speech noting that 'It's not a big leap of the imagination to predict where the talk of "moderate" Muslim leads; in the factory, where they've just hired a Muslim worker, the boss says to his employees: "Not to worry, he's only fairly Muslim". In the school, the kids say: "The family next door are Muslim but they're not too bad". And in the road, as a woman walks past wearing a burqa, the passers-by think: "That woman's either oppressed or is making a political statement"' (Batty 2011). Shryock's argument points to a more complex boundary work at stake in the inscription of good and bad subjects, since both presuppose and inscribe a boundary while invoking its transgression by Muslims. The construction of good/bad Muslims in this sense is not simply about what is inside or what is outside, but rather the process through which these are regulated. Muslim incorporeality – the void without and the excess within – is figured in the very naming of moderate, for it makes no sense to speak of a moderate Muslim unless what is at stake is really moderate Islam, in which case we are speaking of the lack that is the excess; a lack in excess that is not even of the Muslim but rather in the culture (Islam) that is constructed as thoroughly regulating the Muslim. Moderacy provides us no way of moving beyond the Muslim as ontically religious; rather, it only reinforces the reductive hold of ontically pure religion in imaginings about Muslims, and it seeks to institute a subject position based on this. In other words, if we locate ourselves within the discourse on integration to read its central problematic against the grain, the moderate Muslim label creates subject positions from which Muslims can only speak as religious subjects, albeit as the 'right' type of religious subjects. In other words, rather than opening out a broader field of universalisable political possibilities to Muslims, it restricts them.

Shryock's reading is also helpful in drawing our attention to the 'penitential rites' (Shryock 2008: 107–8) expected of all Muslims, irrespective of guilt or innocence; in this he draws our attention to the operation of the moderate/extremist binary as a way of responding to the threats posed by the terrorists, the anti-Semites, the homophobes by acting on all Muslims. Penitence thus implies a collective request for purification that works on two levels. On one level it inscribes collective responsibility for the hatred and murder of the few and as such it belongs in the wider context of calls made upon Muslims to repudiate violence and extremism that had the effect of compressing the difference between ordinary non-violent Muslims and violent extremists; for example, even though Muslim leaders and theologians condemned the 9/11 atrocities, former British Prime Minister Baroness Thatcher criticised them for failing to criticise them (Allison 2001). Responsibility here recalls Connolly's reading of Sartre:

A Jew in a world of anti-Semitism is constantly pressed to observe himself from the perspective of the other, to regulate his demeanor and behavior so that he is not vulnerable to the panoply of accusations the anti-Semite is all too ready to bring against him ...

Everyone could become 'a witness against himself': everyone could
be subjected to the terms of self-examination Sartre so deftly exposes
as the condition of the assimilating Jew in a world of anti-Semitism.
(Connolly 1991: 106)

This witnessing conjures forth the metaphor of Agamben's (1999)
notion of *Muselmann* as witness and bearer of testimony. Penitence as
purification also belongs in the wider context of the discourse of the war
on terror with the repeated calls for an Islamic reformation; witness the
words of former US Deputy Defence Secretary Paul Wolfowitz as the
invasion of Iraq was about to begin: 'We need an Islamic reformation'.
I am not concerned here with debating the helpfulness or not of this
observation, but rather with the reductive routing of Muslim politics
and history through religion, and the way in which it temporalises
Muslim alterity to a point in the West's own pasts. In other words,
within the context of a discourse that problematises Muslims as
potentially undemocratic, as presenting certain kinds of threats, the
ways in which we frame the question of Muslim politics themselves
inscribe certain kinds of subject positions from which Muslims can
enter politics: as ontically religious and yet, because they are ontically
religious, there is the simultaneous inscription of non-raciality that
is deployed in parallel as a limit on Muslim participation in the
public sphere. As Butler (1991: 133) reminds us, abjection involves
'boundary-constituting taboo'; the boundaries maintained through
the inscription of abject difference are also reworked through purifying
acts; the expulsion of the Other demanded by the extreme right is one
such border practice, though there are others, and they frequently take
the form of purification as ritual. Ritual is important in restoring myths
and symbols in the face of a presence that seems to undo and interrupt
boundaries and symbolic frameworks. The rituals of purification bring
to mind the case of the compulsive; as Evans (1996: 126) notes, the
obsessive-compulsive ritual is an act intended to overcome the lack
in the Other; our acting out of this on the Other (rather than on the
self) speaks of anxiety, but it is not really a purification of the Other,
but of the self (our nation which is polluted by the threat of terrorism
or the threat of difference). In this, Elia (2006: 158) notes how, in the
context of immigration sweeps and mass arrests that figured Muslim
men in the United States as a threat, Muslim women were represented

as 'redeemable', the element that could be purified because of common representations of them as devoid of agency (cf. Steans 2008) – the perfect void within. And purification also works as in another way, as a moment of reintegration, but also as a cognate to exorcism itself.

Islamophobia emerges in the wake of a symbolic problem and an inscription of Muslims as an adequately racialised/incompletely realised subject, predicated on the quest for the ontically pure racial subject that ensures Islamophobia can never be read as racism and Muslims can only be read as subjects thoroughly regulated by culture (Islam). The construction of the moderate cannot take us beyond this impasse because it is contingent upon a certain type of purification that will forever conjure forth the Muslim as the ontically pure religious subject (to be purified from the distorted culture [Islam] of the terrorists, homophobes, misogynists and anti-Semites who got us into the war on terror in the first place), and thus incompletely racial. But in spite of this performative purification it does not actually reconfigure what 'Muslim' means and nor does it open out a new field of political possibilities or viable political subject positions. The usefulness of moderate Muslim is thus restricted to its polemical invocations, or as a naming for projects that seek to 'deradicalise' the 'radical'; what it cannot provide is a basis for incorporation into wider modes of democratic politics. What I am trying to suggest is that, like members of all other social groups, the kind of things that most Muslims are likely to want are fairly predictable – a better life, for example. The moderate subject position does not necessarily help them to pursue this through democratic politics because through its inscription of its opposite (extremism) and its inscription of Muslims as ontically pure religious subjects (and thus, incompletely racial in societies in which subjecthood, raciality and recognition have long been imbricated), it positions them at the limits of democracy itself. In doing so, it does not open up a viable range of political identities, and in failing to actually transform what Muslim comes to mean in public discourse, it feeds wider Islamophobia, fears and anxieties about Muslims while failing to institute alternative political or democratic possibilities for Muslims.

In other words, one of the biggest ironies in the discussions about Muslim moderacy is that they have the effect of instituting a subject position from which Muslims can enter politics, but which is entirely predicated on religion. This seems counter-intuitive, but also counterproductive, if the aim is to open up spaces and identities capable of sustaining liberal democratic encounters. It now behoves us to consider what sort of subject positions are instituted around reductionist readings of Islamophobia as simply a matter of religious offence.

Islamophobia and the Politics of Offence

At this point it is helpful to broaden the discussion to consider what is at stake politically in how we define Islamophobia. As I noted in Chapter 1, this question is important because those who oppose the notion of Islamophobia often claim that it enables the advancement of a particular type of religious politics that can both prevent open criticism and discussion of religion, and progress the cause of Islamism. It seems that what is at stake in these claims is actually a reflection of the problematic naming and conception of Islamophobia as simply religious. How we name a particular problem has a direct bearing on how we can understand it, and on the political possibilities that will ensue. If we view Islamophobia as an essentially religious problem, then it necessarily follows that our emphasis will privilege certain kinds of concerns over others. In this it is helpful to note the idea that criticism of religion is necessarily Islamophobic only follows from the problematic understanding of Islamophobia as religious, but this also complicates our understanding of Muslim politics. Remaining with the metaphor of ritual and taboo, it is interesting to consider another performative encounter through which Muslims have been repeatedly engaged in what Sarah Dornhof (2011) terms a politics of offence with increasing frequency during the war on terror. Here, the Rushdie affair can be located outside the context of this politics of offence, for while it was a precursor to cases such as the Danish cartoons affair, I would like to suggest that the Rushdie affair was the political moment after which subsequent appropriations of offence could be named and organised under this rubric. In other words, while offence was clearly at stake in the Rushdie affair, it was only as a result of the debates surrounding it that offence emerged as a framing for making sense of Muslim politics.

As Norton (2011) notes, there is something formulaic about the ways in which these contests over offence and free speech have been played out, yet they are also performative; in this they work almost as a social ritual, as offence is repeatedly invoked on all sides in these encounters. To Norton:

> One might examine how the challenge to freedom of speech by Muslims was made a license for the expression of sentiments calculated not only to offend, but to ensure the continuance of a racial, ethnic, and sexual order. Thus the commemoration of Theo van Gogh's death involved the repeated employment of a sexually explicit ethnic slur for Muslims: 'goat-fuckers.' Muslims were reified in this slur – rendered childlike and amiable by the employment of stuffed-toy goats – as hypersexual rustics, always masculine, never feminine, outside the order of urbanity and civility. One might observe – and critique – the importance of conventional and formulaic narratives (the Rushdie affair, the cartoon controversy) in the construction of the question. (Norton 2011: 68)

To illustrate the complexities of contemporary appropriations of offence it is helpful to consider the case of Theo van Gogh. The product of collaboration between Ayaan Hirsi Ali and Theo van Gogh, *Submission, Part I* was broadcast in 2004, and immediately caused offence among a considerable minority of non-Muslim Dutch people and a majority of Dutch Muslims (Essed 2009: 143). *Submission* is a far more clever film than many give it credit for; Eyerman (2008: 100) notes that its depiction of the corporeal inscriptions of violence and theology on women positioned gender violence as 'expressive of a way of life, not merely a cruel personality or criminal act', although in this Eyerman misses that the very point of the film was to draw attention to the systemic nature of gender violence (which is routinised and normalised in all societies) is precisely that it is frequently unrecognised and treated neither as cruelty nor as criminal. As such, women themselves are the abject. But in its intertextuality *Submission* also came to inscribe the abjection of the racialised; its invocation of veil belongs in the wider context of debates over covering and migrant rights. These debates burst onto the scene in the French *foulards* affair of 1989 and saw contests over the rights of schoolgirls to wear hijab which fed into conflict over the threat of multiculturalism to national identity (Hollifield 2004: 198). Essed (2009: 144) thus reads in *Submission* a dehistoricised, universalist notion of gender emancipation which ignores the ways in which Muslim women face routinised discrimination for wearing hijab; as we have seen, these are not reducible simply to employment discrimination for the far right has mobilised around the spectre of burka as an existential threat. This breaking of taboos is thus more complex than first appears to be the case, where one crossing inscribes another taboo – that of veiling, reflected in various calls and attempts to ban hijab and burka in a number of different countries. As contests over covering play out, they inscribe the abjection of the covered so that as noted earlier, the site of the corporeal An-Sofie Dewinter wearing a burka and bikini ensemble signified a particular way of mediating the border between the proper subject and the abject and incorporeal. Thus, the van Gogh case actually forces us to shift away from the idea that the film had a single, fixed reading, and instead recognise its complexities, and the ways in which it inscribed Muslim abjection.

It is thus helpful to return to draw attention to the framing of his offence by a wider racial politics, as a man wont to describe Muslim immigrants as 'goat fuckers' and who had previously been found guilty of anti-Semitism (Panayiotopoulos 2006: 168). Van Gogh had once said of Jews: 'Fornicating yellow stars in a gas chamber ... What a smell of caramel today. Today the crematoriums burn only diabetic Jews' (Tollenaere 2004). Van Gogh responded to subsequent criticism from the Jewish historian Evelian Gans by writing 'I suspect that Ms Gans gets wet dreams about being fucked by Dr Mengele', and who later expressed hope that the Jewish historian would sue him so 'then Ms Gans will have to explain in court that she claims that she does not get wet dreams about Dr Mengele' (Tollenaere 2004: 6). Gans' (1994) reading of van Gogh's politics was measured and drew attention to his mobilisation of anti-Semitism in the service of free speech (a precursor to his later emphasis on Islamophobia and free speech):

> Cover-up of niet, ook hier bewijst Van Gogh over de juiste seismograaf te hebben beschikt. Juist de koppeling van de roep om vrije meningsuiting aan de (zelf)censuur rond joodse thema's viel op een vruchtbare bodem. Bregstein poneert met recht dat er in Nederland een klimaat is ontstaan waarin er bij de 'weldenkende intellectuele elite' steeds meer irritatie en afweer is gaan broeien ten opzichte van de actieve antisemitisme bestrijding door organisaties

als de Anne Frank Stichting, stiba (De Stichting ter Bestrijding van het Antisemitisme), cidi en ojec (Het Overlegorgaan van Joden en Christenen) en tegen rechterlijke veroordelingen van 'vermeend' antisemitisme. Het nieuwe vaandel dat hierbij geheven wordt heet 'vrije meningsuiting' – bedreigd door pressiegroepen en een door deze gemanipuleerde rechtspraak.

Cover up or not, Van Gogh proves he has the right seismograph. Just linking the call for freedom of speech and (self) censorship around Jewish subjects fell on fertile soil. Bregstein posits that the intellectual élites developed a growing sense of irritation and resistance against the active anti-Semitism fight by organisations such as the Anne Frank Stichting (The Foundation Fighting Anti-Semitism), CIDI and OJEC (Consultative Body of Jews and Christians in the Netherlands) and from court convictions of 'alleged' anti-Semitism. The new flag raised is called free speech which is threatened by pressure groups.' [Trans. Amal Sheiko for the author]

Gans (1994) further described van Gogh as having become a 'cherished enfant terrible. A rebel, one who refused to see that his cause was a bubble and served no purpose other than his own self'. But contra Gans, because van Gogh's interventions were progressing a wider racial politics, it is probably more helpful to suggest that his politics were not simply self-serving, but that they are better read as an intervention on a wider field of racial politics. This point is important, because as we have seen, discussions of Islamophobia tend to disarticulate it from a wider field of racial politics, and recognition of van Gogh's wider history of anti-Semitism helps rehistoricise Islamophobia. In this context we can also locate the case within a wider mode of engaging with racialised and ethnicised communities. For example, an extensive literature has already noted that parodic claims in the right wing press about vexatious bannings by antiracists occurred as a way of trivialising racism and antiracism (cf. Petley 2005: 87; Gaine and George 1999: 74). In a contemporary context, reports surfaced in February 2012 of a court appearance in Lincoln by a former British National Party member who had plastered his windows with notices and leaflets designed to offend Muslims. This is not an isolated case but reflects an increasingly routinised way of addressing the Other. To cite a banal example, there is even a Facebook Group named 'Eating Percy Pigs [a British children's confectionary] outside a mosque to taunt Muslims'. In another case the Italian MEP Mario Borghezio roused supporters by imagining the scenario of 'our grandparents' being told that 'we' would end up banning Christmas songs at the behest of 'a bunch of shit Islamic bastards' (Gazzanni 2011).

At this point it is helpful to turn to the case of the Danish cartoons affair which was set in train by the publication of a series of cartoons in the Danish *Jyllands-Posten* newspaper on 30 September 2005. More than any other case, the furore over the cartoons seems to illustrate the potential for conflict between Muslims and democracy: over one hundred people lost their lives globally in horrifying outbreaks of violence over the cartoons, and although the most serious acts of violence occurred outside Europe and the United States, in Europe they involved plots of murder and terrorism (Patel and Tyrer 2011: 123). Unsurprisingly, the cartoons have often therefore been read as a straightforward conflict between democratic rights such as free speech and the demands of an antidemocratic minority (Patel and Tyrer 2011: 123; Dreier 2011: 177; Rosen 2008: 105). To understand the cartoons we first have to acknowledge that no element in discourse has a single preferred reading. Although often called Muhammad cartoons, they included caricatures drawing from popular stereotypes: Muslims in an identity parade, a bomb in Muhammad's turban, and so on. There are multiple ways of reading the cartoons; for example, if taken out of context, they could equally well function as a comment on Islamophobic stereotypes. Nevertheless, it is fair to suggest that the cartoons were intended to provoke debate, and in this light Ridanpää (2009: 736) suggests that they can hardly be described as innocent. In one sense this is not important, because the ability to speak in ways that might offend is part of political practice and can indicate and facilitate healthy democratic encounters. A more fundamental problem is what can happen when the political itself is displaced and can find no other means of expression other than through discursive appeals to offence. The case of the cartoons is thus interesting because Modood (2006: 4) has located Muslim responses in the West within a wider context of racism against Muslims, and Müller *et al* (2009: 33) have observed that in distinction to responses in the Middle East, European

Muslims viewed the affair as a reflection of the broader social situation and problems facing their communities. The expression of these apparently worldly concerns through a theological register via their conflation with offence complicates our understanding of offence as a straightforward religious question.

One effect of the prominence of the offence framing for Islamophobia is that legitimate and reasonable attempts to engage with and criticise religion become conflated with more problematic expressions of offence, for example at the hands of the far right. But this reductionism is inscribed through the problematic naming and conception of Islamophobia itself, which displaces and privatises the racial politics properly at stake in its expression to a simple notion of religion, privileging the possibility of Islamophobia being expressed and resisted as though it simply is offence. This problem is not peripheral to our understanding of Islamophobia, but it is dependent upon a particular mode of understanding Islamophobia which, by reducing it to a simple question of religion, displaces its racial politics and institutes subject positions through which this can be expressed without the fear of racism (by appealing to offence) and resisted (by appealing to offence). This opens a tension within the idea that the politics of offence centrally concerns free political expression.

In considering this, it is helpful to begin from the distinction between offence and the racial politics at stake in Islamophobia. In other words, offence is not in and of itself Islamophobic, and nor can Islamophobia be reduced to offence. However, while pursuing the politics of offence has not served Muslims' interests well, this problem is framed by a wider displacement of proper political contest over racism. What I want to suggest is that somewhere, in the rubric of offence, its potential political utility has been lost, both because of the ways in which offence is repeatedly appropriated to demonise Muslims (as opposed to extending a substantive politics), and because of the ways in which Muslims have found themselves only able to appeal against Islamophobia by mobilising over offence in the absence of a more helpful definition of Islamophobia. In this, the politics of offence appears increasingly predictable on all sides. In its pastiche nature one is reminded less of Judith Butler's (1990) conception of the political possibilities of pastiche or parody than of a more recent cultural meme involving endless parodies of a scene from Oliver Hirschbiegel's (2004) film *Downfall*. In this, a splenetic outburst by Hitler has been endlessly parodied through the superimposition of subtitles that make it appear as though his rage is directed towards a range of contemporary targets, from underperforming sports teams to the resignation of Sarah Palin, inevitably culminating in a parody in which Hitler discovers all the other *Downfall* parodies. The parody collapses beneath the weight of its own intertextuality, its form having been presaged so many times. In this there is a similarity with the cyclical emergence of ritualistic encounters with Muslims through a politics of offence.

Beyond Displacement

The problem of integration is frequently couched in terms of the problem of Muslim politicality and the perception that Muslims exist as limit figures for democracy itself. This is usually taken not as indicating possible limits for democracy, but as inscribing the abjection of these figures of lack in excess, although the ways in which it manifests tend to construct various limits on the possibility of Muslims engaging in democratic politics. These problems are not peripheral to the wider question of Islamophobia, but are central to it. In societies that have been historically organised on racial terms, formally and informally, the attempt to discern in Muslims an innately religious kernel places them at the borders and the margins in quite specific ways. It institutes certain types of relations with democratic institutions and civil society, as well as with other groups. It also institutes certain types of subject positions from which Muslims can engage in politics. The fetishisation of the ontically pure religious nature of Muslims in turn plays out in modes of politics that simultaneously inscribe Muslim abjection by fetishising the ontic religious purity. In fact, what we see occurring are various forms of performative purification; the purification of Muslims to rid them of extremism, and the equally performative purification that comes with the politics of offence; the release that comes with expressing my democratic right to free speech in spite of the feelings of the Other.

The moderate Muslim subject position does not serve those who want to see Muslims expressing more liberal democratic politics because it institutes a marginal subject position that might be a useful site from which to engage in politics in a world without race, but in a world in which race retains its hold, it merely positions them into a religious subject position that embodies their difficult alterity and institutes a subject position from which they cannot speak of experiencing Islamophobia as racism, because they are marginalised as inadequately racial, while possibilities of challenging Islamophobia without appeals to religious metaphors – for example, by challenging it on grounds of racism – are foreclosed by its ambiguous positioning as a post-racial racism that is not recognised as such. More importantly, it institutes a political subject position that privileges the invocation of religious metaphors. The politics of offence, on the other hand, is somehow playful and yet as with all ritual performativities it can be turgid and predictable, so we know all along what will happen: somebody will write or print something to precipitate a Muslim response, a militant Islamist somewhere or other will respond with violence and death threats, the case will be mobilised as an instance to illustrate the essential nature of the conflict between Muslims and democratic rights, and at some stage in the encounter, Muslims will protest. Once offence shifts from being one possibility within a wider political repertoire to being a fundamental stratagem for the encounter it becomes post-political, and in this sense the politics of offence acts as a cover for a wider condition of post-politics, so that we can see democracy is alive and being defended even though the reality may be a masked, turgid neo-liberal consensus politics in the mainstream. This, too, emerges from the subject positions instituted by a problematic misconception of Islamophobia, and it is striking that this subject position also privileges appeals to religious metaphors.

In other words, the irony of the emphasis on suspending Muslims in a state of radical alterity in order to emphasise the importance of their democratic integration is this: within the terms of the dominant framings for debates about Muslims, it is not possible to institute subject positions from which they can straightforwardly enter into a secular politics. On the one hand, the emphasis on 'moderacy' privileges the notion of a purely religious subject that runs counter to the stated ambition of promoting integration into secular democratic institutions, and instead privileges their mobilisation only as religious actors. On the other hand, the refusal to conceive of Islamophobia as a form of racism, but instead to reduce it to a simple matter of religious discrimination or offence, means that political claims that could otherwise be articulated through the profane can only be expressed in religious terms (cf. Patel and Tyrer 2011). The obvious implication of this is that it is not simply some essential Muslim difference based around a hostility to secularism that lies at the heart of this, but rather that this problematic is underwritten by a hegemonic refusal to conceive of Muslims as anything other than religious subjects, and that this refusal in turn forecloses access to the profane and privileges appeals to religious metaphors. The question of whether Islamophobia can most helpfully be understood as religious discrimination or racism is therefore not merely of abstract academic significance. Rather, to recognise Islamophobia as a form of racism could itself represent an important stratagem in seeking to undercut extremism by opening out a broader range of secular political subject positions for Muslims.

6

Islamophobia beyond the war on terror

As a piece of political artwork, Yoko Ono's *White Chess Set* (1966) engaged with troubled questions concerning agency, power, subjectivity and antagonism, and involved dissolving the difference between antagonists, thus causing the game itself to collapse (Danto 2007: 75). This metaphor helps illustrate the epistemic conditions that underwrite the emergence of Islamophobia. Within the terms of a game – and for the sake of argument, let us call it biopolitics – that institutes a binary inside/outside the nation fracture within human populations and gives way to modes of governance that institute ascribed subject positions elaborating this division, a contemporary condition in which race appears to bleed across its traditional boundaries gives rise to particular anxieties. This problem is radicalised during the war on terror. With the problem of 'sleeper cells', clean skins, the green menace has come to replace the reds under the bed as an invisible threat – one that cannot be recognised and as a result that needs the insertion of a new politics to fix the difference between antagonists. We can call that politics Islamophobia, and this chapter considers its relationship to the war on terror, or, more accurately, whether we can disarticulate it from various attachments to the war on terror, and whether by doing so we can more clearly establish its place in a wider field of racial politics.

As we have seen, Islamophobia emerges in the wake of a Muslim identity politics that is played out against a wider field of racial politics. One of the problems this presents is that it leaves us to assume that Muslim identities are somehow fixed and pre-existing; that they have a certain ontic purity. In other words, they exist prior to, and in spite of, the emergence of Islamophobia. There is thus a tendency to assume that the ways in which Muslims are represented are somehow detached from the realities of Muslim lives, so that while the representations themselves might be stereotyped or incorrect, there is still a 'real', 'authentic' Muslim against whom their inaccuracy can be gauged. This assumption is not unproblematic. The subject positions constructed through a problematic definition of Islamophobia demonstrate to us that the ways in which particular categories are constructed discursively does not only involve setting up a construction which is ultimately false, but rather that it has implications for the ways in which subjects can identify and position themselves. It is possible to pursue this line of reasoning one stage further by suggesting that it therefore also follows that perhaps the discourse on Muslims does not just take Muslims as its objects, but rather that it constitutes Muslim identities in specific ways. In other words, that if Islamophobia acts as a response to an identity politics through which more and more racialised and ethnicised subjects began naming themselves in ways that disrupted racial logics, then perhaps it is also the case that the discursive practices through which Muslims are spoken of have also contributed to this process in some way – in other words, that particular ways of narrating Muslims do not simply speak about or to members of this group, but that they also constitute them. In this chapter I want to explore this question by considering the case of the war on terror. This seems a useful move to make in two respects: first, research has shown that Islamophobia existed prior to the war on terror but that it intensified after 9/11 (cf. Allen and Nielsen 2002; Sheridan 2006) and in response to key subsequent events such as terrorist attacks. Second, in spite of this, there is something about the emphasis upon the war on terror that seems to dehistoricise what is at stake in Islamophobia, but also some of the key ways in which we can understand the war on terror itself. With these in mind it is interesting to consider whether we can see Muslims constituted in the war on terror in particular ways that shed light on a wider historicisation.

From Exceptionalism to Exception

One of the curious features of discussions about Islamophobia, and about relations between Muslims and Western states in particular, is the ways in which they frequently exceptionalise Islamophobia, disarticulating it from a wider field of racial politics. This is reflected in discussions about Islamophobia in a number of ways, but most notably through the contests over whether Islamophobia should be understood as merely a form of religious discrimination or criticism rather than racism. Islamophobia has also been exceptionalised through the emphasis placed on the war on terror within discussions of Islamophobia. These wider discussions of the war on terror have continued to exceptionalise it, in part through the emphasis upon its role in defending democracy and freedom, which has helped frame the increased surveillance and intensification of state powers during the war on terror as being entirely compatible with liberal democracy, rather than undermining its fundamental values.

The extent of this exceptionalisation is reflected in the privatisation of the strategy and aims of the war on terror that has been witnessed in the criticism for which former US President George W. Bush and former British Prime Minister Tony Blair have been singled out. In the case of the latter, who led Britain to war in Iraq in pursuit of the war on terror despite massive and concerted popular protests against the war, the invasion of Iraq came to be overshadowed by contested claims that Blair had misled Parliament over the extent of Saddam's threat. In spite of the fact that a majority of elected Members of Parliament voted to invade Iraq, the war has therefore been exceptionalised as 'Blair's war' to many: for example, as early as 2003 the BBC broadcast a *Panorama* documentary titled 'Blair's war' (BBC 2003), while media coverage of the controversial decision frequently referred to the invasion inter-changeably as 'Blair's decision' and 'Blair's war', while 'Blair's war' has figured in the titles of books by Coates, Krieger and Vickers (2004) and Stothard (2003). This helps fix the war on terror as exceptional in a rather different sense, through the implicit assumption that, in spite of the nebulous nature of the state and security industries, the presence of pro-war media supporting the invasion, and the active support of members from all parties, the personalisation of the war exceptional-ises it as having little to do with wider policy shifts or transformations in state power, and little to do with a broader political field, but rather as simply the assumed work of one individual.

This kind of exceptionalism is clearly unhelpful, but it has also been a feature of discussions about the role of the Bush presidency in pursuing the war on terror. One manifestation of this is in the emphasis that has frequently been placed on Bush's personal convictions, and the assumption that these had a direct bearing on the ways in which the war was pursued. A particularly prevalent feature of this has been the ways in which liberal political commentators, left-wing opponents, and satirists have drawn attention to Bush's religious beliefs. The unhelpfulness of such exceptionalisation is reflected in the fact that Bush's successor, President Obama, is widely acknowledged not to share Bush's fundamentalist convictions – and indeed, is popularly attacked by the Christian right as a secret Muslim – and yet in spite of this difference in personal conviction, in the words of Nancy Murray (2011), Obama has 'embraced' Bush's agenda on security. Nevertheless, much has been made of the seeming exceptionalism of the Bush administration's rhetoric during the war on terror, and this disarticulates the war itself from wider logics of state practice (and the wider development of the security-industrial complex). For example, much continues to be made of Bush's Christian fundamentalist sensibility, and that of the neo-conservative right. Noting the media reliance upon expert knowledge during the war on terror, Croft cites a media intervention by a contributing editor to a religious journal, who argued:

A falling civilisation can't be argued out of its failings ... when a culture is tumbling downward, all its truths and facts – indeed, the whole idea of truth and fact and argument are exactly what its people increasing [sic] disbelieve. Does anyone doubt that western Europe is tumbling downward? It cannot summon the will to reproduce itself. It has aborted and contracted its birthrate down toward demographic disaster ... it has proved supine in the face of those [Islamic] immigrants' anti-Semitism, anti-Christianism, and even anti-Europeanism. (Croft 2006: 234)

Commenting on the intervention, Croft notes that it reflected a Christian evangelical position which was reflected in many of the expert commentaries offered during the war on terror. Indeed, there is also no doubt that the Bush rhetoric on the war on terror was suffused with religious metaphors. Goy et al (2008: 115) note the delivery of religious services by Bush following the 9/11 atrocity and go further still, to analyse Bush statements during the 9/11 period, finding that nearly a quarter of 60 paragraphs coded and analysed for religion focused on the President's references to a religious enemy (Goy *et al* 2008: 127). These references constructed the religious enemy through a lengthy list of characteristics; Goy *et al* (2008: 127–8) note the construction of this enemy as hijackers of a great religion; loving only power; celebrating death; despising choice and creativity; not having a place in faith; hating America; being the heirs to fascism; forcing on humans a grim conformity; encouraging murder and suicide; destroying religious symbols of other faiths... The extensive list identified by Goy *et al* continues at some length. In their analysis, Goy *et al* (2008: 125) establish a very particular framing for Bush's post-9/11 discourse, suggesting that the simple certainties and binaries around which he expressed his politics are consistent with some forms of religious fundamentalism. The most infamous of Bush's apparently religious references occurred during a press conference on 16 September 2001, when President George W. Bush invoked the word 'crusade' in response to a question concerning civil liberties, saying: 'This is a new kind of – a new kind of evil [...] And the American people are beginning to understand. This crusade, this war on terrorism is going to take a while' (Suskind 2004). The ensuing international furore led to immediate damage limitation exercises by the US Secretary of State and by British Prime Minister Tony Blair, who defended the war on terror by pointing out that it was not an attack against Islam, noting that the vast majority of Muslims are 'decent' and 'law-abiding' (Vallely 2004: 48).

Vallely has suggested that 'there is more to the casual use of a word like "crusade" than merely letting loose the doggerel of war' (Vallely 2004: 48). Vallely does not, of course, ascribe to Bush the motivation of crusade any more than Goy *et al* do, but still, there is something in the elevation of a banalised reference to religion that interests me. One of the paradoxes of Bush is the tendency among political satirists and commentators on the left to lampoon him on account of his capacity to stumble over his words at times, often with hilarious results, but despite this the one area of his discourse that they have taken literally has been his use of religious metaphors, as though this might reveal something of the kernel of Bush the fundamentalist. At stake in this amplification of the role of Bush's fundamentalism in shaping the war on terror is a wider question of historicisation – namely, whether the practices associated with the pursuit of the war on terror can be seen as reflecting simply the exceptional visions of a fundamentalist Baptist leader with a neo-conservative advisor base, or whether they should instead be framed within a wider series of shifts in state power. One way of approaching this is to read Bush's utterances literally, but as we have seen, it is not necessarily helpful to reduce the meanings of a broader discourse to a literalist reading of the metaphors it appropriates and organises in certain articulations through particular nodal points. Rather, it is more helpful to first historicise and de-literalise our readings of Bush's fundamentalism. In this, Croft (2006: 24) notes that Bush's utterances reflected a 'culture war' through which neo-conservatives were engaging with liberal and counter-cultures. In this sense, Bush's invocation of religious metaphors in the war on terror was organised under a more parochial horizon, which also goes some way to explaining his apparent inability to grasp from the outset that these might have been read by international audiences and understood within a rather different framing. Indeed, as a result, from 2005 onwards, the rhetoric of the Bush administration began to shift, referring to the war as one waged against militant and extremist Islam (Shapiro 2011: 169).

The paradox of Bush's banalised appeals to religious metaphors is that the responses to which they have been met have helped exceptionalise the war on terror as being a function of a particular neoconservative-Christian fundamentalist alignment and individual convictions, but that they themselves also worked to exceptionalise the war on terror to domestic audiences, by seeking to avoid fixing it for what it was: a reflection of wider shifts in state power. In this light it is helpful to consider one of the more widely publicised invocations of religious metaphor by the Bush administration, when it emerged that the war on terror would be organised under the naming of Operation Infinite Justice. That the operation was renamed Enduring Freedom after it was noted offence might be caused to Muslim beliefs since only god can hand out infinite justice (Roy 2003: 92–3) is perhaps somewhat ironic, for on the same grounds, one could suppose some fundamentalist Christians might also have been troubled by the naming. This also exceptionalised the war on terror with a further irony – the idea that Muslims might have been more concerned about a theological concern than about how innocent people might be caught up in the crossfire. In other words, the incident cements the attempt to exceptionalise the war on terror by placing it into a parochial fundamentalist framing.

Porttikivi draws upon Rancière to observe that infinite justice signifies a demand for a justice without any bounds or limitations placed upon it, and that such a justice is an 'assertion of a right identical to the omnipotence hitherto reserved for the vindictive God' Porttikivi (2010: 200). In this Porttikivi actually opens the way for a split reading of this inscription, by noting that infinite justice can perhaps better be understood as a move through which distinctions between law, politics, ethics and religion are erased (Porttikivi: 2010). This does not necessarily mean that religion has overcome all barriers and overtaken law, politics and ethics, but rather that the systems through which limits can be placed upon the exercise of sovereign power, whether through juridical means or an appeal to ethics or traditional regulatory frameworks, have been placed into question. In other words, far from invoking infinite divine power, it is organised under a horizon of infinite sovereign power in a world in which distinctions are being dissolved. That is to say, it is not about a theological ontology, but about an ontology of pure life itself. To speak of infinite justice as the possibility of unbounded sovereign authority is contingent upon a wider shift, and of the ability to act over life and death in another way, even to constitute subjects in all kinds of ways, though especially to take life in its most pure forms (and yet at its most abject). To speak of infinite justice is to speak of the power to inscribe pure life, *homo sacer* (Agamben 1998); forms of life that are just life, that do not have the political trappings of subjecthood and citizenship, and to perform these under the horizon of sovereign power seemingly unbounded by traditional legal distinctions. To speak of infinite justice is thus not to speak of a world of stable boundaries, but one constituted through zones of indistinction, 'being outside and yet belonging' (Agamben 2005: 35). Infinite justice is better understood as a reference to the increasing use of exceptional powers by states in the context of a shift during the twentieth century from provisional use of exceptional measures (e.g. states of emergency) to their routinisation as a paradigm of government (Agamben 2005). The various attempts to exceptionalise the war on terror are thus unhelpful, and they fail to account for the fact that the various modalities through which it was waged were not a pursuit of neo-conservative agendas, Christian fundamentalism, or even the consciences of individual leaders and the 'cabals' said to have influenced them (to use a term increasingly deployed with anti-Semitic overtones in reference to closed circles of power and influence). Rather, the war on terror has simply reflected a routinised logic of contemporary state power. In this, we are forced to shift our attention from the supposed exceptionalism of the war on terror to its use of exception.

In this the exception is a form of exclusion, though one to which the rule still applies (Agamben 1998: 17), so just as the exception is external to the juridical order it remains internal to it (because it is enshrined legally). The state of exception is thus to Agamben 'an attempt to include the exception itself within the juridical order by creating a zone of indistinction in which fact and law coincide' (Agamben 2005: 26); existing at the nexus between life and law this enables the object of power itself to be life in its most pure. The form of life inscribed through such exercises is life at its most pure, *homo sacer* (Agamben 1998), a form of life that is just life, that does not have the political trappings of subjecthood and citizenship. That is to say, this exercise of power constitutes subjects simply as beings without the political value attendant upon subjecthood or citizenship. Agamben (2005: 3) cites the war on terror as having provided an important exemplification of this process in the form of the USA Patriot Act.

In the context of the exceptional powers deployed during the war on terror, Muslims are conjured in a number of ways; through the racial profiling and immigration sweeps that took place, organised under the horizon opened by the PATRIOT ACT, for example, when large numbers of Muslim men were incarcerated in high security facilities. Meeropol (2005: 148) notes that those detained in the streets were categorised as being 'high interest', 'interest' or, very significantly, 'interest undetermined' by the FBI, and those detained in the MDC ADMAX Special Housing Unit were denied communication with the outside world, often prevented from receiving visitors, and frequently subjected to verbal and physical abuse (Meeropol 2005: 151–2). The post-9/11 sweeps conflated immigration and counter-terror-ism knowledges and enforcement, so many of those swept up were placed into an indeterminate status as non-citizens that compounded the position in which they were placed in high security detention as terrorist suspects, many of whom had been swept in on the basis of informal tip-offs from concerned citizens. The post-9/11 sweeps did not result in any convictions for involvement in the terrorist attacks, but they did constitute Muslim detainees as a form of pure life, detained under exceptional measures and with indeterminate status, lacking the formal rights of citizenship or subjecthood. Similar exceptional measures have been used in a range of other contexts, and the large scale use of stop and search practices in the United Kingdom (cf. Pantazis and Pemberton 2009), constructing the racialised as non-subjects and potential terrorists, even in the absence of any terrorism convictions resulting from such practices. Although stop and search practices under the Section 44 of the Terrorism Act (2000) were, until ruled unlawful by the European Court, hugely controversial, the passage of the Act actually preceded the war on terror. Subsequent British anti-terror legislation saw the creation of 'control orders' under the Prevention of Terrorism Act (2005). These measures were created in order to police the threat of terrorism by imposing a range of stringent conditions on those suspected of acts of terrorism; these could range from conditions akin to house arrest to restricted access to communication equipment (Patel and Tyrer 2011: 86). Although it is important to note that applications for control orders were only made for a small number of cases involving people strongly suspected of posing a serious threat of terrorist violence, they inscribe an indeterminate legal status not least through the use of closed evidence and the difficulty of challenging them through an open legal process, amounting to what Amnesty International (2006: 26) described as 'stripping of a person's right to a fair trial'. Although legal challenges to the process resulted in a decision to replace them with new measures, it is worth noting that the use of control orders had its parallels in other practices such as Anti-Social Behaviour Orders (Lynch 2008; MacDonald 2007) which were introduced in Britain to deal with problems such as nuisance youths and noisy neighbours through civil orders (thus requiring lower levels of evidence), but for the breaching of which criminal sanctions could be imposed. In this, even the most seemingly exceptional of the exceptional powers deployed during the war on terror have their roots in a routinised biopolitical logic.

In this, Daulatzai (2007) draws our attention to a peculiar feature of the carceral archipelago in current times, for this is a global archipelago, and one that Daulatzai argues is organised against global carceral imaginary that collapses and compresses distinctions between home and overseas (Daulatzai 2007: 137), so that carceral practices in the United States and those overseas are connected. Still more parallels emerge, as Daulatzai notes the Abu Ghraib prisoner abuses scandal; Daulatzai (2007: 139) notes that one of the guards involved in the abuses had previously worked at a US prison in which guards had been charged with acts ranging from naked prisoner searchers to sodomy with a weapon and had scrawled 'KKK' on the floor in a prisoner's blood. In an almost obscene twist that lays bare the discursive field on which the incidents took place, Daulatzai notes that a US prison official present at the opening of Abu Ghraib declared it to be 'the only place that we agreed as a team was truly closest to an American prison' (Daulatzai 2007: 138). Here is a further clue to the genealogy of some of the excesses of the war on terror; as Puar (2007: 73) has noted, the violence of Abu Ghraib was organised by a discourse of US queer exceptionalism that worked transnationally through the violence and abuse of the bodies that Puar describes as being 'perversely racialized'. We can thus locate 'infinite justice' in a wider political context, so that it is not simply a further example of the religious discourse that has permeated the war on terror, but rather it is the inscription of a mode of government that is entirely concerned with power over life itself. This does not just shift our reading of the war on terror outside the framing of its exceptionalisation, but it also shifts it outside the framing of war on terror itself. In other words, the war on terror is not the pure object of reason at stake in the exercise of such power, but rather it has reflected a wider logic. But this still does not fully account for how the war on terror relates to racism, or to the conjuring of Muslims as the phantasmatic creatures associated with Islamophobia.

Once we liberate the war on terror from its exceptionalised framing, then in its domestic pursuit its practices entail an elaboration of the logics of exception and intensified exercises of biopower. To establish the relationship between the war on terror and racism is therefore contingent upon also shifting away from privatised, exceptionalised readings of racism, and elaborating how such practices are structured by racism.

Muslims could also be conjured forth as a pure life thanks to the increasing links between state discourse on the war on terror and anti-Muslim racism (cf. Frost 2008: 567), as the construction of Muslims as a suspect population threatening to democracy came to frame wider racisms (Pantazis and Pemberton 2009). To Poynting and Mason (2006: 377), the state 'induces' and 'models' hate crime. Citing police raids by the Australian Federal Police and New South Wales police in the wake of 9/11, and further raids in Sydney, Perth and Melbourne following the 2002 Bali atrocities, arguing that these worked through a logic of ethnic profiling to maintain a particular hegemony; 'the coercion behind the consent' (Poynting and Mason 2006: 379). The effects were terror among Muslims, and in a climate of already existing fear, they faced further, privatised boundary policing through racist violence, so that in a context of unacknowledged state crimes against Muslims, 'perhaps white-thinking citizens feel justified in personally attacking this enemy' (Poynting and Mason 2006: 379). Thus, while the UK and Australia are criticised for failing to take Islamophobia properly, the 'state terror' through which the war on terror is pursued domestically and overseas provides a 'moral licence and impetus' (Poynting and Mason 2006: 384) to Islamophobic violence. The shooting of Jean Charles de Menezes under the shoot-to-kill rules of Operation Kratos is another reflection of the ways in which, during the war on terror subjects can find themselves in zones of indistinction in which there is no law and yet there is only law (Vaughan-Williams 2009), but cases such as the extraordinary rendition of Maher Arar and the arrests of innocent terrorism suspects noted in Chapter 2 also illustrate how the invisible can be conjured forth as forms of pure life, lacking the political trappings and value of citizens.

Islamophobia and the Postcolonial in a World Without Borders

But the idea of a crisis in disciplinary institutions also manifests in other ways. Disciplinary societies were not simply predicated on the ability to confine the mad and the bad into stable disciplinary institutions such as hospitals, schools, factories, or prisons, but also on the discursive construction of subjects in particular ways. The close relationship between emergence of the modern logics of race and the practice of biopower is an example of this; racialisation does not simply facilitate the exercise of biopower but is also bound up with disciplinary practices. In this sense, the decentring of modern notions of phenotypal racial difference are bound up with crisis of disciplinary institutions (Tyrer 2011). The intensification of racial biopolitics amid wider shifts in capital accumulation and the routinisation of exceptional logics – emerges in part in a response to the ways in which the logics and practices through which racial boundaries are regulated are problematised. To illustrate this it is helpful to turn to one of the 'doves' of the administration, Secretary of State Colin Powell, who said in 2001:

> Look, 9/11 was a huge traumatic shock … But the Cold War is gone. All the theologies and ideologies that were going to supplant ours are gone. The communists, the fascists – get serious! The few authoritarian regimes that are left around are peanuts! … We can't let terrorism suddenly become the substitute for Red China and the Soviet Union as our all-encompassing enemy, this great Muslim-extremist, monolithic thing from somewhere in Mauritania all the way through Muslim India. They're all different. It's not going to come together that way. (Little 2008: 320)

Powell's words are revealing, not so much about the war on terror itself than about the political field that made it possible, in which a particular post-Westphalian way of understanding the relationship between sovereignty and territoriality was ruptured and enemies could no longer be ascribed to particular territorially bounded units. Another way of looking at this is to note that Westphalian logics did not simply reflect a means of inscribing sovereignty, but also provided a rubric for organising traditional modes of determining between inside/outside and constituting and regulating populations through the deployment of racial logics. The concerns expressed through the war on terror have not simply reflected attempts to protect and preserve human populations, but have sought to respond to circumstances in which the bordering acts through which they have been constituted have been complicated.

For example, the securitisation of Muslim populations during the war on terror finds its parallels in the treatment of asylum seekers; humans constituted as abject, who 'cannot be either naturalized or repatriated … in a condition of de facto statelessness' (Agamben 2000: 22). Anti-asylum measures such as offshore border policing and immigrant detention without trial (Garner 2010: 156) in centres outside the normal rule of criminal law or the oversight that prisons might have create 'spaces which disrupt traditional understandings of the relationship between state power and territoriality' (Vaughan-Williams 2009). Soguk (2007: 304) has noted that the treatment of asylum seekers signals the decline of the legal categories people traditionally occupy; this is abjection in its purest form. But such practices find their parallels during the war on terror in the ways in which such spaces are used to defend national sovereignty, whether through cases such as Guantanamo Bay or practices such as extraordinary rendition. For example, in addition to the case of Maher Arar, a number of CIA officers were sentenced in absentia by an Italian court for the Milan kidnapping and subsequent rendition of an Egyptian suspect (Hooper 2009). At the same time, the war on terror has witnessed an intensification of the processes through which borders are policed and further tightening of immigration, as the wars on asylum and terror have come together.

When people observe that, in its contemporary form, Islamophobia emerged in the wake of the end of the Cold War and the loss of the previous Soviet enemy, they have a point historically. They also have a point politically insofar as the decline of the Soviet threat seems to point to a triumph of neoliberal consumerism over politics itself, and thus establishes a context within which the post-politics that frames Islamophobia can emerge. But the observation also seems to miss the colonial dis/continuities that sutured the Soviet Union into a wider West/rest arrangement; after all the Cold War itself was also fought culturally through a syncretic orientalism (cf. Hammond 2006). As such it was also a geopolitical conflict between the West and the non-West, in which the non-West was not territorially bounded to the Soviet Union, but also pursued through other proxies (Cuba, Korea ...). The end of the Cold War did not mark the loss of an Other (for there are always Others), but what it did mark was the loss of defining West through its opposition to a non-West that in some way appeared territorially bounded even as it spilled out of any convenient spatial organisation. The end of the Cold War thus collapsed a historically contingent way marking territorially the boundary between the West and the non-West. Following the end of the Cold War the distinction between the West and the non-West persisted as a cultural residue, and its deployment during the war on terror did not mark a replacement for the Cold War, but rather it represented a different mode of expressing this boundary. However, what did change was that the current conflict against terrorism could not be so straightforwardly inscribed territorially. Even as Afghanistan was invaded to destroy the infrastructure that had supported bin Laden and Iraq was attacked in the hunt for WMD, Western leaders made it clear that the hunt for terrorism was not an attack against the Muslim world and emphasised the importance of their allies in the non-West. Instead, this was a global fight against terror, a war with no boundaries. In this sense, infinite justice is not simply a reference to sovereign power unfettered by traditional juridicial restraints, but it was spatialised around a recognition that traditional ways of instituting and regulating geopolitical borders and social boundaries – both of which are imbricated in the regulation of human life – have been problematised by wider geopolitical shifts.

In other words, the post-Westphalian connection between statehood and bounded territoriality was ruptured; this was not a war in a conventional sense but one in which boundaries were mobile and could be collapsed and reinstated in all kinds of novel ways and at all kinds of unexpected sites. For example, Vaughan-Williams (2009) has written of the new bordering practices that emerge under such a horizon, so that the shooting of Jean Charles de Menezes in an anti-terror operation in London in 2005 is read as an example of the kind of bordering practices that occur in the context of a world in which traditional borders and boundaries appear to be in crisis and their traditional relationship to sovereign entities is disarticulated. This condition also finds its expression within Western states through the presence of postcolonial populations – that is, the presence of people formerly categorised from afar. The threat of terrorism, then, is not just read within this discourse as a problem of fighting an invisible enemy that is not territorially bounded, but also as a problem that through its mobility and invisibility, such an enemy can also appear within the nation itself. During the war on terror this discourse was reflected in a range of ways; in a US context we see the emergence of the framing of 'sleeper cells' in reference to a dormant, invisible threat that can be awakened on instruction from afar at any moment to unleash further horrors. In a UK context we see the emergence of the term 'clean skins' following the 7/7 atrocities in a reference to terrorists previously unknown to security services. But both terms present a further difficulty insofar as the crossing of borders is also conflated with the crossing of racial boundaries inscribed through bordering acts, so that the term 'clean skins' can also be read against the grain as an inscription of the wider problem of the racial unknowability of Muslims. In this sense, then, the postcolonial problem posed by Muslim identity politics comes to infuse a key problematic of the war on terror – namely, how can one recognise one's adversaries. Colin Powell's words thus speak on one level of the need to avoid opening a particular cultural front, but on another level they speak of the conflation between a political problem (terrorism) and a postcolonial question (in turn transformed into a political question – how to manage the racialised). The problem is thus not identifying a territorial adversary, but identifying those who lack such territoriality; it might involve wars with states but generally involves individuals who problematise boundaries.

Symbolic Problems and Indeterminate Subjects

This complexification of traditional boundaries is a symbolic problem and a problem for the regulation of bodies (cf. Tyrer and Sayyid 2012). Its dislocating effects are exacerbated by the wider debunking of ideas about race as phenotypal. This has been manifested in the ambiguous positioning of disciplinary institutions in relation to race: states which might on the one hand institutionalise means of challenging racism, but at the same time employ practices that perpetuate its hold. This is based in part on the problematic genealogies of modern definitions of racism (cf. Hesse 2004), and it is reflected in a range of ways: for example, Meer (2007) notes that in spite of the debunking of phenotypal race, UK race relations legislation continues to privilege biological definitions of race as the basis for determining whether or not racism can be said to have been experienced. As such, Muslims are positioned as non-subjects by dint of the ways in which their presence disrupts racial logic and draws attention to the contingency of the operations of biopower. As a result, there is a more banal way in which the phantasmatic are conjured forth as pure beings in the war on terror. This is a result of the indeterminate status of Muslim within Western racial formations: somehow non-racial, and thus within the terms of race, incompletely subjectified. Yet we see a process throughout the war on terror by which states have precisely sought to hail Muslims as Muslim, conjuring forth from their indeterminate raciality a pure ontic kernel of religiosity. The same processes are played out in Islamophobia, where these acts of making the invisible hypervisible also inscribe the problematic status of Muslims in which Islamophobia is not viewed as racist. In other words, there is also a process afoot by which the discourse on the Muslim question seeks to constitute the very Muslims it problematises.

To understand this we need to acknowledge that it is played out on a wider postcolonial field of racial politics, not religion, but that in turn, a move in this racial politics involves the ascription of the subject position Muslim. This is helpful because it enables us to shift beyond the assumption that Muslims somehow pre-exist Islamophobia but that Islamophobia is merely a way of talking about Muslims (as opposed to bringing them into being). For example, even though the war on terror has frequently been read as problematising Muslims and been associated with increasing attacks and Islamophobia against Muslims, a curious trend has been that rather than becoming less visible, Muslims seem to be more visible than ever. There are different ways of looking at this. One way of reading Muslim agency into the process is by suggesting that in the context of Islamophobia that asserts binary them/us distinctions, Muslims in turn become aware of their identity through their Otherness, and thus mobilise around that identity. This illustrates the extent to which the question of Muslim identity politics (contingent upon agency) and the problem of Islamophobia (contingent upon denying the Other's agency by naming) become intertwined, so that with each invocation of the name Muslim in public discourse, Muslims in fact do become consolidated as a distinct population group through the interplay between, and contests over, such inscriptions. Mandaville (2009: 505) reads a Muslim observation of foreign policy as alienating Muslim males in Britain as indicating the irony that '[r]ather than affirming notions of integration and citizenship, such politicies facilitate instead the imagination of broader global Muslim solidarity'. But there is a broader operation at work, through which whether young or old, alienated or integrated, radical or moderate, secular or religious, one of the effects of the discourse on Muslims has actually been a set of struggles over what Muslim actually means, and that this is not simply a question of reading fictive constructions against a real form, but rather it has been about constructing Muslim identities and constructing the Muslim community as a bounded population group.

In other words, the discourse on Muslims plays out in a wider field of racial politics in which their invisibility, border crossings, and mongrelising properties are problematised, and involves a response concerned with making them visible. Thus, one increasingly sees populations previously described as 'Turkish', 'Pakistani', 'Arab', increasingly spoken of as 'Muslims', 'Muslims in Europe', 'Muslims of Europe', and so forth. One of the forms that this has taken has been the positioning of Muslims as though they have an ontically pure form as religious subjects. I have already noted that this is effected through the misconception of Islamophobia as simply religious. However, it has also been effected through the general addressing of Muslim populations in the context of the war on terror. What is interesting is that the effects of trying to fix the ontological properties of Muslim as being purely religious also have the effect of disarticulating Islamophobia from a wider field of racial politics. In this light it is worth noting that in the wake of 9/11, Muslim civil rights groups became increasingly active in challenging what they saw as negative and inaccurate portrayals of Islam and Muslims. In this, they were contesting the terms on which Muslim was constructed by dominant media narratives and the expert commentators upon which the media called to explain the differences between Islam and democracy, and so on. But within these Muslim responses, we witness attempts to occupy the ascription of Muslim as a simply religious identity through appeals to Islamophobia as a form of essentially religious discrimination. However, even through these moves we can see the ways in which Islamophobia is rearticulated within a wider field of racial politics. For example, Woehrle *et al* (2008: 106) note the case of an interfaith memorial organised by the Council on American-Islamic Relations (CAIR) to 'challenge those who seek to divide America along religious or ethnic lines'. The implication was thus that, once Muslims are constituted and spoken of as a human population in a particular way, this cannot be seen outside the context of a wider play of identities that are at stake in particular racialised social settings. In other words, we return to the problematic of whether Islamophobia is racial or religious by being forced to acknowledge that once Muslims are constituted in a particular way, certain kinds of identities and social relations are instituted; this is a function not simply of Islamophobia as a populist racial politics that emerges in the wake of a disruption to the racial symbolic, but also in relation to state discourse. Another statement issued by the Black Radical Congress on 20 March 2003 is even more revealing of the attempt to rearticulate the problem of Islamophobia on a wider field of racial politics:

> The Black Radical Congress opposes the war against Iraqi people and call on all black, brown, red, yellow, and white people (in short, the majority of the peoples of the world) to oppose this war. The attempts to use religion to divide the *non Islamic* peoples of the U.S.A. from the peoples of the Islamic faith must be opposed. Peoples of all religious faith and all spiritual orientation must call on their innermost powers to oppose the war. (Woehrle *et al* 2008: 106)

Although this appeal was couched in terms of religion and spiritual orientation, the juxtaposition of a grammar of colour and a grammar of race is again important. The implications of this are twofold: first, we have to reject the idea that Islamophobia can be located as essentially religious, and second, we have to reject the idea that it can be localised and exceptionalised within the dominant framing of the war on terror, because it actually reflects a wider politics. More curiously, it also enables us to locate the war on terror both outside of religion, and outside the war on terror itself. Still, this postcolonial condition appears to be embodied in the figure of the Muslim, at once racially unrecognisable and yet somehow excessively different, and yet this problem is radicalised within the war on terror because of the threat of terrorism that knows no boundaries, as the official discourse reminded us. The war on terror did not produce Islamophobia, but it provided a discourse and a series of techniques through which Muslims could be constituted in particular ways, and made visible in spite of their invisibility. The emergence of a Muslim subject position unsettles attempts to manage human populations based on the deployment of race, because by selecting their preferred modes of subjectifica-tion outside racial logics, they place into question the continued capacity of a strategy predicated upon racialisation. In this context the emergence of Islamophobia as a site for condensation of a range of anxieties and tensions around the management of populations in seemingly post-racial and post-political times thus illustrates the importance of placing racisms into proper historical context since it is only by recognising the epistemic and political conditions that frame the emergence of Islamophobia that we can gain sufficient analytical purchase to engage with its specific expressions as anti-Muslim racism and with its broader articulations.

This is the wider context in which Islamophobia emerges, but it is also the context in which the war on terror played out. The fundamental problem in fighting a war against enemies who cannot be easily seen or recognised is precisely that they need to be seen and recognised. Here an interesting aside by Alsultany in a discussion of the abjection of Arab-Americans in a post-9/11 context marked by increasing racism, racial profiling and so forth, introduces an interesting dimension. Discussing the problem of anti-Arab racism, Alsultany notes:

> So long as Arab-Americans remain racially illegible within the US racial terrain, and without the appropriate language to address their exclusion, the inclusion of Arabs into the conception of American citizenship will remain problematic. Racial ambiguity did not rid Arabs of racist experiences, but only allowed them to be masked and go unacknowledged. (Alsultany 2006: 141–42)

This speaks to a paradox of racialisation; that while on the one hand it represents an expression of power and underwrites modes of governing bodies (formally but also informally through violence, harassment ...), on the other hand acceptance into (and of) its logics also provides certain guarantees that some degree of protection might be offered against the exceptionalised forms of racism recognised within liberal regimes. In this there is a further parallel, because within the colour grammar of modern racism, Arabs are figured as an indeterminacy, neither White nor Black within the terms of the colour grammar. For example, Nagel (2001) notes that Arab is improperly inscribed in the formal ethnoscape of Britain. This is interesting, for even when Muslims have what might be termed a raciality with some kind of common-sense connection with Islam, they remain racially indeterminate and defiant of corporeal inscription. Here Alsultany's observation poses an uncomfortable question, a centrally political question: should Arab Americans, then, be more concretely racialised in order to seek some redress within the terms of racial biopolitics itself? This is the double-edged nature of liberal racism where the iron hand and the velvet glove come to fit, for just as racialisation opens up a particular racial politics, it also comes with a solution provided through the terms of racial politics itself.

Here we find perhaps the most crucial feature of the (bio)political problem presented in an age of war against terror on the one hand and Islamophobia on the other. This is to say, the abject status of the Arab American is performed through a double inscription: on the one hand, as Arab s/he is racially illegible; an in-between subject, neither one nor the other, though still racially *something*. As a Muslim, s/he is only legible through religion, and thus not only not legible racially, but more than this, incorporeal – a non-subject within the terms of the racial formation. Here we have site of purification, which is the point at which the Muslim is conjured forth in the context of a particular racial (bio)politics, and this is a purification contingent upon the operation of a racial grammar. In this it is helpful to recall that no identities exist outside of discourse, but they are created and struggled over through the exercise of power (discourse). The implication of this is that it was not only a Muslim identity politics that brought forth a Muslim subject position, but also that Muslim identities have been struggled over and constituted through other discursive acts too.

To illustrate how such purifications operate, let us consider the logic of racial profiling. Racial profiling operates as what could be termed within Barnor Hesse's (1997) definition White (or racialised) governmentality. It is, as Laura Khoury (2009) notes, a technology of power; it works through surveillance, rendering subjects visible, classifying them, and a performative spatial organisation. Muslims are conjured in quite specific ways through the logic of racial profiling. For example, after 9/11 the Federal Bureau of investigation used data mining techniques as part of its profiling repertoire, identifying Arab and Muslim foreign nationals lodged on immigration records: 80,000 were forced to register, 8,000 were interviewed, and 5,000 held in preventive detention although no terrorist convictions resulted (Open Society Institute 2009: 69). Here the object of the search is Muslims, the incorporeal, so the pragmatic informal construction of a kind of pastiche Arab-Muslim-Middle Eastern-non National profile that is constructed (cf. Semati 2010) is really a way of drilling through the corporeal excess, dissolving it, to find the excess and the lack within. In this way race acts as a primary marker of who *might* be a Muslim, but not an ultimate guarantor, so the attempt ultimately has to dissolve away the outer shell, to turn it into a void, in order to trace the excess. The threat is thus at once visible and invisible insofar as the African American male conjured into hypervisibility might carry the invisible excess within; the African American citizen *may* also be a Muslim (Daulatzai 2007). There is, in this, another twin inscription through which post/colonial dis/continuities become enmeshed in the regulation of life. If, in contrast to the colonial corporeal inscription (in Fanonian terms) of Blackness as a monstrous excess without that conceals a void within, Islamophobic discourse constructs Muslims as a void without that conceals an excess within, in racial profiling the excess without (Blackness) can also conceal the excess within (Muslimness); either can be purified into hypervisibility or dissolved into invisibility. In this the corporeal inscription of Blackness and suspicion give way to a discursive act which betrays Islamophobia's genealogies in racism, for the raciality of the Other is always constructed as an impurity, so racism works through a perverse purifying logic. In racial profiling, this purification works in a number of ways; on one level it works through spatial purification, divining matter out of place, in the wrong neighbourhood. But here it also works as the corporeality without is dissolved into the search for the excess within; a doubling of racism's terms in which the (assumed) racially pure form which is also held as impurifying is dissolved in the quest for the excess within, yet this also takes the form of an attempt to conjure forth the Muslim as a religiously pure (incorporeal) form. If the stop is accurate and the suspect *is* a Muslim, the pure form has been discerned; if not, its ontic racial purity (Blackness, its very source of impurity), can be restored. This purifying works through the notions of Blackness as impurity, and of Muslimness as impurifying, bleeding out across racial borders to undo the work of race. Yet at the same time, its racial logics are disavowed, for this is just a search for Muslims.

Such practices purify against risk, and thus the immigration sweeps and arrests that followed 9/11 (cf. Meeropol 2005) targeted the racialised to find the incorporeal. But finding the incorporeal is difficult. A 2008 case which perfectly illustrates this problematic perfectly is that of an American citizen of Portuguese heritage named John Cerquiera. Having been removed from an aeroplane on security grounds – he claimed on the basis of his appearance, although airline staff reportedly noted his suspicious and odd behaviour – he sued the airline concerned for damages, although on subsequent appeal the decision was granted in favour of the airline. Throughout the war on terror there have been numerous similar cases of Arabs and South Asians being removed from aircraft on security grounds, and even of passengers refusing to take-off without the removal of a suspicious Other (cf. Leake and Chapman 2006) – but this case illustrates the problem of racial illegibility, and why it is that wider discourse has thus sought in its own ways to constitute Muslims as a distinct group. Semati (2010: 256) notes, for example, the removal of six Muslim imams from a flight within the United States because people were fearful; when the innocent passengers subsequently noted their intention to litigate, a Minneapolis lawyer noted 'When you drive up the road towards the airport, there's a big road sign that says, "Report suspicious behaviour,"' adding that 'There's no disclaimer that adds, "But beware if you do that, you might get sued"' Racial profiling demonstrates the forms that can be taken by these modes of purification in the attempt to conjure forth the Muslim, and the ways in which Muslims can be constituted, rendered hypervisible or invisible. In this way it is possible to suggest that certain kinds of discursive practices have indeed produced Muslims during the war on terror because of the ways in which they have taken Muslims as their objects. This returns us to the question of the place of religion in the state talk of the Bush administration during the war on terror. It would clearly be absurd to suggest that the war on terror can be exceptionalised and particularised based on a literal reading of Bush's rhetoric and his references to religion. However, one effect of its couching in such terms was the constitution of Muslims as the objects of a particular discourse, and it constituted them in very specific terms: as a religion, and thus as illegible within the terms of a racial grammar that is at once formally rejected by Western states and yet informally invoked as a criterion for proper subjecthood and protection from racism.

Constituting Muslims

Having begun this chapter with a chess metaphor, it is helpful to close it with an alternative elaboration. In 'Checkmate', the ninth episode of the dystopian TV series *The Prisoner*, a game of human chess is played out in which seemingly indistinguishable pieces move as they are bid. One of the pieces makes a move outside the terms of the game and this unusual display of agency sees him taken away by ambulance and pathologised as having succumbed to a dangerous cult of individuality. After the game, an exchange takes place in which number six learns that these seemingly indeterminate pieces can actually be distinguished as white or black by 'their disposition. By the moves they make'. This episode has been read as an interrogation of the terms on which antagonisms could be made during the Cold War (Luft 2009: 309), but it can just as fruitfully be appropriated to illustrate a biopolitical answer to the postcolonial problem of how to manage populations that seem ghostly and phantasmatic. Even if the hold of a colour-based racial grammar has been broken, problematising racial inscription through the difficulty of borderlessnes, mobility, and incorporeality, racial logic can still fall back upon cultural registers for determining the distinctions between subjects. In other words, in the absence of the excess without and its replacement by a void space, the excess that is also a lack within can still be identified as a pure ontic form of life through which boundaries can be reinstated, borders regulated, and inscriptions made. This is a postcolonial problem not localisable to the war on terror, but bounded by a wider set of shifts and the routinisation of exceptional powers. The war on terror did not produce Islamophobia, but it provided a discourse and a series of techniques through which Muslims could be constituted in particular ways, and made visible in spite of their invisibility. The implications of this are straightforward: Islamophobia does not owe its emergence to the war on terror, but the war on terror expresses a wider logic which predates its own emergence.

The war on terror transformed Islamophobia in two key ways. Throughout the war on terror appeals were made to a range of master-signifiers in order to retroactively fix the slippery significations at stake in the discourse. These master signifiers included 'freedom' – deployed, in this context, as a completely empty master-signifier through President Bush's words that freedom itself had been attacked – and 'democracy'. This convergence of the political problem of terrorism and the postcolonial question of how to recognize the racialised in a (supposedly) post-racial world quilts wider discussions about minorities and Muslims, in turn framing the emergence of a discourse that does not simply problematise Islamist terrorism, but minorities, and particularly Muslims, more broadly. This context marked a particular shift in the ways in which the Muslim question came to be rearticulated as it provided a vocabulary around which Islamophobia could make it from the extremes into the mainstream of political discourse and emerge as a populist racial politics, not only through the rise of street gangs such as the English Defence League, but also in the routine demonisation of Muslims as the limit figures for democracy. At a time when freedom and democracy were being reworked through post-political modes of biopolitics and increasing use of exceptional powers, these master signifiers became sites at which particular fantasies could emerge, and these took the form of fantasmatic conjurings of Muslim Others that enabled the continued belief that democracy was unaffected by the war on terror through the continued engagement with the anti-democratic Muslim other on a range of fronts. Second, Islamophobia also provided a discourse that could constitute Muslim subjects and conjure them forth in particular ways, purifying them of race and viewing them as ontically pure religious subjects, thus disarticulating Islamophobia from the field of racial biopolitics that had created it. But although the war on terror intensified Islamophobia, it is only possible to understand how this occurred by removing the war from its exceptionalised, self-referential frame in order to point to the ways in which it is cross cut by a postcolonial question and the emergence of a particular biopolitical horizon, under which residues of prior hegemonic inscriptions of race – superstitions – resurfaced and were rearticulated around the constitution of threatening religious subjects.

7

Questions, questions, questions: reframing Islamophobia

Islamophobia emerges as a provisional solution to the problem of how to name a people that interrupt racial namings. The problem with self-ascription is that it is a fundamental challenge to symbolic authority; it does not only challenge the terms on which society has come historically to be organised (formally and informally), but it also forges new allegiances between groups previously divided by institutionalised racial and ethnic lines, and fractures other prior allegiances. It institutes new subject positions that transform the relationships of groups to each other, to civil society, and to the state. In the case of Muslims, it fundamentally problematises the terms on which previous racial ascriptions occurred. Islamophobia emerges as an expression of post-political racial biopolitics as a response to these challenges. The war on terror draws upon and quilts existing racial signifiers; a range of studies have considered the ways in which the war on terror drew upon orientalist metaphors (cf. Porter 2009; Steuter and Wills 2008), in ways that produced certain kinds of knowledges about the Other. This is illustrated in one of the great controversies of the war on terror, the sexual abuse of prisoners in Abu Ghraib prison. Following an article by the investigative journalist Seymour Hersh, Patai's orientalist text *The Arab Mind* became widely criticised for its influence on pro-war neo-conservative strategists as well as military and intelligence staff on the ground, leading to further media debate about its value (cf. Whitaker 2004). Of particular issue were readings of the book's apparent emphasis on force and essentialist caricatures about Arab sexual taboos (Klein 2010: 113). Such claims have been challenged, and in reprinting a foreword to the book, the Editors of *The Middle East Quarterly* also wrote a Preface repudiating the claim that the work had been widely used and influential (*Middle East Quarterly* 2004). González (2010: 104) suggests that while there is no direct evidence of systematic use of the book, neoconservative planners were aware of it and similar texts, as were staff on the ground in Iraq. In fact, it does not actually matter whether or not the book was used systematically, for one would expect military and political strategists to be drawing upon a range of sources and expertise. The more important point, as Armour (2008: 180) notes, is that the ease with which the images of sexual abuse in Abu Ghraib could be read demonstrates the very hold of orientalist representations of the Other.

But the images of abuse in Abu Ghraib do not simply speak to us of the traces of orientalism, but of its complex rearticulation in contemporary postcolonial Western states. Noting the photograph of Lynndie England that became the iconic image in the Abu Ghraib scandal, Norton (2011: 70) suggests that it presents an 'architecture of abjection', and of the modes through which the Muslim question is worked through intersections of gender, race, class and religion, in which the question of human rights is rearticulated as a means of re-establishing hierarchies and inscribing abjection. As Norton (2011: 70) notes, 'affirmations of the equality of women are diverted into supports for a system that renders Arabs and Muslims abject'. In this the Abu Ghraib images belong in a wider context, one that links the attempts to couch the war on terror in terms of a defence of women's rights and democracy with the attempts of the extreme right to couch its Islamophobia as a defence of women's rights and democracy. The quilting of Islamophobia around the master-signifier democracy creates Muslim abjection; in the appropriation of progressive political metaphors in the service of justifying the exclusion of Muslims, the Muslim is fixed as the Other to the progressive West, and as a form of life that exists at best at the limits of democracy, and at worst outside it. The far right's conjurings of the phantasmatic burka-clad woman as a warning of what will happen to Europe is not a straightforward appeal to human rights, for it renders the burka-clad woman herself just a void, an absence, a symptom of the phantasmatic green menace.

The war on terror has thus had a significant effect upon Islamophobia. While much emphasis has been placed on the circulation of orientalist metaphors during the war on terror (cf. Zine 2006), others have spoken of the emergence of a post-orientalism (cf. Dabashi 2009). The important distinction is not between colonialism or imperialism or post-imperialism, or between orientalism and post-orientalism, because it would be impossible to escape the residual traces of past discourse. Rather, what the discourse of the war on terror achieved was to frame the expression of Islamophobia in ways that emphasised the idea of a threat to democracy itself. As Ash Amin notes:

> Past and new portrayals of threat and contamination [by Muslims] are being given bite by states hastily cobbling together emergency powers permitting intrusive surveillance, arrest without warrant, illegal detention, foreign rendition, supported by hysterical media commentary calling for vigilance regarding veils, rucksacks, Urdu, gatherings in mosques, Islamic organization, the behaviour of Muslim-looking people in public and private. (Amin 2010: 10)

Most importantly, with the phantasmatic Other constructed as haunting democracy itself, this lack in excess is represented by the ways in which Islamophobia also sees a shift in its stereotyping of Muslims, from representing them as all being fundamentalists (a cultural excess) to all being extremists (a political excess). For example, in March 2011 the *Guardian* (2011) newspaper printed a letter of resignation sent by journalist (Richard Peppiatt) to his former employer, a national tabloid newspaper. In his letter Peppiatt accused the newspaper of propagandising for a far-right street movement, and claimed that his journalistic role had involved 'stirring up a bit of light-hearted Islamaphobia [sic]' by inventing or exaggerating stories about Muslim excess. Such stories, he claimed, included assertions that Muslim-only toilets were being provided at taxpayer expense, and in the course of obtaining them he claimed to have used a range of methods from taking to the streets disguised in a burka to contacting the Islamist extremist Anjem Choudary for comment, knowing the sort of Muslim comment they would then receive. Peppiatt's letter climaxed with the assertion that the stories he was writing about Muslims had the power to cause racial violence. The newspaper immediately issued a statement denying Peppiatt's allegations.

While Islamophobia emerges prior to the war on terror, its modes of expression do shift during the war on terror. These shifts also reflect a wider framing for Islamophobia as a postcolonial problem. But if we are to understand Islamophobia we have to recognise that it might have been heightened and quilted in particular ways during the war on terror, but its roots actually lie in certain ontological investments in race, as a result of which Muslims will always appear as the unsettling presence that disrupts the attempt to arrive at a stable play of differences. This is a postcolonial problem that cannot be localised solely to the war on terror. Despite this, there is a tendency to privilege certain historical moments and continuities within accounts of contemporary Islamophobia. This is perhaps best illustrated by the notion of the Muslim question, which in recent years has emerged as an object of particular concern as Muslims have been increasingly securitised and their allegiances scrutinised. The Muslim question forces open wider questions concerning the tendency to historicise Islamophobia within the war on terror, and in relation to its relationship to other forms of racism.

Although the Muslim question is not clearly defined, among others, Meer and Modood (2009), Norton (2011), Parekh (2008), Ramadan (2012) have given the question as it plays out in Europe a scholarly treatment, while Shani (2010) has covered it in an Indian context. The University of Birmingham have organised a 2012 workshop on the Muslim question and multiculturalism, and it has been the subject of numerous op-ed pieces (cf. Ahmed 2011; Nawaz 2011). Somehow the Muslim question has come to be associated both with the political challenges posed by Muslim minorities in postcolonial contexts, and with Islamophobia. The Muslim question seems to evoke so much while conveying little of any specificity. Its circulation and exchange, its displacements and logic of repetition appear to be the wages of a neoliberal problematisation of difference, and of politics itself, yet they also imply that this is a question without an answer, and possibly one without even a specific object of inquiry. It seems that in order to think through the Muslim question it is necessary to tease out its entanglement in racism and Islamophobia on the one hand, and its imbrication in changing forms of political mobilisation by Muslims on the other. But this still leaves open this question without answers.

Framing the Muslim Question

One way of fixing the Muslim question might be to locate it as a series of contemporary questions concerning security, integration and integrability, that is, to locate the question internally to contemporary state practices since 9/11. This seems superficially helpful, for the questioning of the nature of Muslim identities and their place in Western states has intensified since 9/11 as Muslims have been securitised, as De Genova notes:

> This operationalisation of suspicion with regard to Muslim identities has effectively reduced any and all Muslim persons into potential targets for the activation of a question, to be examined and cross-examined, inspected and interrogated, in an unrelenting quest to discern the fatal difference between the 'good' ones and 'bad' ones. In this respect, all Muslim particularities came to be pressed into the service of reiterating a generic conundrum concerning the identification and detection of Muslim 'enemies' this is what I have designated here to be *the Muslim Question*. Thus, the United States' unabashed domestic profiling and selective persecution of Muslims, particularly non-citizen men, as alleged terror 'suspects' was a decisive and defining feature of the new racial project of antiterrorism and the dire need to produce 'culprits' in its amorphous and borderless war. Indeed, 'detentions' – which is to say, more precisely, *indefinite* imprisonment without formal charges or any semblance of due process of law – have truly been the hallmark of the Homeland Security State, with male Arab and Muslim non-citizens overwhelmingly figured as its special targets. (De Genova 2010: 627)

This seems helpful in relating wider discussions about Muslims to specific state practices in the context of the war on terror. However, while state practices might bring into play a range of political questions, the state can neither establish nor exhaust all the possibilities for politics. It is also helpful to situate the Muslim question in a wider context, not with the intention of tracing out straightforward continuities, but rather with the aim of identifying precursors for its contemporary expression.

One way of doing this might be to trace the emergence of the Muslim question in wider histories of racism. In their discussion of 'Refutations of racism in the "Muslim question"' Meer and Modood (2009) choose not to elaborate a definition of what is meant by the Muslim question, thus implicitly recognising that the political work of the question is not contingent on its literal reading, but rather indicating the metaphorical use of the question. Meer and Modood implicitly frame their discussion in relation to racism against Muslims. In light of public questions over the loyalties of Muslims, the usefulness of this is clear. However, what Meer and Modood are arguably considering is not the denial of racism in the Muslim question, but the denial of racism in discussions about Islamophobia. This is only sustainable if one is able to demonstrate that the Muslim question is reducible to its particular articulation with Islamophobia or liberal citizenship more broadly at a moment in time. It is also worth noting that Meer and Modood (2009: 339) offer a more limited reading of racism which privileges hostility, but which does not elaborate on the possibility that racism might be understood in a less privatised sense in relation to its functions in the regulation of bodies.

Meer and Modood also set the Muslim question against older articulations of the Jewish question, noting (2009: 336) that representations of Jews have become increasingly normalised in Europe in contrast to representations of Muslims. This is not unproblematic. First, it implicitly reads the Muslim question in terms of an Islamophobia that is itself read through anti-Semitism. Second, it is important to note the obvious question of whether this involves a reading of anti-Semitism that reduces all anti-Semitism to a particular mode of nineteenth-century expression, in other words whether representations of Jews have normalised or whether anti-Semitism has simply been rearticulated in different ways. In fairness, Meer and Modood do acknowledge (2009: 336) that it would be problematic to assume that anti-Semitism has been banished from Europe. But their reading implicitly dehistoricises both anti-Semitism and Islamophobia by adopting a reading of anti-Semitism as the basis for a comparative reading of Islamophobia (2009: 337).

This move reflects a wider tendency to situate Islamophobia in relation to anti-Semitism. For example, Norton's (2011) discussion of the Muslim question also opens by exploring the parallel between that and the Jewish question. More widely, a superficial reading of the similarities between anti-Semitism and Islamophobia has led some even to draw comparisons between the holocaust and contemporary Islamophobia (Sardar 2005), while others have even described Muslims as the 'new Jews' (Hellyer 2009: 112; Ma'oz 2010: 24). For example, British Labour Member of Parliament Shahid Malik has made such comparisons (Doughty 2008), while Yasmin Alibhai Brown wrote in *The Independent*:

Since the organised massacres of Muslim males in Bosnia, we 16 million European Muslims live with a menacing whirr at the back of the head, ghostly fears that the fires next time will burn with our bodies. We are today's despised 'other', blamed for all the ills of the world which is still largely controlled by Christians. We have to atone ceaselessly for the Taliban and al-Qa'ida and home-grown men of violence. We are expected – just as Jews were in the thirties – to bend our heads and take the slurs, looks of hatred, to accept the burden of shame. By remembering the Holocaust with past victims, we remind ourselves of what could happen in the future [...] When the boots kick down the doors and they come for us Muslims or our children, perhaps good Jews will not speak up and we will rue the day we callously refused to pray for their lost generations. (Alibhai-Brown 2006)

Such arguments have been problematised on a number of grounds, including that aside from the family resemblances between structurally embedded racisms, it is difficult not to take into account the very differing political contexts; for example, Cesarani (2008) has suggested that this contextual difference is marked in the case of Islamophobia by the emergence of Islamist terrorism. In a further complication, Tibi (2008: 212) notes that Muslim descriptions of themselves as the 'new Jews' reveals hypocrisy in the face of Muslim silences over (and sometimes acceptance of) Islamist anti-Semitism. Indeed, Alibhai-Brown's (2006) comparison between Islamophobia and anti-Semitism was bound up with criticism of a refusal by the Muslim Council of Britain to participate in a Holocaust Remembrance Day service.

A further difficulty emerges from this dehistoricisation: if the Muslim question is the new Jewish question, and Muslims are the new Jews, then whatever happened to the old Jews? Clearly they did not just vanish, and nor did they become Muslims. This notion of Muslims as the new Jews introduces a rupture into our understanding of Jewish identities that problematises the basic premise that today's Islamophobia is analogous to yesterday's anti-Semitism. Of course, the old Jew does not disappear in such accounts, but continues to haunt them. At stake in the description of Muslims as the new Jews is a double violence through which the old Jews (whoever they are) are written out as subjects, instead inscribed only as the objects of anti-Semitism. In other words, they are not narrated through Jewish traditions of remembrance and commemoration of the humanity of victims of pogroms and the shoah, but rather they are narrated only through a vocabulary of gentile anti-Semitism. Meanwhile, new Jews are also written out as subjects through the inscription of new Jews as Muslims. In turn, we lose sight of Jewish humanity during the Holocaust, while the agency and specificity of the Muslim question is also erased. If Muslims are the new Jews, then are we also to assume that there were no Muslims prior to the Holocaust?

Reframing the Muslim Question

If it is problematic to frame the Muslim question through its dehistoricisation, Norton's (2011) reading of the question in relation to anti-Semitism opens an alternative possibility through her recourse to Marx on the Jewish question. But might there be a more apposite Marxian detour that can shed light on the emergence of this question? In an essay printed in the *New York Tribune* (15 April 1854) on the English declaration of war with Russia, Marx noted the challenges presented by the articulation of Islam with politics, writing that '[t]he Koran and the Mussulman legislation emanating from it reduce the geography and ethnography of the various people to the simple and convenient distinction of two nations and of two countries; those of the Faithful and of the Infidels. The Infidel is *"harby,"* i.e., the enemy. Islamism proscribes the nation of the Infidels, constituting a state of permanent hostility between the Mussulman and the unbeliever' (Marx 1994: 316). This intervention was part of a considerable body of writing devoted by Marx to the Eastern question, and it is helpful in establishing another moment in the genealogy of the Muslim question. Indeed, to Al-Azmeh (2003), the Muslim question is analogous to the earlier Eastern question.

If the Muslim question appears to have some relationship to the Eastern question, the roots of the Eastern question itself are not entirely straightforward. One could, for example, trace the origin of the Eastern question to the Kuchuk Kainarji Treaty of 1774, which marked the end of Russo-Turkish war and began the long process of Ottoman disintegration (cf. Karcic 2002: 635). But the limits of Ottoman power were themselves highlighted in earlier encounters which played key roles in constituting Europe: one could, for instance, point to the 1571 Battle of Lepanto, when the defeat of Ottoman forces marked the high tide of Islamic naval capacity for European incursion. Neumann and Welsh (1991: 340) note that the Battle of Vienna was decisive in shifting the relationship between Europe and the Ottoman Empire, a shift formalised in the 1699 Treaty of Karlowitz. This was not simply a change in the balance of power, but one that went hand in hand with wider transformations, also marking the start of a European age of imperial conquest. This was the time at which the identity of Europe was being fixed, both in relation to its Others, and internally; not only did the Battle of Vienna enable the redrawing of political maps within Europe to consolidate Habsburg power, but it also occurred in a period marked by the consolidation of modern state forms following the 1648 Treaty of Westphalia. Thus, while Neumann and Welsh note the hardening of relations between Europe and 'the Turk' following the Battle of Vienna, they also note that the increasing appropriation of 'barbarian' as a description for the Ottoman enemy differed from religious labels such as 'infidel' and thus reflected the growth of an increasingly secular Westphalean state system (Neumann and Welsh 1991: 340). Thus, to Buzan (1995: 390), the main seventeenth-century landmarks in the emergence of Western domination included 'the consolidation of European control over Asian shipping trade, the steady colonisation of the Americas, the occupation of Siberia by the Russians; and, in the Treaty of Westphalia, the triumph of the sovereign territorial state as the basic form of European political organisation'.

To read the Muslim question through its relationship to the Eastern question opens possibilities for situating it within the context of the constitution of European modernity itself, and attempts to regulate the relationship between Europe and its others. Even if one reads the Eastern question in relation to the nineteenth-century erosion of Ottoman power and the disintegration of the Ottoman Empire, this simultaneously brings into play both questions about colonial geopolitics and the implications of these for pan-Islamic politics. To read the Muslim question through the Eastern question is not therefore to trace a moment of origin or a linear history, but rather to situate the articulation of both of these questions within the contexts of particular exercises of power; as Vakil (2011) notes, it is not to read a genealogy backwards, but contrapuntally through relations of government and moments of institution and rearticulation.

In this light it is also worth noting that the Muslim question has been given to various rearticulations in different contexts. Here Elena Campbell offers an interesting reading of its expression in imperial Russia, noting that it emerged as one of a series of 'alien questions' (inorodcheskie voprosy) rehearsed in Russian politics of the late nineteenth century, along with the Jewish question, the Ukrainian question, and the Baltic question (Campbell 2007: 320). Campbell's reading is interesting insofar as it overcomes the problematic of reducing discussions about Muslims simply to religion, but instead traces the ways in which the Muslim question came to be read through a range of questions such as the compatibility of Muslim culture with the Russian state and indeed with Europe (Campbell 2007: 326). In this reading, the Muslim question is not reducible to the state, and nor can it be dehistoricised to a particular mode of politics at a particular point in history. Rather, Campbell's work demonstrates the ways in which specific articulations of the Muslim question in nineteenth-century Russia were shaped by particular hegemonic relations in a given context, and how they drew upon particular cultural resources rooted in Russian traditions which gave the Muslim question a particular inflection in regulating the relationship between Muslims and Russia and, indeed, between Muslims and Europe in differing ways as the question played out. Campbell's reading is therefore helpful not simply in drawing attention to the problems of reducing the Muslim question to a particular form of politics, but rather in opening it out and historicising its varying articulations and dis/continuities.

From Muslim Question to Muslim Policy

But there is more to the Muslim question than simply the Eastern question. Possibly the earliest reference to the Muslim question can be found in an article in 1900 by Gabriel Hanotaux, who served as France's Minister of Foreign Affairs between 1894–1895 and between 1896–1898. Here a minor difference over the citation of Hanotaux's work might be revealing: to Wilfred Cantwell Smith it was 'Face à face de l'Islam et la question Musulmane' (Cantwell Smith 1981: 304n), to Nader (2003: 132) it was 'Face à face avec l'Islam et le problème Musulmane', and to the librarian at the Bibliothèque nationale de France who assisted me in my search for the piece, it was simply 'L'Islam'. Published in *Le Journal* in two parts on 2 March 1900 and 28 March 1900, Hanotaux's piece belonged in the context of concerns about the maintenance of colonial power which were not simply couched in terms of religion, but race, positing Aryan and Semitic religious traditions and mindsets in opposition to each other (Haj 2009: 91), and led to a series of published responses by Muhammad 'Abduh (Haj 2009: 91). Hanotaux's writings – which also included, for instance, a later piece on the 'yellow peril' in *Le Journal* – belong in the context of attempts to deal with pressing political concerns facing colonial rulers.

While it would be problematic to establish a linear relationship between these early expressions of the Muslim question and its contemporary articulation, it is striking that the question finds its precursors in the politics of colonial knowledge production and administration. Naomi Davidson (2012) has explored the ways in which understandings of the name Muslim in twentieth-century France were structured by colonial practices and concerns about both the place of Islam and Muslims globally and within the metropole, noting that these concerns were played out in attempts to create a Muslim policy (*politique Musulmane*) (Davidson 2012: 16). Hanotaux's piece therefore belongs in the context of a series of attempts to deal with what were felt to be pressing political concerns facing colonial France at the turn of the century. Such attempts were not simply ways of responding to particular political problems, but rather, they involved government. Here, the Muslim question is articulated through *la politique Musulmane*. In this context, Hanotaux's piece was one of a number written in the same period which called for systematic investigation and production of knowledge on Islam and Muslims in order to produce a handbook – a sociology of the Muslim world (Laurens 2004: 219). This helps reframe *la question Musulmane* in the context of *la politique Musulmane*, a response not only to moves made by Muslims which posed challenges for colonial powers (e.g. the emergence of pan-Islamism), but also colonial anxieties around the balance of power and influence. To Henry Laurens (2004: 57), *la politique Musulmane* was not a policy in favour of Muslims, but rather an attempt to account for Muslims externally and within the metropole, and took the form of an assemblage of institutionalised sites of knowledge production including ministries, pressure groups, those representing trade interests, and academics, and it emerged simultaneously into 'a political slogan, an institutional reality and a subject of debate' (Laurens 2004: 59) which provided a means of dealing with Muslims. A bibliographic note on Arthur Pellegrin's *L'Islam Dans Le Monde* in *Races et Racisme* (No. 6, December 1937, p. 18) is here interesting, noting that '[t]he colonial expansion of Europe placed most Muslims in the world under the aegis of England, France, Holland, Italy, etc. Each country has applied a specific policy... Of this, the term "Muslim policy" was used to describe the ensemble of rules, methods and means, empirical or rigorously derived, which governed relations between Europeans and Muslims, for a century and more of colonization'. The politics of knowledge production was central to this enterprise, as can be witnessed not only in the preoccupation with knowledge about Muslims, but also through its embodiment in the figure of the colonial scholar-administrators who delivered public lectures and produced books and articles discussing such questions.

Muslim policy emerged as a means of producing knowledge about Muslims in order to regulate their relationship vis-à-vis the West and was closely associated with a particular articulation of the Muslim question. At the end of the nineteenth century and in the first years of the twentieth century a number of preoccupations and concerns were expressed by French colonial administrators, ranging from such questions as the extent of the spread of Islam among 'les noirs' to the extent to which Islam presented a threat. One feature of these questions was that they concerned the problem of how to deal with Muslim agency. Another feature of them was that they reflected anxieties about the limits of the colonial project and of the vocabulary by which colonial relations were narrated and managed.

Muslim policy and the Muslim question were not restricted to French colonial policy, but demonstrate a wider colonial investment and took different articulations in different contexts. For example, in a 1910 lecture delivered for the French Colonial Union, the German orientalist Carl Heinrich Becker advocated adoption of French Muslim policy by the German government, further claiming that '[t]his problem, like Islam, is by its nature an international problem ... Agreement on a uniform attitude vis-à-vis Islam is in the interests of all governments. The fear that one power could ally itself with Islam to thwart the designs of another seems baseless for if the solidarity of Islam is a ghost, the solidarity of the white race is a reality' (Becker 1910: 23). If reference to the spectrality of Muslim identities is worthy of note, its contrast against the supposed materiality and permanence of race place this articulation of the Muslim question (and Muslim policy) within particular epistemic and political circumstances. In fact, Becker's position on the phantom-like nature of a transnational Muslim identity only makes sense in a context in which such identifications were possible. The period was marked by increasing resistance to colonial rule, but the nature of these projects was not entirely clear; from the 1890s onwards, decolonial and anticolonial politics were increasingly articulated with nascent nationalisms in many colonial contexts, but colonial administrators were faced on the one hand by the possibility of nationalist challenges and on the other hand by the prospect of a Muslim politics that appeared to cut across ethnic and racial distinctions, and even geopolitics.

For example, Louis Vignon, a professor at the École Coloniale, argued in 1919 against the adoption of a uniform Muslim policy for Tunisia, Morocco, and Algeria, arguing that '[y]es, these three countries are populated by Muslims, but the ethnic composition of the population is not the same, their faith is different, as are their practices, religious and political authorities' (Vignon 1919: 223) [author's translation]. In west Africa, questions arose over the ways in which Islam articulated with African cultures to produce a syncretic, impure 'black Islam'.

The appeal of Islam to large numbers of geographically dispersed peoples of diverse ethnic, cultural and linguistic backgrounds posed questions that were not simply abstract theoretical concerns about the relationship between Islam and race (or ethnicity), but distinctly practical questions that emerged from its interruption of the politics of colonial knowledge production. For example, Lebovics (1992: 113) notes that Becker's conservative approach to the Muslim question, which fetishised primordial ethnic differences steered as clear of the promotion of Frenchness in the interests of avoiding creating resentment among the colonised as it did of Muslimness, was to set the scene for French colonial policy during the interwar years. Again, this only makes sense within the context of debates over the Muslim question that were framed by the possibility of Muslim agency, the specific articulations of Muslim identities (and of Islam with politics) possible within that context, and specific articulations of Muslim policy as a relationship of government.

The Muslim Question and Islamophobia

The origins of the Muslim question lie in concerns over the management of Muslim populations and attempts to regulate the relationship between the idea of Europe and the idea of Muslims. In this sense, to speak of its contemporary expression as rearticulations of the Jewish question elides the colonial precursors of modern invocations of the question. But if the earliest expressions of the Muslim question emerged in the context of debates about Muslim policy, so too did Islamophobia. The earliest print references to Islamophobia can possibly be dated to 1910, and indicate a colonial context. Commenting in the May issue of *Revue du Monde Musulman* that '[w]hatever is said by those for whom Islamophobia is a principle of native administration', Maurice Delafosse (1910: 53) suggested that 'France has nothing more to fear from Muslims in West Africa than non-Muslims'. This refutation of presuppositions about the Muslim threat places Islamophobia in the context of contests over colonial Muslim policy.

But if Islamophobia belongs in the context of contests over colonial knowledge about Muslims and growing anticolonial resistance, it also depoliticises the latter, reading it as an anti-foreign impulse. In this there is a parallel with the earlier term xenophobia. Conventional accounts of the origins of xenophobia indicate that it came into print use with the publication of Anatole France's *M. Bergeret à Paris* in 1901 (Berezin 2006, Villard 1984), but it was already in print use a year earlier in the context of the Boxer rebellion. Its use was also bound up with attempts to privatise and pathologise anti-colonial resistance as aberrant, lacking proper politics and instead being based simply on dislike of foreigners, a usage that simultaneously elided the matter of racism against colonial subjects. For example, in 1925 M. Cognacq, the Lieutenant-Governor of Cochinchina, related the growth of xenophobia in south-east Asia to a wave, in China, of 'deadly contagion that threatens to overwhelm the incessant effort of Western civilization' (*République Française* 1926: 7). Yet there is also a tension in this use, which cast colonisers as foreigners, rather than 'natural' rulers. It reflected growing awareness of increasing anti-colonial resistance overseas.

If xenophobia both offered means of depoliticising anti-colonial resistance, the emergence of the term Islamophobia in the context of specific contests over Muslim policy lent it a sharper focus on the politics of colonial knowledge production, thereby opening a de/colonial tension within its use evident in Alain Quellien's (1910) *La Politique Musulmane dans l'Afrique Occidentale Française*:

Islamophobia. –
There has always been, and remains, a prejudice against Islam prevalent among people of Western and Christian civilization. For some, the Muslim is the natural and irreconcilable enemy of the Christian and the European, Islam is the negation of civilization and barbarism, cruelty and bad faith are all that one can expect of most Mohammedans. For Dr Oskar Lenz 'in the current circumstances, the Christian powers represent civilization and progress, Islam is, however, identical to stagnation and barbarism.' It cannot result in intolerance, greed, murder, theft and systematic killings. The same ideas are also contained in a letter from Count de Saint-Vallier, Ambassador to Berlin, to the Minister of Foreign Affairs following a conversation with the famous Austrian traveler: 'Besides the very interesting stories of Mr Lenz ... our conversation was focused on the business of Tunisia and the massacre of the mission of Colonel

Flatters. Messrs Lens and Nachtigal reported of their stay in central Africa, a profound contempt for the races that inhabit it, especially for the many branches of the Arab race that they see as absolutely resistant to all civilization; dishonesty, barbarism, savage and cruel instincts of the African muslims …' […] It seems that this warning about Islam might be rather exaggerated, the Muslim is not the born enemy of the European, though he can become one due to local circumstances and particularly when he resists conquest. (Quellien 1910: 133–4)

Quellien's use also indicates a colonial context, and in this case his reference to the Flatters case also invokes the contextual effects of a complicated twist by which the Dreyfus affair impacted on representations of Touareg 'barbarism' (Brower 2009: 243). It also revealed the potential for a political reading of anti-colonial resistance by Muslims that might otherwise be rendered through Islamophobic stereotyping as innate to Islam and Muslim cultures. However, Quellien's use indicates a narrow focus on Islamophobia *qua* fear, so to dispute Islamophobia in this sense simply means to dispute the notion that Western colonial powers need to fear Muslims as implacable enemies (López 2011: 563). While this usage again situates Islamophobia in the context of the Muslim question, the potential of the term to open a more radical critique of colonial power was reflected by later works which, as Vakil (2011) notes, saw it being used by Muslims in the early post-World War I years. As Vakil notes, this usage signalled Muslim agency and the expression of a critique of colonial knowledge production through Islamicate registers. Discussing two works by Dinet and Ibrahim – *L'Orient vu de l'Occident* (1925) and *Le pèlerinage à la maison sacrée d'Allah* (1930) – López (2011: 561) notes that the latter established an early classification of Islamophobia which distinguished between clerical and pseudo-scientific forms. To López, the latter could be read as a reference to certain forms of orientalism.

López draws upon these early engagements with Islamophobia to suggest that Islamophobia is not necessarily racism, concluding that 'approaches to the term and the phenomenon in the early twentieth century leave no doubt that the term "Islamophobia" should be applied only to denote a hostile attitude towards Islam and Muslims based on the image of Islam as the enemy and as a vital, irrefutable and absolute threat to "our" well-being and even to "our" existence, irrespective of how Muslims are identified, whether on the basis of religious or ethnic criteria' (López 2011: 570). However, this ignores a crucial aspect of the debates over *la Politique Musulmane* that framed the emergence of these debates about Islamophobia. References to Muslim hostility in such accounts cannot be viewed outside the context of the colonial milieu through which they were expressed, since antipathy to the West was a signifier for broader anti-colonial resistance. In this sense, to reject the idea of an innate Muslim hostility to the West is not in itself unproblematic, but also reflects wider exercises of power, as can be seen when Delafosse argued of Muslims that:

> All see us as teachers sometimes irritating, sometimes useful, generally benevolent, and we endure with more or less ease according to the diversity of their characters or their interests. Those among them who most ardently wish to see us leave the country ... desire this, not because we are not of their faith, but simply because we are not of their race or their mentality or their soil, because we are foreign. (Delafosse 1910: 53)

This challenged the construction of Muslims as innately threatening only insofar as it depoliticised their resistance to colonial domination and constructed them as colonised subjects and elided their agency. The term Islamophobia did not simply emerge as a result of straightforward disputes over whether or not Muslims presented a fundamental threat to Westerners, but rather, in response to concerns about the colonial administration of populations that were increasingly given to anti-colonial sentiment and resistance. The challenges this posed did not simply concern attempts to narrate and depoliticise the interruption to hegemonic ideas of the inevitability of colonial mastery that was presented by such challenges, but they also brought into question colonial knowledges in other ways. The second half of the nineteenth century had seen France positioned through its colonial policy as if it were a major Muslim power by dint of the large numbers of Muslims subjected to French rule (Robinson 1999). Many of these lived beyond the traditional heartlands of Islam, for example in West Africa. This presented a number of tensions including the ability of a transnational Muslim identification to override other ethnic and racial ascriptions.

The Tension of Islamophobia

The attempt to read the Muslim question through the Jewish question involves an attempt to read a straightforward historical continuity between early- and mid- twentieth-century anti-Semitisms and contemporary Islamophobia. This has the effect of distancing contemporary anti-Semitism from Islamophobia, but it also has the effect of eliding the colonial precursors of contemporary Islamophobia that can be read through dis/continuities rather than straightforward historical analogy which may be superficially appealing. But such strategies also illustrate another issue at stake in the tension that is often held to exist between Islamophobia and the idea of racism itself insofar as they establish anti-Semitism as the template for contemporary racism.

This is not, in fact, novel to the discussions of the Muslim question. For example, Hesse (2004: 144) has noted that a genealogy of the idea of racism itself points to the emphasis on the 'discredited fascist excesses of nationalism' in its conception. In fact, the term Islamophobia appears to have been in print use for longer than the term racism, which is often said to have emerged following the publication (in English) of Magnus Hirschfeld's *Racism* in 1938. But the term racism was in fairly widespread use prior to Hirschfeld, though almost exclusively in relation to fascism. Taguieff (1984: 88) notes that the 1932 edition of *Larousse du XXe siècle* had entries for racism and racist, the former being defined in terms of the doctrine held by racists, and the latter as the name given to German national socialists.

One of the difficulties we face in reading Islamophobia as a derivative concept is that such readings tend to privilege a particular moment of anti-Semitism as foundational, in turn eliding earlier or later forms of anti-Semitism and also eliding other expressions of racism. In doing so they also play upon an exceptionalised reading of racism that works against recognition of the daily grind of racialised governmentality and its colonial precursors (Hesse 2004). Nevertheless, the argument pervades. Zizek, for example, has argued that anti-Semitism provides a template for racism itself. In this I am not interested in his conceptualisation as such, but rather in what is at stake in his reading of anti-Semitism as a template for contemporary racisms:

In classical racism, anti-Semitism functions as an exception: in Nazi discourse, for example, the attitude towards Jews (who are the unheimlich double of the Germans themselves and, as such, have to be annihilated) differs radically from the attitude towards other 'inferior' nations, in whose case the aim is not their annihilation but only their subordination – they have to assume their 'proper place' in the hierarchy of nations. Jews are the disturbing element that incites other inferior nations to insubordination, so that it is only through the annihilation of Jews that other nations will accept their subordinate place. Here also, however, a specific inversion is taking place today: we are dealing with universalised anti-Semitism – that is, every ethnic 'otherness' is conceived of as an unheimliches double that threatens our enjoyment; in short, 'normal', non-exceptional, non-anti-Semitic racism is no longer possible. The universalisation of the Holocaust metaphor (apropos of every ethnic cleansing it is asserted that it is comparable to the Nazi Holocaust), excessive as it may appear, is therefore founded in the inherent logic of the thing itself, in the universalisation of anti-Semitism. (Zizek 2005: 79).

One could substitute anti-Semitism with Islamophobia in this account, and replace Jew with Muslim, and also replace the historical references with a contemporary framing and it might be possible to read from this a condition of banalised contemporary anti-Muslim racism. Indeed, Zizek has elsewhere noted that 'today it is the Muslims, not the Jews, who are perceived as a threat and an obstacle to globalization' (Zizek 2006: 257). This confronts us with the problem of historicity: anti-Semitism as a modern form, and Islamophobia as a postmodern emergence. A superficial means of reconciling this difficulty might be to posit Islamophobia as a dislocated modern anti-Semitism; this, however, still leaves us with the difficulty that by establishing anti-Semitism as the template for another form, we either risk losing specificity of anti-Semitism or that of Islamophobia (or both), and reducing the analytical purchase of both concepts.

When modernity has presented us with so many variations on a centrally racist theme – genocide in the Americas, millions killed in the Bengal famine thanks in part to colonial policy, extinction of the Tasmanian Aborigines ... – we can also ask why Zizek selects anti-Semitism as the defining form of racism. Ignoring the underlying conceptual points, something that really differentiates anti-Semitism to Zizek is the representation of Jewish people as 'the disturbing element that incites other inferior nations to insubordination' (Zizek 2006: 257). More importantly, anti-Semitism emerges within Europe in contrast to other racist forms; it takes the neighbour as the object. In this there is an obvious further parallel with contemporary Islamophobia, which emerges through the possibility of proximity, but also through the role of fantasy in structuring all racisms. In both of these we can find a parallel between anti-Semitism and Islamophobia. It seems fair to suggest that the extent of Islamophobia today and the status of Muslims is rather different to the conditions of the Holocaust, even if we take into account increasing Islamophobia and extreme cases such as ethnic cleansing in Bosnia. Even if we ignore this difficulty, by noting that the extent of racisms is not the arbiter of a similar form, can we conflate the two modalities of racism? In other words, does Islamophobia follow the template of a generalised anti-Semitism?

An obvious parallel lies in the ways in which both anti-Semitism and Islamophobia are expressed through the metaphor of a haunting presence in Europe. Ghostliness is a helpful metaphor for thinking through the constitution of Muslim subjects (Tyrer and Sayyid 2012). The phantasmatic excess of the other figures in wider discussions about Muslim identities (Daulatzai 2007: 135), whether in relation to the fantasy projections of Islamic conspiracy and Islamisation (Geisser 2003: 82; Rivera 2005: 33–34), or the spectral, problematic visibilities through which these are imagined. To be ghostly is also to be orientalised; Mirzoeff (2002: 243) notes that the ghostly are constructed in opposition to Western reason, and that the problematic figure of the ghost was a staple of colonial discourse on the illicit spirituality and nebulous threat posed by others. To Mirzoeff:

The Jewish ghost is the vantage point of this hauntology, not because Jewishness is claimed as a new paradigm, but precisely because of its ambivalences and ambiguities. Jewishness, like the ghost, is an identity that is not identical to itself. How is Jewishness even to be defined: as a religion – but what of secular Jews? As an ethnicity – but isn't that the Nazi game? As a nation – but what of anti-Zionist Jews? [...] the Jew is literally a ghost, something that resembles the human even as it is not human, rather like the cyborg of our own time. Like the Terminator, the ghost says: 'I'll be back'. (Mirzoeff 2002: 244)

To Mirzoeff, this hauntology establishes the ghost as in a liminal space between the visible and the invisible. But visibility is the work of biopower; even in the panopticon 'the prisoner could neither be perfectly visible nor be constantly aware of disciplinary surveillance. Consequently, they were not disciplined, but simply punished: they became ghosts' (Mirzoeff 2002: 241). The establishment of ghosts is not simply a result of the lacuna at the heart of governmentality, but rather it emerges from the prior work through which subjects are themselves brought forth into the world. The ghost is the remainder left over in the interval between *zoe* and *bios*, between pure life and life that has been made the object of politics. In this sense, in spite of the differences between Islamophobia and anti-Semitism there is a parallel between Jewish and Muslim minorities, both of whom occupy an indeterminate position in relation to raciality. In the case of Muslims, this problem is exacerbated since anti-Semitism is more widely recognised as a form of racism than is Islamophobia, based on the recognition of Jews as racial. In contrast, Muslims are simultaneously fixed as improperly racial (Tyrer 2010), as religious, and yet as improperly religious. This places Muslims in a peculiar and indeterminate position; while their construction as religious positions them as inadequately racial, in wider terms their putative religiosity is frequently constructed as an aberration from what religion should properly mean. For example, the Swiss ban on minarets was based on the logic that minarets were not a religious expression, but a political one. Muslims are ghostly, not because they are invisible, but rather because they are indeterminate beings whose very modes of being appear through the cracks between pure life and politically qualified life.

One of the implications of this is that if Muslim identity politics interrupt biopolitical racial categories, they also interrupt other modes of constituting subjects through classifying practices. Notably, Muslim identities interrupt Western modes of constructing a clear distinction between the secular and the religious (cf. Sayyid 1997). In doing so, they do not only interrupt racial, but also religious classifications. The problematic visibilities of Muslims emerge because Muslim identities cannot be classified as purely racial or purely religious within the terms of the Eurocentric grammar on which such categories are based, and the subsequent attempts to discipline Muslims can be read on one level as a series of attempts to reinstate the hold of such categories of race (and religion). Muslims therefore seem somehow incorporeal and ghostly, slipping through the cracks between categorisations of political forms of life. If modern racism constitutes the racialised as being marked by a libidinal lack (Marriott 2005: 160) so that in Fanonian terms the Other is an absence within and an exaggerated form without, Islamophobia reverses this, constituting Muslims as possessing a lack without (incorporeality) and an excess within (Islam). Muslims are not constituted as excesses (bodies) without souls, but rather as excesses (souls) without bodies. Excess figures in contemporary Islamophobia in various ways: excessive difference, excessive politicality, and excessive/deviant religiosity, and the practices for regulating life which emerge as a consequence of these centrally concern the attempt to tame this excess. As such Muslims take the form of the ghostly. However, although contemporary Islamophobia takes specific and recognisable forms, its precursors are colonial.

Epilogue

Everything was beautiful, and nothing hurt.
Kurt Vonnegut, *Slaughterhouse Five*

If Islamophobia's antecedents are colonial, then its expression takes the form of postcolonial racism. Hesse notes that postcolonial racism 'describes the continuing incidence of an (un)acknowledged White racism in contemporary Western cultures, together with a constitutive disavowal of its antecedents in liberal-colonial doubleness and its liberal-democratic configuration of imperial discontinuities' (Hesse 2000: 111–112). Islamophobia is attendant upon a series of shifts such as the ways in which ideas about racial difference which homogenised populations at arm's length in colonial times are retraced and reworked domestically in the postcolonial West. The emergence of Muslim identity politics shows the contingency of the political practices through which populations have been named racially, and the wider cultural and political problems it presents are not reducible to the war on terror. An over-emphasis upon the war on terror as a framing for the emergence of Islamophobia operates as a further disavowal of Islamophobia's antecedents. Islamophobia is *not* the war on terror. Nor is it religious discrimination.

Nor even is Islamophobia religious criticism; there is not necessarily anything problematic about criticising or debating Islam. To reduce the racial politics at stake in Islamophobia simply to religion conflates questions such as critique, or even offence, with the wider manifestations of Islamophobia and makes it difficult to effect a distinction between them in analysis or political practice. The subject positions instituted by the problematic misconception of Islamophobia privilege certain kind of modes of engaging in, or resisting, Islamophobia. Debates about Islamophobia inevitably concern struggles and contests over what 'Muslim' means and how it can be constituted as a viable identity. 'Muslim' to the extremist right and 'Muslim' to the extremist Islamists might bear some similarities (violence...) but also, one supposes, some differences. To the Demokratiske Muslimer movement in Denmark or the Quilliam Foundation in Britain, or any of the countless variations between them and the Islamists will also mean different things. Islamophobia tends to construct Muslim identities through reference to an essentialist notion of culture as lack in excess, this forecloses the possibility of contesting what Muslim means and leaves us with only one solution to the Muslim problem: that its surplus be either excised or tamed. It thus takes us beyond any possible political solution to the problem of Islamist extremism, and only opens an ultra-politics.

We can only access the real through language, and since each signifier only directs us to other signifiers, meanings are unstable. In Lacanian terms meaning is retroactively fixed through quilting points which structure the discursive field. A master-signifier is empty in that it does not refer to any signified other than itself. This allows the master-signifier to organise the other signifiers that float around it. For example, the war on terror was organised through appeals to the master-signifier of democracy, at a time when the emptiness of the master-signifier was radicalised through the dominance of a post-political logic that empties the democratic vision (Stavrakakis 2007) around what might be termed post-democracy (Rancière 1995), and through formal and informal practices such as rendition, detention without trial, and increasing racism that might be termed anti-democratic. The emptiness of the master-signifier presents a problem of its own: it needs to be filled. It thus comes to be a site for the inscription of fantasies that can fill the void (Zizek 2006: 373). The Other – the *objet a* – thus becomes a substitute for the Real, and a way of populating the gap in the master-signifier, so that the Other can be 'jettisoned into an abominable real, inaccessible except through jouissance' (Kristeva 1982: 9). The abject figure of the Muslim, the lack in excess, exists in fantasy as the means of filling out the emptiness of the master-signifier, providing us with the fantasmatic figures on whom we can project the impossibility of closing the gap.

Muslims, not Islam, are the objects of these fantasies. Islam is superficially problematised, but only as a metaphor to draw upon in narrating these stories about excess; it is not the fundamental problem of Islamophobia. Islam only figures insofar as it operates as a substitute for subjecthood and corporeality, and this is in turn figured in the problematic naming and conception of Islamophobia which renders Muslims invisible, inscribing their haunting and unknowable presence. In this Islam plays the role of culture, so that in the wake of its nominal elision of Muslim subjects, we can only figure in the Muslim if we can use Islam as both a shorthand for Islam and Muslims and, since it figures as a comment on the lack of raciality, it also acts as a substitute for race. The Islam in Islamophobia is not, therefore, a religion. What I understand as Islamophobia has little or nothing to do with religion, and everything to do with race. By Islamophobia I refer not to critiques of religion, but rather to those practices by which Muslims are constituted and essentialised as a bounded group in order to manage the relationship between the idea of the West and its Others or its outsiders. Islam here simply figures as a cultural formation that is thoroughly regulative, so we can understand the Other as improperly realised and inadequately racialised and lacking agency, yet as also having excessive difference/politicality. This is not fundamentally about Islam; it is about using Islam as a metaphor to narrate a particular story about a human population. Yalçin-Heckmann (1998: 168) notes that Muslims 'are perceived as Muslims more at certain moments of political and historical development than others'. Muslim identities are not uniformly visualised or constituted. They are inscribed in public discourse as non-racial (even though they are racialised), and this non-raciality is contingent on the absence of ontic racial purity. This displaces resistance to Islamophobic racism into religious registers and constitutes Muslim subject positions in the public sphere as essentially religious, foreclosing other modes of politicisation.

Umberto Eco reminds us of Gladstone's suggestion that Greeks could not tell blue from yellow, and of other claims that speakers of Latin had no means of drawing a distinction between blue and green (Eco 1985: 158; see also Deutscher 2011). One way of approaching this is to suggest that the signifiers we use are not unproblematic mirrors of nature, but that they provide a set of conventions which enable us to organise external phenomena. As such, we do not only know how to name a given colour, but we also know how to treat it, how to visualise it, how to work with it, and how to understand its relationship to other colours ... That such conventions become naturalised to the point at which, within a given cultural formation, we may become unaware of them, does not mean that they are absent, but simply indicates the success of a given ontology. Where a difficulty might arise is the point at which some unforeseen occurrence interrupts these discursive operations to demonstrate their contingency and limits. Much of the time it seems unlikely that this will happen; for example, the prospect of a Welsh uprising against the naming of green grass as *glaswellt* (blue grass) (or even to challenge its Anglocentric naming as 'green') appears remote. But once we accept that the language of colours is not innate to the objects it describes, then we also have to accept the possibility that terms for colours can also be deployed in other ways. In other words, what happens when a sedimented label such as 'green' is suddenly applied to institute a new set of social relations around the naming of something that has not hitherto been named as such?

Such acts of institution can be understood as being fundamentally political (cf. Laclau and Mouffe 1985), and this metaphor helpfully illustrates the problem of race insofar as the grammar of colours that has been so central to modern racial discourse can often appear natural and unproblematic, even though the shoehorning of a great range of human diversity into categories such as 'black', 'red', 'white', 'brown', or 'yellow' is the product of a discursive operation which was centrally political. Not insignificantly, contemporary Islamophobia has been associated with the idea of a green menace (Abu Sway 2006: 17; Cole 2011: 127; Haddad 2004: 99; Husain and Rosenbaum 2004: 171). 'Black menace' (hooks 2004: 241); 'yellow peril' (Clegg 1994; Ono and Pham 2009); 'green menace': the greening of Muslims resonates. It is a provisional naming that points to the racial and post/colonial dis/continuities. But even as it renders undeniable Islamophobia's place on a wider field of racial politics, it points to the ways in which the identities to which it is ascribed appear to disrupt racial politics. If Islamophobia has been able to thrive in 'post-racial' times in part through its disarticulation from other racisms, the greening of Muslims opens new possibilities for contesting Islamophobia by and forging new alliances in challenging this racial politics. This is because this colour coding of Muslims helps draw attention to the ways in which Muslimness is positioned within a wider racial politics. Green might be an unlikely colour, but as a suitably lurid marker for such phantasmatic conjurings, it is no more or less contingent than 'white', 'black' or any other racial ascription. Challenging Islamophobia is contingent on our recognition that Islamophobia racialises Muslims, and is also contingent on our recognition of the ways in which the constitution of Muslim subjects unsettles a wider field of racial politics.

Islamophobia is a barometer; it can tell us something of the atmospheric conditions in our epistemic universe. Through its naming we can also confront the contingency of the phantasmatic conjurings through which particular images of others are being produced and in turn, to appropriate from Zizek, to traverse the fantasy of our worst fears. Islamophobia is a reminder of the contingent and political nature of racism in a world in which it is alternately naturalised, denied, or exceptionalised. In this, it also needs to be named as a reminder to us that, in contrast to the promise of the post-politics, not everything is beautiful, and some things hurt.

Bibliography

Abu Sway, M. (2006) 'Islamophobia: *Meaning, Manifestations, Causes*', in Schenker, H. and Abu-Zayyad, Z. (eds) *Islamophobia and Anti-Semitism*, (Princeton, NJ: Markus Wiener Publishers), pp. 13–24.

Adams, S. (2010) 'Ian McEwan: Criticising Islam is not racist', *Daily Telegraph*, 13 March 2010, at: www.telegraph.co.uk/culture/books/booknews/7428769/Ian-McEwan-Criticising-Islam-is-not-racist.html

Agamben, G. (1998) *Homo Sacer: Sovereign Power and Bare Life* (Stanford: Stanford University Press).

—— (1999) *Remnants of Auschwitz: The Witness and the Archive* (New York: Zone Books).

—— (2000) *Means Without End: Notes on Politics* (Minneapolis: University of Minnesota Press).

—— (2005) *State of Exception* (London: University of Chicago Press).

Ahmed, A. (2011) 'The Muslim Question: An understanding for difficult times', *Foreign Policy Journal*, 1 August 2011, at: www.foreignpolicyjournal.com/2011/08/01/the-muslim-question-an-understanding-for-difficult-times/

Ahmed, S. (2004) 'Affective Economies', *Social Text*, 22 (2): 117–139.

Al-Azmeh, A. (2003) 'Postmodern Obscurantism and "The Muslim Question"', *Socialist Register*, 39: 28–50.

Alibhai-Brown, Y. (2006) 'Why Muslims must remember the Holocaust', *The Independent*, 23 January 2006, at: www.independent.co.uk/opinion/commentators/yasmin-alibhai-brown/yasmin-alibhaibrown-why-muslims-must-remember-the-holocaust-524187.html

Allen, C. (2010) *Islamophobia* (Farnham: Ashgate Publishing).

—— and Nielsen, J.S. (2002) *Summary Report on Islamophobia in the EU after 11 September 2001* (Vienna: European Monitoring Centre on Racism and Xenophobia).

Allievi, S. (2002) 'Islam in Italy', in Hunter, S.T. (ed.) *Islam, Europe's Second Religion: The New Social, Cultural, and Political Landscape* (Westport CT: Praeger Publishers), pp. 77–95.

—— (2005) 'Sociology of a Newcomer: Muslim Migration to Italy Religious Visibility, Cultural and Political Reactions', in Al-Shahi, A. and Lawless, R. (eds) *Middle East and North African immigrants in Europe* (Abingdon: Routledge), pp. 43–56.

Allison, R. (2001) 'Muslim leaders condemn Thatcher attack', *The Guardian*, 4 October 2001, at: www.guardian.co.uk/politics/2001/oct/04/uk.september11

Alsultany, E. (2006) 'From ambiguity to abjection: Iraqi-Americans negotiating race in the United States', in Smail Salhi, Z. and Netton, I.R. (eds) *The Arab Diaspora: Voices of an Anguished Scream* (Abingdon: Routledge), pp. 127–142.

Altheide, D.L. (2006) *Terrorism and the politics of fear* (Lanham, MD: AltaMira Press).

Amin, A. (2010) 'The Remainders of Race', *Theory, Culture, Society*, 27 (1): 1–23.

Amnesty International (2006) *UK: Human Rights: A Broken Promise* (London: Amnesty International).

Andersen, N. (2010) 'Meet Denmark's Sarah Palin', *PoliticsUSA*, at: www.politicususa.com/en/denmark-sarah-palin

Andreassen, R. (2011) 'Sing a Song, but Stay Out of Politics: Two Cases of Representations of Racial/Ethnic Minorities in the Danish Media', in Eide, E. and Nikunen, K. (eds) *Media in motion: cultural complexity and migration in the Nordic region* (Farnham: Ashgate Publishing), pp. 163–180.

Archer, L. and Bawdon, F. (2010) *Ricin! The Inside Story of the Terror Plot That Never Was* (London: Pluto Press).

Armour, E.T. (2008) 'Visual Theology: Diagnosing Postmodernity', in Boeve, L. and Brabant, C. (eds) *Between Philosophy and Theology: Contemporary Interpretations of Christianity* (Farnham: Ashgate), pp. 175–192.

Art, D. (2011) *Inside the Radical Right: The development of anti-immigrant parties* (Cambridge: Cambridge University Press).

Barnard-Wills, D. (2012) *Surveillance and Identity: Discourse, Subjectivity and the State* (Farnham: Ashgate Publishing).

Batchelor, D. (2000) *Chromophobia* (London: Reaktion Books).

Batty, D. (2011) 'Lady Warsi claims Islamophobia is now socially acceptable in Britain', *Guardian*, 20 January 2011, at: www.guardian.co.uk/uk/2011/jan/20/lady-warsi-islamophobia-muslims-prejudice

BBC (2003) *Panorama: Blair's war*, broadcast Sunday, 23 March 2003 at 21:15 GMT on BBC One.

BBC (2004) '9/11 violence "stalks UK Sikhs"', at: http://news.bbc.co.uk/1/hi/uk_politics/4017161.stm

BBC (2005) 'Britons warned over "segregation"', 22 September 2005, at: http://news.bbc.co.uk/1/hi/uk/4273414.stm

BBC News (2010) 'Belgian lawmakers pass burka ban', 30 April 2010, at: http://news.bbc.co.uk/1/hi/8652861.stm

BBC News (2010) 'Merkel says German multicultural society has failed', 17 October 2010, at: www.bbc.co.uk/news/world-europe-11559451

BBC News (2011) 'Profile: Anders Behring Breivik', at: www.bbc.co.uk/news/world-europe-14259989

Becker, C.-H. (1910) *L'Islam et La Colonisation de L'Afrique* (Paris: Union Coloniale Francaise).

Berezin, M. (2006) 'Xenophobia and the New Nationalisms', in Delanty, G. and Kumar, K. (eds) *The Sage Handbook of Nations and Nationalisms* (London: Sage), pp. 273–284.

Betz, H. (2003) 'The Growing Threat of the Radical Right', in Merkl, P.H. and Weinberg, L. (eds) *Right-Wing Extremism in the Twenty-First Century* (London: Frank Cass Publishers), pp. 74–93.

—— (2005) 'Mobilising Resentment in the Alps: The Swiss SVP, the Italian *Lega Nord*, and the Austrian FPO', in Caramani, D. and Meny, Y. (eds) *Challenges to Consensual Politics: Democracy, Identity, and Populist Protest in the Alpine Region* (Brussels: P.I.E.-Peter Lang S.A./Presses Interuniversitaires Europeennes), pp. 147–166.

—— (2007) 'Against the 'Green Totalitarianism': Anti-Islamic Nativism in Contemporary Radical Right-Wing Populism in Western Europe', in Liang, C.S. (ed.) *Europe for the Europeans: the Foreign and Security Policy of the Populist Radical Right* (Aldershot: Ashgate Publishing Limited), pp. 33–54.

Blumenthal, R. and Mowjood, S. (2009) 'Muslim Prayers Fuel Spiritual Rebuilding Project by Ground Zero', *New York Times*, 8 December 2009, at: www.nytimes.com/2009/12/09/nyregion/09mosque.html?pagewanted= all

Bommes, M. (2010) 'Migration Research in Germany: The Emergence of a Generalised Research Field in a Reluctant Immigration Country', in Thränhardt, D. and Bommes, M. (eds) *National Paradigms of Migration Research* (Osnabrück: Universität Osnabrück Institut für Migrationsforschung und Interkulturelle Studien [IMIS]), pp. 127–186.

Brower, B.C.A. (2009) *Desert Named Peace: The Violence of France's Empire in the Algerian Sahara, 1844–1902* (New York and Chichester: Columbia University Press).

Bunglawala, I. (2008) 'Zero tolerance of religious discrimination', *The Guardian*, 18 September 2008, at: www.guardian.co.uk/commentisfree/2008/sep/18/ islam.religion

Butler, J. (1990) *Gender Trouble: Feminism and the Subversion of Identity* (London: Routledge).

Buzan, B. (1995) 'The Present as a Historic Turning Point', *Journal of Peace Research*, 32 (4): 385–398.

Buzan, B., Waever, O. and De Wilde, J. (1998) *Security: A New Framework for Analysis* (Boulder, CO: Lynne Rienner Publishers).

Caeiro, A. and Peter, F. (2007) 'Ham, Mozart, & Limits to Freedom of Expression', *ISIM Review*, 19 (Spring 2007): 26–27.

Cameron, D. (2011) PM's speech at Munich Security Conference, at: www. number10.gov.uk/news/pms-speech-at-munich-security-conference/

Campbell, E. (2007) 'The Muslim Question in Late Imperial Russia' in Burbank, J., von Hagen, M. and Remnev, A. (eds) *Russian Empire: Space, People, Power, 1700–1930* (Bloomington, IN: Indiana University Press), pp. 320–347.

Cantwell Smith, W. (1981) *On Understanding Islam: Selected Studies* (The Hague: Mouton Publishers).

Carpentier, N. and De Cleen, B. (2007) 'Bringing discourse theory into Media Studies: The applicability of Discourse Theoretical Analysis (DTA) for the Study of media practises and discourses', *Journal of Language and Politics*, 6 (2), pp. 265–293.

Cesarani, D. (2008) 'Muslims the "new Jews"? Not by a long way', *The Jewish Chronicle* 17 January 2008, at: www.thejc.com/comment/comment/ muslims-new-jews%E2%80%99-not-a-long-way

Cherribi, S. (2010) *In the House of War: Dutch Islam Observed: Dutch Islam Observed* (Oxford: Oxford University Press).

—— (2011) 'An Obsession Renewed: Islamophobia in the Netherlands, Austria, and Germany', in Esposito, J.L. and Kalin, I. (eds) *Islamophobia;*

The Challenge of Pluralism in the 21st Century (Oxford: Oxford University Press), pp. 47–62.

Chiantera-Stutte, P. (2005) 'Leadership, Ideology, and Anti-European Politics in the Italian *Lega Nord*', in Caramani, D. and Mény, Y. (eds) *Challenges to Consensual Politics: Democracy, Identity, and the Populist Protest in the Alpine Region* (Brussels: P.I.E.-Peter Lang S.A./Presses Interuniversitaires Européennes), pp. 113–129.

Clegg, J. (1994) *Fu Manchu and the Yellow peril: the making of a racist myth* (Stoke-on-Trent: Trentham Books).

Clough, P.T. (2003) 'Affect and Control: Rethinking the Body "Beyond Sex and Gender"', *Feminist Theory*, 4 (3): 359–364.

Coates, D. and Krieger, J. with Vickers, R. (2004) *Blair's War* (Oxford: Polity).

Cohen, T. (2005) *Hitchcock's Cryptonymies* (Minneapolis, MN: University of Minnesota Press).

Cole, J. (2011) 'Islamophobia and American Foreign Policy Rhetoric: The Bush Years and After', in Esposito, J.L. and Kalin, I. (eds) *Islamophobia: The Challenge of Pluralism in the 21st Century* (Oxford: Oxford University Press), pp. 127–142.

Connolly, W.E. (1991) *Identity/difference: democratic negotiations of political paradox* (Ithaca: Cornell University Press).

Croft, S. (2006) *Culture, Crisis and America's War on Terror* (Cambridge: Cambridge University Press).

d'Appollonia, A.C. and Reich, S. (2010) 'Conclusions: Lessons Learned and Their Policy Implications', in d'Appollonia, A.C. and Reich, S. (eds) *Managing Ethnic Diversity After 9/11: Integration, Security, and Civil Liberties in Transatlantic Perspective* (Piscataway, NJ: Rutgers University Press), pp. 276–284.

D'Souza, D. (2010) *The Roots of Obama's Rage* (Washington: Regnery Publishing, Inc).

Dabashi, H. (2009) *Post-Orientalism: Knowledge and Power in Time of Terror* (New Brunswick, NJ: Transaction Publishers).

Danto, A.C. (2007) *Unnatural Wonders: Essays from the Gap Between Art and Life* (New York: Columbia University Press).

Daulatzai, S. (2007) 'Protect Ya Neck: Muslims and the Carceral Imagination in the Age of Guantánamo', *Souls* 9 (2): 132–147.

Davidson, N. (2012) *Only Muslim: Embodying Islam in Twentieth-Century France* (New York: Cornell University Press).

Deaux, K. (2006) *To Be an Immigrant* (NY: Russell Sage Foundation).

De Genova, N. (2010) 'Antiterrorism, Race, and the New Frontier: American Exceptionalism, Imperial Multiculturalism, and the Global Security State', *Identities: Global Studies in Culture and Power*, 17, (6): 613–640.

de Tollenaere, H. (2004) 'Theo van Gogh: Hero, Anti-Semite, Misogynist or Islamophobe?', *What Next?*, No. 29, at: www.whatnextjournal.co.uk/Pages/Back/Wnext29/Vangogh.html

Delafosse, M. (1910) 'L'Etat actuel de l'Islam dans l'Afrique occidentale française', *Revue du Monde Musulman*, XI (V): 32–53.

Deleuze, G. (1992) 'Postscript on the Societies of Control', *October,* vol. 59 (Winter 1992): 3–7.

Deleuze, G. and Guattari, F. (2004) *A Thousand Plateaus* (London: Continuum Books).

Deltombe, T. (2007) *L'Islam Imaginaire: La construction mediatique de l'Islamophobie en France, 1975–2005* (Paris: La Decouverte).

Deutscher, G. (2011) *Through the Language Glass: Why the World Looks Different in Other Languages* (London: Arrow Books).

Die Standaard (2012) 'Dochtor van Filip Dewinter is een booerkababe', 4 February 2012, at: www.standaard.be/artikel/detail.aspx?artikelid=DMF 20120203_148

Diken, B. and Laustsen, C.B. (2005) *The Culture of Exception: Sociology Facing the Camp* (Abingdon: Routledge).

Dobratz, B.A. and Shanks-Meile, S.L. (1997) *The White Separatist Movement in the United States: "White Power, White Pride!"*, (Maryland: Johns Hopkins University Press).

Doe, N. (2011) *Law and Religion in Europe: A Comparative Introduction* (Oxford: Oxford University Press).

Dolar, M. (1992) 'Hitchcock's Objects', in Zizek, S. (ed.) *Everything You Always Wanted to Know about Lacan (But Were Afraid to Ask Hitchcock)* (London: Verso), pp. 31–46.

Donnell, A. (2003) 'Visibility, Violence and Voice? Attitudes to Veiling Post-11 September', in Bailey, D.A. and Tawadros, G. (eds) *Veil: Veiling, Representation and Contemporary Art* (London: Institute of Visual Arts), pp. 120–135.

Dornhof, S. (2011) *Reading Practices, Visuality and Moral Offense in the Case of Salman Rushdie's 'The Satanic Verses'*, paper presented to Configurations of Muslim Traditions in European Secular Public Spheres conference on Memory and Image of Islam, Friday 14 October 2011, Casa Arabe, Cordoba.

Doughty, S. (2008) '"We Muslims are the new Jews" says MP who has been victim of a hit-and-run and a firebomb attack', *Daily Mail*, 4 July 2008, at: www.dailymail.co.uk/news/article-1031697/We-Muslims-new-Jews-says-MP-victim-hit-run-firebomb-attack.html

Eco, U. (1985) 'How Culture Conditions the Colours We See', in Blonsky, M. (ed.), *On Signs* (Baltimore: Johns Hopkins University Press), pp. 157–175.

El-Tayeb, F. (2011) *European Others: Queering Ethnicity in Postnational Europe* (Minneapolis MN: University of Minnesota Press).

Elia, N. (2006) 'Islamophobia and the "Privileging" of Arab American Women', *NWSA Journal* 18 (3): 155–161.

Erickson, C. (2010) *The Poetics of Fear: A Human Response to Human Security* (London: Continuum).

Esposito, J.L. and Kalin, I. (eds) (2011) *Islamophobia: The Challenge of Pluralism in the 21st Century* (Oxford: Oxford University Press).

Essed, P. (2009) 'Intolerable humiliations', in Huggan, G. and Law, I. (eds) *Racism Postcolonialism Europe* (Liverpool: Liverpool University Press), pp. 131–147.

Evans, D. (1996) *An Introductory Dictionary of Lacanian Psychoanalysis* (London: Routledge).

Eyerman, R. (2008) *The Assassination of Theo van Gogh: From Social Drama to Cultural Trauma* (Durham: Duke University Press).

Fairclough, N. (1995) *Critical Discourse Analysis: The Critical Study of Language* (New York: Longman).

Faris, S. (2011) 'In the Burqa Ban, Italy's Left and Right Find Something to Agree On', *Time*, 4 August 2011, at: www.time.com/time/world/article/0,8599,2086879,00.html

Fekete, L. (2012) 'The Muslim conspiracy theory and the Oslo massacre', *Race and Class*, 53 (3): 30–47.

Fleras, A. (2009) *The Politics of Multiculturalism: Multicultural Governance in Comparative Perspective* (Basingstoke: Palgrave Macmillan).

Fortier, A.-M. (2008) *Multicultural Horizons: Diversity and the limits of the civil nation* (Abingdon: Routledge).

Foucault, M. (2004) *Society Must Be Defended* (London: Penguin).

Friedlander, B. (2011) 'An Interview with a Madman: Breivik Asks and Answers His Own Questions', *Time*, 24 July 2011, at: www.time.com/time/world/article/0,8599,2084895,00.html

Frost, D. (2008) 'Islamophobia: examining causal links between the media and "race hate" from "below"', *International Journal of Sociology and Social Policy*, 28(11/12): 564–578.

Gaine, C. and George, R. (1999) *Gender, 'Race' and Class in Schooling: A New Introduction* (London: Falmer Press).

Gans, E. (1994) 'Theo van Gogh als fenomeen', at: www.dbnl.org/tekst/gans007gojs01_01/gans007gojs01_01_0005.php

Garner, S. (2007) *Whiteness: An Introduction* (Abingdon: Routledge).

—— (2010) *Racisms: An Introduction* (London: Sage).

Gazzanni, C. (2011) 'Lega Nord/Meridionali, stranieri e omosessuali: fuori dai coglioni! Siam leghisti, siam razzisti', *infiltrato.it*, at: www.infiltrato.it/inchieste/italia/lega-nord-meridionali-stranieri-e-omosessuali-fuori-dai-coglioni-siam-leghisti-siam-razzisti

Geaves, R., Gabriel, T., Haddad, Y. and Smith, J.I. (eds) (2004) *Islam and the West Post 9/11* (Aldershot: Ashgate).

Geisser, V. (2003) *La Nouvelle Islamophobie* (Paris: La Decouverte).

Gillborn, D. (2008) *Racism and Education: Coincidence or Conspiracy?: Understanding Race Inequality in Education* (Abingdon: Routledge).

Gillingham, J. (2003) *European Integration, 1950–2003: Superstate or New Market Economy?* (Cambridge: Cambridge University Press).

Gilman, S. (1991) *The Jew's Body* (London: Routledge).

—— (2006) 'Can the Experience of Diaspora Judaism Serve as a Model for Islam in Today's Multicultural Europe?', in Schenker, H. and Abu-Zayyad, Z. (eds) *Islamophobia and Anti-Semitism* (Princeton, NJ: Markus Wiener Publishers), pp. 59–74.

Glaberson, G. (2010) 'Newburgh Terrorism Case May Establish a Line for Entrapment', *New York Times*, 15 June 2010, at: www.nytimes.com/2010/06/16/nyregion/16terror.html

Glynos, J. and Howarth, D.R. (2007) *Logics of Critical Explanation in Social and Political Theory* (Abingdon: Routledge).

Gohil, N.S. and Sidhu, D.S. (2008) 'The Sikh Turban: Post-911 Challenges To This Article Of Faith', *Rutgers Journal of Law And Religion* 9 (2), at: http://org.law.rutgers.edu/publications/law-religion/articles/sidhu.pdf

Gold, T.W. (2003) *The Lega Nord and Contemporary Politics in Italy* (Basingstoke: Palgrave Macmillan).

Goldberg, D.T. (2009) *The Threat of Race: Reflections on Racial Neoliberalism* (Oxford: Blackwell).

González, R.J. (2010) *Militarizing Culture: Essays on the Warfare State* (Walnut Creek: Left Coast Press).

Goodwin, M. (2011) *Right Response: Understanding and Countering Populist Extremism in Europe* (London: Chatham House).

Gottschalk, P. and Greenberg, G. (2008) *Islamophobia: Making Muslims the Enemy* (Plymouth: Rowman and Littlefield Publishers).

Goy, P.G., Maney, G.M. and Woehrle, L.M. (2008) 'Blessing war and blessing peace: religious discourses in the US during major conflict periods, 1990–2005', *Research in Social Movements, Conflicts and Change*, 29: 113–150.

Grayson, J. (2011) 'Are the main parties just taking on BNP policies?', *Institute of Race Relations*, 3 November 2011, at: www.irr.org.uk/news/are-the-main-parties-just-taking-on-bnp-policies/

Greenberg, K. (2011) 'The FBI's synagogue bomb plot', *The Guardian*, 30 June 2011, at: www.guardian.co.uk/commentisfree/cifamerica/2011/jun/30/fbi-terrorism

Grillo, R. (2007) 'An excess of alterity? Debating difference in a multicultural society', *Ethnic and Racial Studies* 30 (6): 979–998.

Haddad, Y. (2004) 'The Shaping of a Moderate North American Islam: Between "Mufti" Bush and "Ayatollah" Ashcroft', in Geaves, R., Gabriel, T., Haddad, Y. and Smith, J.I. (eds) *Islam and the West Post 9/11* (Aldershot: Ashgate), pp. 97–114.

Haj, S. (2009) *Reconfiguring Islamic Tradition: Reform, Rationality and Modernity* (Stanford: Stanford University Press).

Hall, S. (2000) 'Conclusion: The multi-cultural question', in Hesse, B. (ed.) *Un/Settled Multiculturalisms: Diasporas, Entanglements, "Transruptions"* (London: Zed Books), pp. 209–241.

Hammond, A. (2006) *Cold War Literature: Writing the global conflict* (Abingdon: Routledge).

Hansard (2005) House of Commons Hansard Debates for 21 June 2005 (Part 12), (accessed August 2005) at: http://www.publications.parliament.uk/pa/cm200506/cmhansrd/cm050621/debtext/50621-12.htm#50621-12_spnew6

Hari, J. (2008) 'Ken Livingstone: The Interview', at: www.johannhari.com/2008/04/13/ken-livingstone-the-interview

Hellyer, H.A. (2009) *Muslims of Europe: The 'Other' Europeans* (Edinburgh: Edinburgh University Press).

Hervik, P. (2011) *The Annoying Difference: The Emergence of Danish Neonationalism, Neoracism and Populism in the Post-1989 World* (New York: Berghahn Books).

Hesse, B. (1997) 'White governmentality: Urbanism, nationalism, racism', in Westwood, S. and Williams J.M. (eds) *Imagining Cities: Scripts, Signs, Memory* (London: Routledge), pp. 85–102.

—— (2000) 'Introduction: Un/Settled Multiculturalisms', in Hesse, B. (ed.) *Un/Settled Multiculturalisms: Diasporas, Entanglements, "Transruptions"*, (London: Zed Books), pp. 1–30.

—— (2004) 'Discourse on Institutional Racism, the Genealogy of a Concept', in Law, I., Phillips, D. and Turney, L. (eds) *Institutional Racism in Higher Education*, (Stoke-on-Trent: Trentham), pp. 131–148.

—— (2011) 'Self-Fulfilling Prophecy: The Postracial Horizon', *The South Atlantic Quarterly*, Winter 2011, 110 (1) : 155–178.

Hewitt, R. (2005) *White Backlash and the Politics of Multiculturalism* (Cambridge: Cambridge University Press).

Heyer, J.A. and Traufetter, G. (2011) 'Norway Massacre Suspect Reveals All But Motive', *Spiegel*, 26 October 2011, at: www.spiegel.de/international/spiegel/0,1518,793923-3,00.html

Hollifield, J.F. (2004) 'France: Republicanism and the Limits of Immigration Control', Cornelius, W.A. (ed.) *Controlling immigration: a global perspective*, pp. 183–214.

Hook, D. and Neill, C. (2008) 'Perspectives on "Lacanian subjectivities"', *Subjectivity*, 24 (1): 247–255.

hooks, b. (2004) 'Reflections on Race and Sex', in Darder, A., Baltodano, M. and Torres, R.D. (eds) *The Critical Pedagogy Reader* (New York: Routledge), pp. 238–245.

Hooper, J. (2009) 'Italian Court Finds CIA Agents Guilty of Kidnapping Terrorism Suspect', *Guardian*, 4 November 2009, at: www.guardian.co.uk/world/2009/nov/04/cia-guilty-rendition-abu-omar

Howarth, D.R., Norval, A.J. and Stavrakakis, Y. (eds) (2000) *Discourse Theory and Political Analysis: Identities, Hegemonies and Social Change* (Manchester: Manchester University Press).

Husain, Z. and Rosenbaum, D.M. (2004) 'Perceiving Islam: The Causes and Consequences of Islamophobia in the Western Media', in Saha, S.C. (ed.) *Religious Fundamentalism in the Contemporary World: Critical Social and Political Issues* (Oxford: Lexington Books), pp, 171–206.

Huysseune, M. (2006) *Modernity and Secession: the social sciences and the political discourse of the Lega Nord in Italy* (New York: Berghahn Books).

Independent Police Complaints Commission (2007a) *Stockwell One: Investigation into the shooting of Jean Charles Menezes at Stockwell underground station on 22 July 2005* (London: IPCC).

Independent Police Complaints Commission (2007b) *Stockwell Two: An investigation into complaints about the Metropolitan Police Service's handling of public statements following the shooting of Jean Charles Menezes on 22 July 2005*. (London: IPCC).

Insdorf, A. (1994) *Francois Truffaut* (Cambridge: Cambridge University Press).

Ishii-Gonzáles, S. (2004) 'Hitchcock with Deleuze', Allen, R. and Ishii-Gonzáles, S. (eds) *Hitchcock: Past and Future* (London: Routledge), pp. 128–145.

Jackson, P. (2011) 'The EDL: Britain's "New Far Right" Social Movement', (Northampton: RNM Publications/University of Northampton), at: www. radicalism-new-media.org/wp-content/uploads/2011/09/The_EDL_ Britains_New_Far_Right_Social_Movement.pdf

Jackson, R.L. (2006) *Scripting the Black masculine body: identity, discourse, and racial politics in popular media* (Albany, NY: State University of New York Press).

Jayadev, R. (2003) 'Cab Wars: Sikh cab drivers in San Jose say racism and recession have put their lives in danger', *Metro*, 6–12 November 2003, at: www.metroactive.com/papers/metro/11.06.03/sikhs-0345.html

Jonker, G. and Amiraux, V. (2006) *Politics of Visibility: Young Muslims in European Public Spaces* (Bielefeld: Transcript).

Karcic, F. (2002) 'The Eastern Question – A Paradigm for Understanding the Balkan Muslims' History in the 20th Century', *Islamic Studies* 41:4 (2002): 635–650.

Karpf, A. (2012) 'Don't be fooled. Europe's far-right racists are not discerning', *Guardian*, 27th March 2012, at: www.guardian.co.uk/commentisfree/2012/ mar/27/far-right-philozionism-racism

Katz, C. (2007) 'Banal Terrorism', Gregory, D. and Pred, A. (eds) *Violent Geographies: Fear, Terror, and Political Violence* (Abingdon: Routledge), pp. 349–362.

Khoury, L. (2009) 'Racial Profiling as Dressage: A Social Control Regime!', *African Identities*, 7 (1): 55–70.

Kim, S.M. (2012) 'King: I'm continuing Muslim radicalisation hearings', 2 September 2012, at: www.politico.com/blogs/on-congress/2012/02/ king-im-continuing-muslim-radicalization-hearings-114062.html

Klandermans, B. and Mayer, N. (2006) 'Links with the past', in Klandermans, B. and Mayer, N. (eds) *Extreme Right Activists in Europe: Through the Magnifying Glass* (Abingdon: Routledge) pp. 16–27.

Klausen, J. (2005) *The Islamic Challenge: Politics and Religion in Western Europe* (Oxford: Oxford University Press).

Klein, W. (2010) *The Inside Stories of Modern Political Scandals* (Santa Barbara: Praeger).

Koff, H. (2008) *Fortress Europe or a Europe of Fortresses?*, (Brussels: P.I.E. Peter Lang S.A. / Editions scientifiques internationals).

Kristeva, J. (1982) *Powers of Horror: An Essay on Abjection* (New York: Columbia University Press).

Kundnani, A. (2009) *Spooked: How not to prevent violent extremism* (London: Institute of Race Relations).

Kurzman, C. (2012) *Muslim–American Terrorism in the Decade Since 9/11*, Triangle Center on Terrorism and Homeland Security.

Lacan, J. (1972) 'Seminar on "The Purloined Letter"', *Yale French Studies* No. 48, *French Freud: Structural Studies in Psychoanalysis* (1972), pp. 39–72.

Laclau, E. (2000) 'Constructing University', in Butler, J., Laclau, E. and Zizek, S. (eds) *Contingency, Hegemony, Universality: Contemporary Dialogues on the Left* (London: Verso), pp. 281–307.

Laclau, E. and Mouffe, C. (1985) *Hegemony and Socialist Strategy* (London: Verso).

Laurens, H. (2004) *Orientales II. La IIIe République et l'Islam* (Paris: CNRS editions).

Law, I., Phillips, D. and Turney, L. (eds) (2004) *Institutional Racism in Higher Education* (Stoke-on-Trent: Trentham Books Ltd).

Lazzarato, M. (2006) 'The Concepts of Life and the Living in the Societies of Control', in Fugslang, M. and Sorenson, B.M. (eds) *Deleuze and the Social* (Edinburgh: Edinburgh University Press), pp. 171–190.

Leake, C. and Chapman, A. (2006) 'Mutiny as passengers refuse to fly until Asians are removed', *Daily Mail* 20 August 2006, at: www.dailymail.co.uk/news/article-401419/Mutiny-passengers-refuse-fly-Asians-removed.html

Lemke, T. (2011) *Bio-Politics An Advanced Introduction* (London: New York University Press).

Lebovics, H. (1992) *True France: The Wars Over Cultural Identity* (New York: Cornell University Press).

Le Figaro (2011) 'Sarkozy: le multiculturalisme, "un échec"', 10 February 2011, at: www.lefigaro.fr/flash-actu/2011/02/10/97001-20110210FILWWW00731-sarkozy-le-multiculturalisme-un-echec.php

Lentin, A. and Titley, G. (2011) *The Crises of Multiculturalism: Racism in a Neoliberal Age* (London: Zed Books).

Lindow, J. (2001) *Norse Mythology: A Guide to the Gods, Heroes, Rituals and Beliefs* (Oxford: Oxford University Press).

Little, D. (2008) *American Orientalism: The United States and the Middle East Since 1945* (Chapel Hill, N.C.: University of North Carolina Press).

Logan, E.L. (2011) *'At This Defining Moment': Barack Obama's Presidential Candidacy and the New Politics of Race* (New York: New York University Press).

López, F.B. (2011) 'Towards a definition of Islamophobia: approximations of the early twentieth century', *Ethnic and Racial Studies* 34 (4): 556–573.

Luft, E. (2009) *Die at the Right Time! A Subjective Cultural History of the American Sixties* (NY: Gegensatz Press).

Lynch, A. (2008) 'Control Orders in Australia: A Further Case Study in the Migration of British Counter-Terrorism Law', *Commonwealth Law Journal*, 8 (2): 159–185.

MacDonald, S. (2007) 'ASBOs and Control Orders: Two Recurring Themes, Two Apparent Contradictions', *Parliamentary Affairs*, 60 (4): 601–624.

Ma'oz, M. (2010) 'Introduction', in Ma'oz, M. (ed.) *Muslim Attitudes to Jews and Israel: The Ambivalences of Contempt, Antagonism, Tolerance and Cooperation* (Eastbourne: Sussex Academic Press), pp. 1–28.

Mahmood, S. (2006) 'Secularism, Hermeneutics and Empire: The Politics of Islamic Reformation', *Public Culture* 18 (2): 323–347.

Malik, K. (2005) 'The Islamophobia Myth', at: www.kenanmalik.com/essays/prospect_islamophobia.html

Mandaville, P. (2009) 'Muslim Transnational Identity and State Responses in Europe and the UK after 9/11: Political Community, Ideology and Authority', *Journal of Ethnic and Migration Studies* 35 (3): 491–506.

Marchetti, S. (2011) 'La sorelli di Mario Balotelli: <<Potrei votare Lega>>', *VanityFair.it*, at: www.vanityfair.it/people/italia/2011/08/10/abigail-balotelli-diva-e-donna-intervista-lega-nord#?refresh=ce

Marriott, D. (2005) 'En moi: Frantz Fanon and Rene Maran', in Silverman, M. (ed.) *Frantz Fanon's Black Skin White Masks: New interdisciplinary essays* (Manchester: Manchester University Press), pp. 146–178.

Martin, P.L. (2002) 'Germany: Managing Migration in the 21st Century', *Comparative Immigration and Integration Program, Institute of European Studies* (UC Berkeley), at: http://escholarship.org/uc/item/1gb6j203

Marx, K. (1994) *The Eastern Question A Reprint of Letters Written 1853–1856 Dealing with the Events of the Crimean War* (London: Frank Cass).

Mason, D. (2003) 'Changing ethnic disadvantage: an overview', in Mason, D. (ed.) *Explaining Ethnic Differences: Changing patterns of disadvantage in Britain* (Bristol: The Policy Press), pp. 1–8.

Massari, M. (2006) *Islamofobia: la paura e l'islam* (Roma: Laterza).

Mathur, S. (2006) 'Surviving the dragnet: "special interest" detainees in the US after 9/11', *Race and Class* 47 (3): 31–46.

Mayr, W. (2011) 'Austria's Freedom Party Goes from Strength to Strength', *Spiegel*, 14 July 2011, at: www.spiegel.de/international/europe/0,1518,774255,00.html

McClure, K. (1992) 'On the Subject of Rights: Pluralism, Plurality and Political Identity', in Mouffe, C. (ed.) *Dimensions of Radical Democracy: Pluralism, Citizenship, Community* (London: Verso), pp. 108–127.

Meer, N. (2007) 'Less equal than others', *Index on Censorship*, 36 (2): 114–118.

—— (2008) 'The politics of voluntary and involuntary identities: Are Muslims in Britain an ethnic, racial or religious minority?', *Patterns of Prejudice* 42 (1): 61–81.

Meer, N. and Modood, T. (2009) 'Refutations of racism in the '"Muslim question"', *Patterns of Prejudice,* 43(3–4): 335–354.

Meeropol, R. (ed.) (2005) *America's Disappeared: Detainees, Secret Imprisonment, and the 'War on Terror'* (New York: Seven Stories Press).

Miller-Idriss, C. (2009) *Blood and culture: youth, right-wing extremism, and national belonging in contemporary Germany* (Durham: Duke University Press).

Mirzoeff, N. (2002) 'Ghostwriting: working out visual culture', *Journal of Visual Culture*, 1 (2): 239–254.

Modood, T. (2005) *Multicultural Politics: racism, ethnicity and Muslims in Britain* (Edinburgh: Edinburgh University Press).

—— (2006) 'The Liberal Dilemma: Integration or Vilification?', *International Migration,* 44(5): 4–7.

Moeckli, D. (2007) 'Stop and Search Under the Terrorism Act 2000: A Comment on R (Gillan) v Commissioner of Police for the Metropolis', *Modern Law Review*, 70(4): 659–670.

Monahan, T. (2010) *Surveillance in the time of Insecurity* (Rutgers University Press).

Moors, A. (2011) 'Fear of Small Numbers? Debating Face-Veiling', Sayyid, S. and Vakil, A. (eds) *Thinking Through Islamophobia: Global Perspectives* (London: Hurst and Co), pp. 157–164.

Moreau, P. (2012) 'The Victorious Parties – Unity in Diversity?', in Backes, U. and Moreau, P. (eds) *The Extreme Right in Europe: Current Trends and Perspectives* (Göttingen: Vandenhoeck & Ruprecht), pp. 74–148.

Mouffe, C. (1993) *The Return of the Political* (London: Verso).

—— (2005) *On The Political* (London: Verso).

Mullender, S. (2008) 'Vienna Jewish community leader: Strache more dangerous than Haider', *European Jewish Press* 29 September 2008, at: www.ejpress.org/article/30705

Müller, M.G., Özcan, E. and Seizov, O. (2009) 'Dangerous Depictions: A Visual Case Study of Contemporary Cartoon Controversies', *Popular Communication*, 7(1): 28–39.

Murray, N. (2004) 'Profiled: Arabs, Muslims and the Post-9/11 Hunt for the "Enemy Within"', in Hagopian, E.C. (ed.) *Civil Rights in Peril: The Targeting of Arabs and Muslims* (London: Pluto Press), pp. 27–68.

—— (2011) 'Obama and the global war on terror', *Race and Class*, 53 (2): 84–93.

Myers, T. (2003) *Slavoj Žižek* (London: Routledge).

Naber, N. (2008) 'Introduction Arab Americans and U.S. Racial Formations', Jamal, A. and Naber, N. (eds) *Race and Arab Americans Before and After 9/11* (Syracuse NY: Syracuse University Press), pp. 1–45.

Nader, A. (2003) *Courants d'idees en Islam* (Montreal: Mediaspaul).

Nagarajah, S. (2005) 'Mistaken identity', *The Guardian*, 5 September 2005, at: www.guardian.co.uk/world/2005/sep/05/religion.july7

Nagel, C. (2001) 'Hidden minorities and the politics of "race": the case of British Arab activists in London', *Journal of Ethnic and Migration Studies* 27 (3): 381–400.

Nagra, R.K. (2011) 'A Tribute to Sikh Victims of 9/11', *The Sikh Foundation International*, 10 September 2011, at: www.sikhfoundation.org/2011/people-events/a-tribute-to-sikh-victims-of-911/

Nawaz, M. (2011) 'How the government should handle the "Muslim Question"', 5 December 2011, *New Statesman*, at: www.newstatesman.com/religion/2011/12/muslim-groups-nothing

Neiyar, D. (2011) 'Sikhs upset about airport security checks on turbans', BBC Asian Network, 24 February 2011, at: www.bbc.co.uk/news/uk-england-12558996

Neumann, I.B. and Welsh, J.M. (1991) 'The Other in European Self-Definition: An Addendum to the Literature on International Society', *Review of International Studies*, 17 (4): 327–348.

Norton, A. (2011) 'On the Muslim Question', in Mookherjee, M. (ed.) *Democracy, Religious Pluralism and the Liberal Dilemma of Accommodation* (London: Springer), pp. 65–76.

Nouvelle République (2012) 'Jean-Marie Le Pen: "c'était Strauss, sans Kahn"', 30 January 2012, at: www.lanouvellerepublique.fr/France-Monde/Actualite/Politique/n/Contenus/Articles/2012/01/30/Jean-Marie-Le-Pen-c-etait-Strauss-sans-Kahn

O'Driscoll, C. (2008) 'Fear and Trust: The Shooting of Jean Charles de Menezes and the War on Terror', *Millennium – Journal of International Studies*, 36 (2): 339–360.

Omi, M. and Winant, H. (1994) *Racial Formation in the United States: from the 1960s to the 1990s* (London: Routledge).

Ono, K.A. and Pham, V. (2009) *Asian Americans and the Media* (Cambridge: Polity Press).

Open Society Institute (2009) 'Ethnic Profiling In The European Union: Pervasive, Ineffective, and Discriminatory', (NY: Open Society Institute).

Pace, E. (2004) *L'Islam in Europa: modelli di integrazione* (Roma: Carocci).

Page, J. (2006) 'Sikhs head for the barber and turn their backs on tradition: Western intolerance of religious symbols and a series of street attacks are prompting young men to shed their hair and turbans', *Times Online*, 24 November 2006, at: www.timesonline.co.uk/tol/news/world/asia/article648044.ece

Panayiotopoulos, P.I. (2006) *Immigrant Enterprise in Europe and the USA* (Abingdon: Routledge).

Pantazis, C. and Pemberton, S. (2009) 'From the "Old" to the "New" Suspect Community: Examining the Impacts of Recent UK Counter-Terrorist Legislation', *British Journal of Criminology* 49 (5): 646–666.

Papastergiadis, N. (2006) 'Ambient Fears', in Margaroni, M. and Yiannopoulou, E. (eds) *Metaphoricity and the Politics of Mobility* (Amsterdam: Editions Rodopi), pp. 119–140.

Parekh, B. (2008) 'European Liberalism and "the Muslim Question"', *ISIM Papers,* no. 9, (Amsterdam University Press ISIM /Leiden).

Patel, T. and Tyrer, D. (2011) *Race, Crime and Resistance* (London: Sage).

Paterson, T. (2009) 'Swiss move to ban minarets as "symbols of Islamic power"', *The Independent* 14 August 2009, at: www.independent.co.uk/news/world/europe/swiss-move-to-ban-minarets-as-symbols-of-islamic-power-1771879.html

Paul, M. (2009) 'Supporting Diversity - Strenghtening Cohesion – Multiculturalism in Germany', Seminar Paper (Norderstedt: GRIN-Verlag), (accessed June 2013) at: http://books.google.co.uk/books?id=zvq_YCF0M_YC&printsec=frontcover#v=onepage & q&f=false

Peter, F. (2011) 'Government in Visual Space: Image, Spectatorship, Islamophobia', paper presented at conference *Islam-Debatten: Schweiz-Europa 2011*, University of Bern, 30 September 2011.

Petley, J. (2005) 'Hit and Myth', Curran, J., Petley, J. and Gaber, I. (eds) *Culture wars: the media and the British left* (Edinburgh: Edinburgh University Press), pp. 85–107.

Pew Research Center (2011) 'Muslim Americans: No Signs of Growth in Alienation or Support for Extremism: Mainstream and Moderate Attitudes', 30 August 2011, at: www.pewforum.org/Muslim/Muslim-Americans--No-Signs-of-Growth-in-Alienation-or-Support-for-Extremism.aspx

Pieterse, J.N. (2007) *Ethnicities and Global Multiculture* (Plymouth: Rowman and Littlefield Publishers, Inc).

Pitcher, B. (2009) *The Politics of Multiculturalism: race and racism in contemporary Britain* (Basingstoke: Palgrave Macmillan).

Porter, P. (2009) *Military Orientalism: Eastern War Through Western Eyes* (Chichester: Columbia University Press).

Porttikivi, J. (2010) 'What's so funny about Infinite Justice?', Hirvonen, A. and Porttikivi, J., (eds) *Law and Evil: Philosophy, Politics, Psychoanalysis* (Abingdon: Routledge), pp. 199–223.

Poynting, S. and Mason, V. (2006) '"Tolerance, freedom, justice and peace"? Britain, Australia and anti-Muslim racism since 11 September 2001', *Journal of Intercultural Studies*, 27 (4): 365–91.

—— (2007) 'The resistible rise of Islamophobia: anti-Muslim racism in the UK and Australia before 11 September 2001', *Journal of Sociology*, 43 (1): 61–86.

Priest, D. and Arkin, W.M. (2011) *Top Secret America: The Rise of the New American Security State* (New York: Little, Brown and Company).

Prizel, I. (2008) 'Identity Discourse in Western Europe and the United States in the Aftermath of 9/11', in d'Appollonia, A.C. and Reich, S. (eds) *Immigration, Integration, and Security: America and Europe in Comparative Perspective* (Pittsburgh: University of Pittsburgh Press), pp. 23–43.

Puar, J.K. (2007) *Terrorist Assemblages: Homonationalism in Queer Times* (Durham: Duke University Press).

Pugliese, J. (2006) 'Asymmetries of Terror: Visual Regimes of Racial Profiling', *Borderlands*, 5 (1), at: www.borderlands.net.au/vol5no1_2006/pugliese. htm

Purgato, A. (2006) *Fobie. Le Nuove obsession del XXI secolo* (Roma: Alberto Castelvecchi Editori srl).

Quellien, A. (1910) *La Politique Musulmane Dans l'Afrique Occidentale Française* (Paris: Emile Larose).

Quraishi, M. (2005) *Muslims and Crime: A Comparative Study* (Aldershot: Ashgate Publishing Limited).

Ramadan, T. (2012) 'The challenge of being Muslim in an age of globalisation', ABC Religion and Ethics, at: www.abc.net.au/religion/ articles/2012/08/07/3562392.htm

Rana, J. (2007) 'The Story of Islamophobia', *Souls*, 9 (2): 148–161.

—— (2011) *Terrifying Muslims: Race and labor in the South Asian diaspora* (Durham: Duke University Press).

Rancière, J. (1995) *On the Shores of Politics* (London: Verso).

—— (2010) *Dissensus* (London: Continuum).

Ratnesar, R. (2010) 'Ground Zero: Exaggerating the Jihadist Threat', *Time* viewpoint, at: www.time.com/time/nation/article/0,8599,2011400,00. html

République Française (1926) Cochinchine Française/ Proces-Verbaux du Conseil Colonial (Session Ordinaire De 1925), (Saigon: C Ardin).

Richard, A. and Rudnyckyj, D. (2009) 'Economies of affect', *Journal of the Royal Anthropological Institute*, 15 (1): 57–77.

Richardson, J.E. (2004) *(Mis)Representing Islam: The racism and rhetoric of British broadsheet newspapers* (Amsterdam: John Benjamins Publishing Co.).

Ridanpää, J. (2009) 'Geopolitics of Humour: The Muhammad Cartoon Crisis and the Comic Strip Episode in Finland', *Geopolitics*, 14 (4): 729–749.

Rivera, A. (2005) *La guerra dei simboli: Veli postocoloniali e retoriche sull'alterità* (Bari: Edizioni Dedalo srl).

Robinson, D. (1999) 'France as a Muslim Power in West Africa', *Africa Today*, 46 (3/4): 105–127.

Rorty, R. (1989) *Contingency, Irony, and Solidarity* (Cambridge: Cambridge University Press).

Rosen, L. (2008) *Varieties of Muslim Experience: Encounters with Arab Political and Cultural Life* (London: University of Chicago Press).

Roy, A. (2003) 'The Algebra of Infinite Justice', in Gioseffi, D. (ed.) *Women on War: An International Anthology of Writings from Antiquity to the Present* (New York: the Feminist Press), pp. 90–98.

Runnymede Trust (1994) *A Very Light Sleeper: the persistence and dangers of antisemitism* (London: Runnymede Trust).

Runnymede Trust (1997) *Islamophobia: A Challenge for Us All* (London: Runnymede Trust).

Rydgren, J. and van Holsteyn, J. (2005) 'Holland and Pim Fortuyn: A deviant case or the beginning of something new?', in Rydgren, J. (ed.) *Movements of Exclusion: Radical Right-Wing Populism in the Western World* (New York: Nova Science), pp. 41–63.

Sabet, A.G.E. (2008) *Islam and the Political: Theory, Governance and International Relations* (London: Pluto Press).

SALDEF (2010) 'Sacramento Sikh Cab Driver Severely Beaten', 29 November 2010, at: www.saldef.org/news/sacramento-sikh-cab-driver-severely-beaten/#more-4382

Salecl, R. (1998) 'The Silence of the Feminine Jouissance', in Zizek, S. (ed.) *Cogito and the unconscious* (Durham: Duke University Press), pp. 175–196.

Dreier, S. (2010) 'It's Not about Free Expression: A Sociological Examination of the Danish Cartoon Controversy', in Banakar, R. (ed.) *Rights in Context: Law and Justice in Late Modern Society*, (Farnham: Ashgate), pp. 177–192.

Sardar, S. (2005) 'The next holocaust', *New Statesman*, 5 December 2005, at: www.newstatesman.com/200512050006

Sayyid, B. and Zac, L. (1998) 'Political Analysis in a World without Foundations', in Scarbrough, E. and Tanenbaum, E. (eds) *Research Strategies in the Social Sciences: A Guide to New Approaches* (Oxford: Oxford University Press), pp. 249–267.

Sayyid, B.S. (1997) *A Fundamental Fear: Eurocentrism and the Emergence of Islamism* (London: Zed Books).

Sayyid, S. (2004) 'Slippery people: The immigrant imaginary and the grammar of colours', in Law I., Phillips, D. and Turney. L. (eds) *Institutional Racism in Higher Education* (Stoke-on-Trent: Trentham Books), pp. 149–160.

Sayyid, S. and Vakil, A. (eds) (2011) *Thinking Through Islamophobia: Global Perspectives*, (London: Hurst and Co).

Schlag, P. (1998) *The Enchantment of Reason* (Durham: Duke University Press).

Schneider, P. (2010) 'Die Lehren der Geschichte', *Spiegel*, 25 October 2010, at: www.spiegel.de/spiegel/print/d-74735249.html

Seib, P. and Janbek, D.M. (2011) *Global Terrorism and New Media: The post-Al Qaeda Generation* (Abingdon: Routledge).

Semati, M. (2010) 'Islamophobia, Culture and Race in the Age of Empire', *Cultural Studies*, 24 (2): 256–275.

Sennels, N. (2011) 'What is Islamization? An incomplete list', *EuropeNews.dk*, at: http://europenews.dk/en/node/45059

Serwer, A. (2010) 'Majority of GOP thinks Obama wants to impose Islamic Law?', Sargent, G. (ed.) *The Plum Line* blog of *The Washington Post*, 31

August 2010, at: http://voices.washingtonpost.com/plum-line/2010/08/majority_of_republicans_think.html

Shani, O. (2010) 'Conceptions of Citizenship in India and the "Muslim Question"', *Modern Asian Studies*, 44 (Special Issue 01):145–173.

Shapiro, I. (2011) *The Real World of Democratic Theory* (Oxford: Princeton University Press).

Sheehi, S. (2011) *Islamophobia: The Ideological Campaign against Muslims* (Atlanta: Clarity Press).

Shepherdson, C. (2008) *Lacan and the Limits of Language* (New York: Fordham University Press).

Sheridan, L.P. (2006) 'Islamophobia Pre- and Post-September 11th, 2001', *Journal of Interpersonal Violence*, 21: 317–336.

Shryock, A. (2008) 'The Moral Analogies of Race: Arab American Identity, Color Politics, and the Limits of Racialized Citizenship', in Jamal, A. and Naber, N. (eds) *Race and Arab Americans Before and After 9/11* (Syracuse NY: Syracuse University Press), pp. 81–113.

Shryock, A. (2010) 'Introduction: Islam as an Object of Fear and Affection', in Shryock, A. (ed.) *Islamophobia/Islamophilia: beyond the politics of enemy and friend* (Bloomington, IN: Indiana University Press).

Sjölander, A.E. (2011) 'Comparing Critical Discourse Analysis and Discourse Theory', in Sjölander, A.E. and Payne, J.G. (eds) *Tracking Discourses: Politics, Identity and Social Change* (Lund: Nordic Academic Press), pp 13–48.

Smith, A.M. (1998) *Laclau and Mouffe: The Radical Democratic Imaginary* (London: Routledge).

Smith, R.M. (2008) 'Religious Rhetoric and the Ethics of Public Discourse', *Political Theory*, 36 (2): 272–300.

Soguk, N. (2007) 'Border's Capture: Insurrectional Politics, Border-Crossing Humans, and the New Political', in Rajaram, P.K. and Grundy-Warr, C. (eds) *Borderscapes: Hidden Geographies and Politics at Territory's Edge* (Minneapolis: University of Minnesota Press), pp. 284–308.

Spiegel (2008) Spiegel interview with Dutch populist Geert Wilders: 'Moderate Islam is a contradiction', *Spiegel,* 31 March 2008, at: www.spiegel.de/international/europe/spiegel-interview-with-dutch-populist-geert-wilders-moderate-islam-is-a-contradiction-a-544347.html

Squires, P. and Kennison, P.(2010) *Shooting to Kill: Policing, Firearms and Armed Response* (Chichester: John Wiley & Sons).

Stavrakakis, Y. (1999) *Lacan and the Political* (London: Routledge).

—— (2007) *The Lacanian Left: Psychoanalysis, Theory, Politics* (Edinburgh: Edinburgh University Press).

Steans, J. (2008) 'Telling Stories about Women and Gender in the War on Terror', *Global Society*, 22 (1): 85–202.

Steuter, E. and Wills, D. (2008) *At War with Metaphor: Media, Propaganda, and Racism in the War On Terror* (Plymouth: Lexington Books).

Stockwell Inquest (2008a) *Hearing Transcript – 29 October 2008,* at: www.stockwellinquest.org.uk/hearing_transcripts/oct_29.pdf

Stockwell Inquest (2008b) *Hearing Transcript – 4 November 2008,* at: www.stockwellinquest.org.uk/hearing_transcripts/nov_04.pdf

Stothard, P. (2003) *30 days: A Month at the Heart of Blair's War* (London: HarperCollins).

Stychin, C.F. (2003) *Governing sexuality: the changing politics of citizenship and law reform* (Portland: Hart Publishing).

Suskind, P. (2010) *The Pigeon* (London: Penguin).

Suskind, R. (2004) 'Faith, Certainty and the Presidency of George W. Bush', *New York Times*, 17 October 2004, at: www.nytimes.com/2004/10/17/magazine/17BUSH.html

Svendsen, L. (2008) *A Philosophy of Fear* (London: Reaktion).

SVP (2011) Campaigning leaflet, (accessed 27 October 2011) at: http://jsvpbern.ch/downloads/initiativbogen_web.pdf

Swiffen, A. (2011) *Law, Ethics and the Biopolitical* (Abingdon: Routledge).

Taguieff, P.-A. (1984) 'Les présuppositions définitionelles d'un indéfinissable: le racisme', *Mots*, Mars 1984, no. 8, pp. 71–107.

Taguieff, P. (2001) *The Force of Prejudice: on racism and its doubles* (Minneapolis, MN: University of Minnesota Press).

Tambini, D. (2001) *Nationalism in Italian Politics: The stories of the Northern League, 1980–2000* (London: Routledge).

Tamim, F.A. and Smith, M.S. (2010) 'Human Rights and Insecurities: Muslims in Post-9/11 East Africa', in Smith, M. (ed.) *Securing Africa: post-9/11 discourses on terrorism* (Farnham: Ashgate), pp. 99–128.

Terranova, T. (2007) 'Futurepublic: On Information Warfare, Bio-racism and Hegemony as Noopolitics', *Theory, Culture and Society*, May 2007, 24 (3): 125–145.

The Guardian (2011) 'Richard Peppiatt's letter to Daily Star proprietor Richard Desmond', *The Guardian*, 4 March 2011, at: www.guardian.co.uk/media/2011/mar/04/daily-star-reporter-letter-full

The Middle East Quarterly (2004) Editors' Preface to N.B. De Atkine, 'The Arab Mind Revisited', Summer 2004, pp. 47–55, at: www.meforum.org/636/the-arab-mind-revisited

Tibi, B. (2008) *Political Islam, World Politics and Europe: Democratic Peace and Euro-Islam versus Global Jihad* (Abingdon: Routledge).

—— (2010) 'Ethnicity of Fear? Islamic Migration and the Ethnicization of Islam in Europe', *Studies in Ethnicity and Nationalism* April 2010, Vol. 10 (1): 126–157.

Tie, W. (2004) 'The psychic life of governmentality', *Culture, Theory and Critique*, 45 (2): 161–176.

Todorov, T. (2010) *The Feat of Barbarians: Beyond the Clash of Civilizations* (Chicago: The University of Chicago Press).

Topal, C. (2011) 'Surveillance of immigrants from Turkey in Germany: From the disciplinary society to the society of control', *International Sociology*, 26: 789–814.

Torfing, J. (1999) *New Theories of Discourse: Laclau, Mouffe and Zizek* (Oxford: Blackwell).

Toynbee, P. (2004) 'Get off your knees', *The Guardian*, 11 June 2004, at: www.guardian.co.uk/politics/2004/jun/11/religion.world

—— (2005) 'My right to offend a fool', *The Guardian*, 10 June 2005, (accessed June 2011) at: www.guardian.co.uk/politics/2005/jun/10/religion.political columnists

Travis, A. (2009) 'Terror law used to stop thousands "just to balance racial statistics"', *The Guardian*, 17 June 2009, at: www.guardian.co.uk/uk/2009/jun/17/stop-search-terror-law-met

Trevisan Semi, E. (2003) 'Dalla giudeofobia alla islamofobia nei media italiani: il discorso della Lega Nord', in Di Bella, S. and Tomasello, D. (eds) *L'Islam in Europa Tra Passato E Futuro* (Cosenza: Luigi Pellegrini Editore), pp. 282–313.

Tyrer, D. (2010) 'Flooding The Embankments: Race, Bio-Politics and Sovereignty', in Sayyid, S. and Vakil, A. (eds) *Thinking Through Islamophobia: Global Perspectives* (London: Hurst and Co), pp. 93–110.

Tyrer, D. and Sayyid, S. (2012) 'Governing Ghosts: Race, incorporeality and difference in post-political times', *Current Sociology*, May 2012, 60 (3): pp. 353–367.

Vakil, A. (2011) 'Is The Islam in Islamophobia the Same as the Islam in anti-Islam: Or, When is it Islamophobia Time?', in Sayyid, S. and Vakil, A. (eds) *Thinking Through Islamophobia: Global Perspectives* (London: Hurst and Co), pp. 23–44.

Vallely, P. (2004) 'The fifth crusade: George Bush and the Christianisation of the war in Iraq', in Crooke, A., Milton-Edwards, B., Kaldor, M. and Vallely, P. (eds) *Re-imagining security* (London: British Council).

Van Dijk, T. (2008) *Discourse and Power* (Basingstoke: Palgrave Macmillan).

van Driel, B. (2004) 'Introduction', in van Driel, B. (ed.) *Confronting Islamophobia in Educational Practice* (Stoke on Trent: Trentham Books), pp. vii–xiii.

Van Haute, P. (2002) *Against Adaptation: Lacan's 'subversion' of the subject; a close reading* (New York: Other Press).

Vaughan-Williams, N. (2009) *Border Politics: The limits of sovereign power* (Edinburgh: Edinburgh University Press).

Viego, A. (2007) *Dead Subjects: Toward a Politics of Loss in Latino Studies* (Durham: Duke University Press).

Vignon, L. (1919) *Un Programme de Politique Coloniale: Les Questions Indigenes* (Paris: Librarie Plon).

Villard, P. (1984) 'Naissance d'un mot grec en 1900. Anatole France et les xénophobes', *Mots*, Mars 1984, no. 8, pp. 191–195.

Waterfield, B. (2012) 'Norway killer Anders Bering Breivik demands medal for combatting "Islamic colonization"', *Daily Telegraph*, 6 February 2012, at: www.telegraph.co.uk/news/worldnews/europe/norway/9064300/Norway-killer-Anders-Bering-Breivik-demands-medal-for-combatting-Islamic-colonisation.html

Weiner Zeitung (2012) 'Nach "Juden"-Sager: Kein Orden fur Strache', 31 January 2012, at: www.wienerzeitung.at/nachrichten/politik/oesterreich/431932_Nach-Juden-Sager-Kein-Orden-fuer-Strache.html

Weiser, B (2011) '3 Men Draw 25-Year Terms In Synagogue Bomb Plot', *New York Times*, 29 June 2011, at: www.nytimes.com/2011/06/30/nyregion/3-men-get-25-years-in-plot-to-bomb-bronx-synagogues.html

Weller, P. (2006) 'Addressing Religious Discrimination and Islamophobia: Muslims and Liberal Democracies. The Case of the United Kingdom', *Journal of Islamic Studies*, 17 (3): 295–325.

Whitaker, B. (2004) 'Its best use is as a doorstop', *The Guardian*, 24 May 2004, at: www.guardian.co.uk/world/2004/may/24/worlddispatch.usa

Wilders, G. (2009) 'Geert Wilders' speech in Kopenhagen', *Partij Voor De Vrijheid*, at: www.pvv.nl/index.php?option=com_content&task=view&id=2045

Woehrle, L.M., Coy, P.G. and Maney, G.M. (2008) *Contesting Patriotism: Culture, Power, and Strategy in the Peace Movement* (Plymouth: Rowman and Littlefield).

Wright, J. (2011) *The Obama Haters* (Dulles, VA: Potomac Books).

Yalçin-Heckmann, L. (1998) 'Growing up as a Muslim in Germany: religious socialisation among Turkish migrant families', in Vertovec, S. and Rogers, A. (eds) *Muslim European Youth: reproducing ethnicity, religion, culture* (Aldershot: Ashgate), pp. 167–192.

Young, I.M. (1990) *Justice and the Politics of Difference* (Princeton: Princeton University Press).

Zaretsky, R. (2011) 'Send the Marine', *Tablet*, 12 December 2011, at: www.tabletmag.com/jewish-news-and-politics/85828/send-the-marine/

Zine, J. (2006) 'Between Orientalism and Fundamentalism: Muslim Women and Feminist Engagement', in Hunt, K. and Rygiel, K. (eds) *(En)gendering the war on terror: war stories and camouflaged stories* (Aldershot: Ashgate Publishing): 27–49.

Zizek, S. (1997) *The Abyss of Freedom/Ages of the World* (Ann Arbor: University of Michigan Press).

—— (1999) *The Ticklish Subject: the absent centre of political ontology* (London: Verso).

—— (2002) *Welcome to the Desert of the Real* (London: Verso).

—— (2005) *The Metastases of Enjoyment: On Women and Causality* (London: Verso).

—— (2006) *The Parallax View* (Cambridge MA: MIT Press).

—— (2009) *In Defence of Lost Causes* (London: Verso).

Index